DAILY PLANS FOR ACTIVE PRESCHOOLERS

JUDY GALLOWAY · LYNETTE IVEY · GLORIA VALSTER

**THE CENTER FOR APPLIED
RESEARCH IN EDUCATION**
West Nyack, New York 10995

THE CENTER FOR APPLIED
RESEARCH IN EDUCATION
West Nyack, New York

10   9   8   7   6

Library of Congress Cataloging-in-Publication Data

Galloway, Judy, 1950-
   Daily plans for active preschoolers : 80 ready-to-use daily
activity plans for children ages 3-5 / Judy Galloway, Lynette Ivey,
Gloria Valster.
   p. cm.
   Includes bibliographical references.
   ISBN 0-87628-250-8 :
   1. Education, Preschool—Activity programs. 2. Creative
activities and seat work. I. Ivey, Lynette, 1945-
II. Valster, Gloria, 1947- . III. Center for Applied Research in
Education. IV. Title.
LB1140.35.C74G36 1990
372.5—dc20   90-33546
                                                          CIP

ISBN   087628-250-8

**THE CENTER FOR APPLIED
RESEARCH IN EDUCATION**
BUSINESS & PROFESSIONAL DIVISION
A division of Simon & Schuster
West Nyack, New York 10995

About the Authors

The three coauthors of *Daily Plans for Active Preschoolers* have a combined experience of over forty years in early childhood education. They began working together in 1980 when they cofounded The Children's Playshop, a preschool for three-year-olds, in Pella, Iowa.

Judy Galloway, B.S., Southern Illinois University, has been a director and teacher of preschool, day care, and Head Start for more than fifteen years. Currently, she is the director of The Children's Playshop, which is now a preschool and prekindergarten. She is in her 8th year of teaching Early Childhood I and II classes at Central College in Pella.

Gloria Valster, B.A., Central College, taught first grade for three years in Albia, Iowa. For the past eight years, she has been a preschool teacher at The Children's Playshop.

Lynette Ivey, B.S., University of Wisconsin, has taught young children for eighteen years. She was a teacher of grades 1–3 in Wisconsin and Illinois schools for eleven years before cofounding The Children's Playshop, where she taught for seven years. Mrs. Ivey is presently a Chapter 1 reading teacher in Derry, New Hampshire.

Acknowledgments

Specific material was used and permission granted from the following authors:
Carol Beckman, Roberta Simmons, and Nancy Thomas, "Lady Bug Race"
(p. 151) from *Channels to Children: Early Childhood Activity Guide for Holidays and Seasons*, Copyright ©1982.
Phyllis Halloran, "Amazin' " from *i'd like to hear a flower grow and other poems*, Copyright ©1985.
Tamara Hunt and Nancy Renfro, giraffe puppet, from *Puppetry in Early Childhood*, Copyright ©1982.
National Wildlife Federation, "Feely Board" (Series II September issue) from *Your Big Backyard*.
Dick Wilmes, "Ouch" from *Everyday Circle Times*, Copyright ©1983.

Some very special people have helped to make this book possible. We would like to say thank you . . .

. . . to all the children and parents who believed in us as we "founded" The Children's Playshop. Through your encouragement, support, and love for learning these plans evolved.

. . . to Marla Kettler who drew the picture on the front cover.

. . . to Matt and Mark Ivey for the illustrations you drew.

. . . to Evelyn Bandstra for the many hours of typing and computer instruction you unselfishly provided.

. . . to our families and friends for their moral support.

. . . to the "big" people across the hall who patiently and silently listen and watch as our eager "little" people learn!

Enjoy!!

Judy, Lynette, Gloria

About Daily Plans for Active Preschoolers

Dear Early Childhood Educator:

Whether you are a preschool teacher, children's librarian, play group leader, or day care director, you will find our book *Daily Plans for Active Preschoolers* invaluable. The book will save you countless hours by organizing games and activities around daily themes and grouping related daily plans into units. Moreover, we have used these plans successfully in our own classrooms and can virtually guarantee that they will work effectively for *you*!

For easy use, we have followed a uniform format in presenting all of the plans. Each daily plan begins with a PREPARATION section headed "To the Teacher." This is followed by sections for ARRIVAL, OPENING, CRAFT, FREEPLAY, and CLOSING. We realize that you will use these plans to best fit your schedule. However, we like to encourage all children to be in a large group for the OPENING and CLOSING activities. Hopefully, all children will find time and interest to participate in activities offered during FREEPLAY.

The various books and records recommended throughout these daily plans are ones that we have used and found to be favorites. The activities included develop small motor, visual discrimination, listening, shape and color recognition, and cognitive skills and enhance creativity. Our experience is that most early childhood educators want open-ended suggestions and innovative stimulation in order to bring out each child's creativity and uniqueness.

As you review these plans, please notice that the reproducibles are for your use and not the children's. Those that are included at the end of each teaching unit are meant to help you prepare games and visual aids. We have also provided notes to be sent home to parents.

Children aged 3–5 years are eager to try new things, and they learn a great deal from exposure to new thoughts and ideas. Our hope is that these plans will help you find new activities for the children in your class to explore and enjoy. *Daily Plans for Active Preschoolers* is packed full of versatile activities and ideas allowing you to personalize your own program and make both teaching and learning a joy.

> **Judy Galloway**
> **Lynette Ivey**
> **Gloria Valster**

Contents

UNIT 7 REPRODUCIBLES:

UNIT 8 OLD FAVORITES   183

UNIT 8 REPRODUCIBLES:

UNIT 9 THINGS THAT GO TOGETHER 211

UNIT 10 REPRODUCIBLES:

unit 1

HELLO SPRING

Spring is a wonderful time of year. It is the season after winter and before summer. We think of blooming flowers, spring showers, beautiful rainbows, and lots of sunshine. This unit includes all these topics and much more. You will find many hands-on activities, such as science experiments and cooking. There are lots of fingerplays and songs welcoming spring.

Each day, point out any new signs of spring that the children can observe. Grass turning green, gardens being planted, and trees budding are sure indications that it is warmer and spring is here.

The daily activity plans in Unit 1 include:

- Chicken Day
- Butterfly Day
- Bird Day
- Rain Day
- Spider Day
- Bunny Day
- Seed Day
- Spring Day

1

Chicken Day

© 1990 by The Center for Applied Research in Education

PREPARATION _____ To the Teacher _____

The story of *The Little Red Hen*, edited by Nova Nestrick (Platt & Munk, 1961) is the theme of today's activities and craft. As you make the biscuits, be sure everyone helps.
   You will need:

- ingredients for biscuits for Arrival;
- puppets (see pp. 18–19) for Opening;
- puffed wheat and colored paper for Activity 1;
- Listen-and-Do game prepared for Activity 2;
- Chicken and Egg game prepared for Activity 3; and
- pictures or examples of breads for Closing.

ARRIVAL _____ Homemade Biscuits _____

Wheat is a grain. When it is ground very fine, it is turned into flour. From flour we can make bread, cookies, etc. If possible, bring some wheat to show the children. Ask the children to help make biscuits. Serve warm biscuits for snack time.

Rolled Biscuits

2-1/4 cups baking mix
2/3 cup milk

Mix ingredients until dough forms. Beat well for thirty seconds. If the dough seems sticky, add up to 1/4 cup baking mix to make it easy to handle. Turn onto well-floured surface. Shape dough into a ball. Knead ten times. Roll 1/2" thick. Cut into any size or shape biscuit you would like. Bake for ten to twelve minutes at 450 degrees.

OPENING _____ Story _____

Read or tell the story of *The Little Red Hen*. Make puppets (see pp. 18–19) to use while telling the story.
   Lead the children in a thought-stimulating discussion by asking them questions about the story. *Examples:* What lesson do you think the animals in the story learned? Has anyone ever asked you to help do something special? Did you help? Why do you think the animals refused to help? Do you think they wish they would have helped the Little Red Hen? Why?
   Review the story, emphasizing the correct sequence. The children will enjoy dramatizing this story.

CRAFT _____ Little Red Hen _____

Materials Needed:

    picture of hen (see p. 20)
    pieces of straw
    traced ovals to cut
    scissors, crayons, glue

Explanation:
Children use red crayons to color the hen and glue pieces of straw under the hen for a nest. Then they cut out small ovals for eggs to glue in the nest.

FREEPLAY _____ Activity 1 _____

Name Outlines—On a colored sheet of paper, print each child's first name. Have the child outline each letter one at a time with glue and put puffed wheat on the glue.

_____ Activity 2 _____

Listen-and-Do Bread Slices—Cut twenty pieces of paper in the shape of a slice of bread. Write instructions on each slice. A child selects a slice, hands it to the teacher, listens to the instructions, and then does what it says. *Examples:* Place a blue book under the table. Put your finger on your back.

_____ Activity 3 _____

Chicken and Egg Game—One a large piece of cardboard draw a hen. Below the hen, attach a piece of paper with a nest drawn on it. Leave an opening at the top of the nest into which eggs can be inserted. Teacher provides paper eggs of various colors. Ask a child to tell you what color an egg is. As the child tells you, he or she may put the egg in the nest.

CLOSING _____ Bread Talk _____

Biscuits, croissants, and muffins are all types of bread. Name different kinds of bread—raisin, sunflower, banana, French, wheat, pumpkin, poppy seed, etc. Ask a baker to visit your classroom and bring various kinds of bread.

_____ "Old MacDonald Had a Farm" _____

There is a book to go with this popular song. It is published by Child's Play International Limited, 1975.

Butterfly Day

© 1990 by The Center for Applied Research in Education

PREPARATION _____ To the Teacher _____

A large picture of a butterfly, or a real butterfly, will aid in the science lesson in Opening. There are directions in Opening for a caterpillar/butterfly puppet you will want to make.

You will need:

- food and cooking supplies for Arrival;
- sock puppet and felt butterfly for Opening;
- large, white butterflies and tissue paper for Activity 1; and
- felt ovals and triangles for Activity 2.

ARRIVAL _____ Breakfast Butterflies _____

Children help fix scrambled eggs and toast. Eggs are served in the center of the plate to form the butterfly body. The children can add triangle "toast wings" and thin, rectangle "toast feelers."

OPENING _____ Butterfly Talk _____

A butterfly is an insect. Its body is divided into three parts. A butterfly has four wings, three pairs of thin legs, and one large eye on each side of its head. Like all other insects, a butterfly has two feelers, called antennae. A butterfly cannot bite or chew. It sips water and nectar from flowers through a long sucking tube.

There are four stages in the life of a butterfly. They are: the egg, the caterpillar, the resting stage (in a cocoon), and the adult stage—a beautiful butterfly.

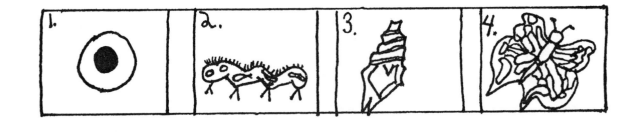

_____ Butterfly Puppet _____

In order to show the children the stages, make a sock puppet. Using a striped tube sock, make a creepy, crawly caterpillar puppet by gluing on felt eyes. Pull the puppet over your arm. The caterpillar then goes to sleep in a cocoon, so pull the sock inside out over the caterpillar's face to form the cocoon. After a long nap, out of the cocoon comes a beautiful butterfly. Pull your hand out of the sock showing the children the felt butterfly that you have been hiding.

4

_____ **Fingerplay** _____

Teach the following fingerplay:

    1, 2, 3, 4, 5—I caught a butterfly alive.

    6, 7, 8, 9, 10—I let him go again.

CRAFT _____ **Foot Butterflies** _____

Materials Needed:

    paper   scissors

    crayons

    pretraced ovals

    glue

Explanation:
The child cuts out an oval to be used for the butterfly's body. Glue the oval in the center of a sheet of paper. Then have the child stand with one foot on each side of the oval so that a teacher can trace around his or her feet to form wings. Use scraps from cutting out the oval to make two antennae. Color the completed butterfly.

FREEPLAY _____ **Activity 1** _____

Colored Butterflies—Draw two or three large, white butterflies for this class project. Children cut small pieces of colored tissue paper and lay them on the wings of these butterflies. When the wings are covered with tissue, the children sprinkle drops of water over the tissue. The colors bleed through the tissue onto the wings, making a beautifully colored butterfly.

_____ **Activity 2** _____

Flannel Board Butterflies—Cut one oval and two triangles out of six colors of felt. Children place matching felt ovals and triangles on flannel board to make butterflies. Let the children practice giving and following instructions.
Example: Make a butterfly with a green body and two orange wings.

CLOSING _____ **Story** _____

Read one of the following stories: *The Very Hungry Caterpillar,* by Eric Carle (Putman Pub. Group, 1981). *Where Do Butterflies Go When It Rains?*, by May Garelick (Scholastic, Inc., 1961). *The Butterfly's Ball,* by William Roscoe (McGraw-Hill, 1967).

Bird Day

PREPARATION _____ To the Teacher _____

Prior to class, make each child an Edible Bird Nest for Arrival. You will need to collect a few mesh bags for Activity 3. Also, note the two-day bulletin board, which you will begin today.

You will need:

- food for the snack for Arrival;
- plastic circles or ropes for Opening;
- plastic forks, circles, and wings (see p. 21) for Activity 1;
- prepared bulletin board
- play dough (see p. 55) for Activity 2; and
- items for birds' nests for Activity 3.

ARRIVAL _____ Edible Nests _____

In advance, prepare a small nest for each child using the following recipe. As children arrive, they name colors of jelly bean eggs as they place them in their nest. They eat the nests during snack time.

> 1/4 cup margarine or butter
>
> 1 pkg. (10 oz.) regular marshmallows
>
> 6 cups crisp rice cereal

Melt margarine in large saucepan over low heat. Add marshmallows and stir until completely melted. Remove from heat.
Add crisp rice cereal. Stir until well coated.
Using wax paper, shape into small bird nests.

OPENING _____ Bird Talk _____

Birds come in all colors, shapes, and sizes from tiny hummingbirds to huge eagles. All birds have two wings, and most birds can fly. Their bodies are covered with feathers. Their bones are hollow and filled with air. A bird's heart beats very fast. It takes a lot of energy to fly. Birds must eat all day to stay strong! Birds that live on or near the water eat small fish. What do other birds eat? (worms, bugs, seeds, fruits, tree sap) What do birds use to build their nests? (yarn, grass, feathers, mud, weeds, hair, string) Name birds of different colors. Some birds migrate (fly south in the winter to be where it is warm and where they can find food).

_____ Record _____

Using rope or plastic circles, have children follow suggestions in the song "Birds in a Circle" on the album _Easy Does It_ (AR 581), by Hap Palmer (Educational Activities, Inc., Freeport, N.Y. 11520). The group will also enjoy "Over the Meadow" on the album _Baby Beluga_ (SL-0010), Raffi with Ken Whiteley (Shoreline Records, 6307 Yonge Street, Willowdale, Ontario, Canada M2M 3X7).

CRAFT _____ Shape Bird Houses _____

Materials Needed:

cardboard shapes to trace   scissors
paper
crayons, glue

Explanation:
Children trace, color, and cut out a square, a triangle, and a small circle. Glue the shapes on a sheet of paper to "build" a bird house.

FREEPLAY _____ Activity 1 _____

Signs of Spring Bulletin Board—Place several trees with nests and bird houses in them on a bulletin board with a light blue background. Children make birds using plastic forks. Trace wing shapes and circles (see p. 21), and have children cut them out. Use the tines of a fork for the bird's tail, and attach the wings and the head with masking tape on the backside. Attach two adhesive eyes. (See Freeplay Activity 3 on Rain Day [p. 9] for an addition to this bulletin board.)

_____ Activity 2 _____

Play Dough Nests and Eggs—Children use play dough (see p. 55) to make bird nests and eggs. Take this opportunity to review counting as they make the eggs.

_____ Activity 3 _____

Donations to a Bird's Nest—Have the children help stuff a mesh grapefruit bag with things (string, yarn, cotton, lint) birds use to build nests. Hang it in a tree by your preschool so the children can watch birds take things from the bag.

CLOSING _____ Story _____

Read one of the following stories: *Are You My Mother?*, by P. D. Eastman (Random House, 1976). *Flap Your Wings,* by P. D. Eastman (Random House, 1977). *Have You Seen Birds?*, by JoAnne Opperheim (Addison-Wesley, 1968).

Rain Day

PREPARATION ———————— To the Teacher ————————————

Peter Spier's wordless book *Rain* (Doubleday, 1982) would be the perfect way to begin this day, as it shows every aspect of rain. Sharing the book with the children and having them describe to you what they see provides a stimulating language experience.

You will need:

- large umbrella for Arrival;
- prism for Opening;
- items for categorization for Activity 1;
- felt shapes for Activity 2; and
- straws, paint and dark blue paper for Activity 3.

ARRIVAL ———————— Who Is Missing Game ————————————

One child leaves the room. While he or she is gone, another child is chosen to hide under an umbrella. When the first child returns, he or she must guess who is missing from the group.

———————————— Fingerplay ————————————

Recite and do the actions of the Eency Weency Spider (see p. 21).

Eency Weency Spider
(Walk index and middle finger up arm.)
Went up the water spout;
Down came the rain
And washed the spider out;
(Hold hands high, bring down, and push to the side.)

Out came the sun
(Make a circle with arms above head.)
And dried up all the rain;
Eency Weency Spider
Went up the spout again.
(Walk fingers back up arm again.)

OPENING ———————— Rain Talk ————————————

When you see a raindrop, do you ever wonder where it comes from? Rain is moisture or water that has evaporated from the ground and from bodies of water. The water vapor collects (condenses) into rain clouds and then falls to the earth in the form of rain. Rain is useful because people, plants, and animals cannot live without water. Rainstorms may also bring beautiful rainbows.

If you go outside on a rainy day, you need to wear a raincoat or use an umbrella. How does a rainy day make you feel? What do you like to do on a rainy day?

———————————— "Clouds" ————————————

Rain on green grass
And rain on the tree
Rain on the roof
But not on me!

On a large sheet of paper, write the poem "Clouds." After you have read it to the children and discussed it, have the children help you illustrate each line. Draw raindrops, grass, a tree, a house, and finally a person sheltered from the rain. Give various ways a person can stay dry other than the obvious—using an umbrella!

© 1990 by The Center for Applied Research in Education

_____ **Make a Rainbow with a Prism** _____

Hang a prism in a window where the sun is shining. Hold a white piece of paper in front of the prism, and you will see a rainbow of colors. Ask the children to identify the colors as they appear. If you do not have a prism, this can be accomplished with a jar of water. Place the jar of water in front of the window. Hold the paper in front of the jar, and as the sun shines through the water and onto the paper, the colors will appear.

CRAFT _____ **Spool Painting** _____

Materials Needed:

blue tempera paint   empty thread spool through which a wire loop

paper   has been strung to make a handle

Explanation:
Children hold onto the wire handle and dip the spool into paint. Then they roll the spool vertically on their paper to make rain. Clouds can be added by gluing cotton balls above the rain.

FREEPLAY _____ **Activity 1** _____

Water Absorption Experiments—Test and categorize to see which objects will absorb water. Use an eyedropper or syringe to drop water on the following items: (1) sock, (2) rubber boot, (3) sponge, (4) Kleenex®, (5) spoon, (6) rock, (7) mitten, (8) plastic boat, (9) raincoat, and (10) shirt.

_____ **Activity 2** _____

Hidden Shapes—Cut felt into different shapes. Also cut out a large cloud and place it on a flannel board. Show the children all the shapes. Have the children close their eyes while you hide one of the shapes under the cloud. When they open their eyes, see if they can tell you which shape is behind the cloud.

_____ **Activity 3** _____

Cloud Shapes—Cut cloud shapes from dark blue paper. Pour a small amount of white tempera paint in the center of each cloud. With plastic straws (cut in 3-inch lengths) have the children blow the paint on the cloud. The clouds can be added to the Signs of Spring bulletin board started yesterday.

CLOSING _____ **Story** _____

Read one of the following stories: *Mushroom in the Rain,* by Mirra Ginsburg (Macmillan, 1974). *Raindrops Splash,* by Alvin R. Tresselt (Lothrop, 1974). *Umbrella,* by Taro Yashima (The Viking Press, 1958).

Spider Day

© 1990 by The Center for Applied Research in Education

PREPARATION _____ **To the Teacher** _____

Along with science facts about spiders, there are many different kinds of activities for this day. Among the unusual items necessary are pizza boards, a rain gutter, and lots of black buttons!
     You will need:

- styrofoam ball, black yarn, pipe cleaners, and wiggly eyes for Arrival;
- rain gutter and plastic spider for Arrival;
- Little Miss Muffet theater for Opening;
- pizza boards and yarn for Activity 1;
- Miss Muffet props for Activity 2; and
- black buttons for Activity 3.

ARRIVAL _____ **"There's a Spider on the Floor"** _____

Play the record _Singable Songs for the Very Young_ (SL-002), by Raffi with Ken Whiteley (Shoreline Records, 6307 Yonge Street, Willowdale, Ontario, Canada M2M 3X7). Make a spider to use with this song: Wrap a styrofoam ball with black yarn, and add black pipe cleaner legs and wiggly eyes.

_____ **Fingerplay** _____

Review the "Eency Weency Spider" taught on Rain Day (see p. 8). Use a piece of rain gutter and a plastic spider on a string as props.

OPENING _____ **Spider Talk** _____

Spiders are not insects. They have eight legs. (Insects have six legs.) A spider has only two body parts, the head and abdomen. (Insects have three body parts—head, thorax, and abdomen.) Spiders spin webs to catch their food. Most spiders are helpful because they catch and eat harmful insects.

_____ **"Little Miss Muffet"** _____

You can tell the story of Miss Muffet using a theater in the round. To construct the theater, slit three holes in the bottom of a pizza board which has been folded in half. Glue a picture or drawing of a little girl, a spider, and a pillow to the ends of three Popsicle® sticks. Slip the other end of the sticks through the holes in the pizza board. Insert the characters as you mention them in the rhyme.

Little Miss Muffet
Sat on a tuffet,
Eating her curds and whey;
Along came a spider,
And sat down beside her
And frightened Miss Muffet away.

CRAFT _____ Marble Paint Spider Webs _____

Materials Needed:

>   marbles
>   brown paper grocery bag
>   black tempera paint
>   white paper

Explanation:
Lay the white paper in the bottom of the grocery bag. Drop marbles that have been dipped in the black paint onto the paper. Children tip the bag to make the marbles roll and create lines resembling a spider web.

FREEPLAY _____ Activity 1 _____

Spider Web—Cut small slits around the edges of a small pizza board. Children can string black yarn back and forth from slit to slit.

_____ Activity 2 _____

Acting Out Miss Muffet—Act out the story of Miss Muffet. *Props:* bonnet, bowl and spoon, pillow. Encourage the children to make facial expressions showing fright and surprise.

_____ Activity 3 _____

Button Spiders—Children glue a black button on a piece of paper. Then they use a black crayon or marker to give the spider eight legs. With different size buttons, you can teach the concept of big, bigger, biggest.

CLOSING _____ Story _____

Read one of the following stories: *The Very Busy Spider,* by Eric Carle (Philomel Books, 1984). *Be Nice to Spiders,* by Margaret Graham (Harper & Row, 1967). *Spider's First Day At School,* by Robert Kraus (Scholastic, Inc., 1987).

Bunny Day

PREPARATION _____ To the Teacher _____

With both holiday and spring themes emphasized, this day could easily be stretched into two days. You will need:

- cake and decorating supplies for Arrival;
- cotton balls and numerals for Activity 1;
- Sound Eggs prepared for Activity 2; and
- mural paper and craft supplies for Activity 3.

ARRIVAL _____ Bunny Cake _____

Children decorate a Bunny Cake. Prepare in advance two layers of white cake (one round and one square) to cut and decorate. Snack time will be such fun!

Decorating Supplies:

    white frosting
    jelly beans
    licorice
    coconut

OPENING _____ Bunny Talk _____

Rabbits are small, furry mammals with long ears and short, puffy tails. They have whiskers by their noses. They live in burrows (holes) under the ground. They eat grass and clover.

_____ Here's a Bunny Fingerplay _____

Teach the following fingerplay (see p. 22):
Here is a bunny with ears so funny
(Hold up index and middle fingers of left hand.)
And here is a hole in the ground
(Make circle with thumb and index finger of right hand.)
When a noise he hears, he pricks up his ears
(Wiggle fingers of left hand.)
And hops into his hole.
(Put fingers into hole made with right-hand fingers.)

_____ "Bunny Hop" _____

Children should be in a single file line as they dance or hop to "The Bunny Hop," found on the album *Preschool Aerobics Fun* (KIM 7052), by Georgiana Stewart (Kimbo Educational, Box 477, Long Branch, N.J. 07740).

CRAFT _____ Tube Bunny _____

Materials Needed:

>   one toilet tissue tube per child
>   pipe cleaners (whiskers)
>   paper (ears)
>   cotton balls (tail)

Explanation:
Children color or paint the tube white if desired. Coding dots or crayons can be used to make eyes. Then children glue on the ears, whiskers, and tail.

FREEPLAY _____ Activity 1 _____

Counting Cotton Balls—Write the numerals 0 through 9 on separate pieces of paper. The child chooses one piece of paper and counts out that many cotton balls (bunny tails).

_____ Activity 2 _____

Sound Eggs—Make a set of four pairs of sound eggs by filling L'eggs® containers half full with different objects. Tape the containers shut. The children try to identify the pairs by shaking and listening to the sounds they make. Examples of things to put in containers are sand, popcorn, paper clips, and pennies.

_____ Activity 3 _____

Rabbit Mural—On a sheet of mural paper, draw the outline of a rabbit and clouds. The children will fill in both by gluing on cotton balls. Have the children cut 3-inch-wide strips of green paper and fringe them. Glue these on the mural for the grass. Make flowers by gluing small cupcake papers onto the mural and adding leaves and stems. Shade in the sky with blue chalk.

CLOSING _____ Story _____

Read one of the following stories: *Little Rabbit's Loose Tooth,* by Lucy Bate (Scholastic, Inc., 1975). *Peter Rabbit,* by Beatrice Potter (Putman Pub. Group, 1981). *The Bunny Who Found Easter,* by Charlotte Zolotow (Houghton-Mifflin, 1959).

_____ Recording _____

Children sing along with or act out "Here Comes Peter Cottontail," found on the album *Peter Cottontail* (1947, Peter Pan Records, Newark, N.J. 07015).

Seed Day

PREPARATION ——————— To the Teacher ————————————

Spring means gardening. Gardening means seeds. Start collecting seed catalogs, as you will need several for Activity 1. A note asking each child to bring a package of seeds should be sent home prior to this day (see p. 22).

You will need:

- egg cartons and seeds for Arrival;
- seed catalogs for Activity 1;
- seed packages for Activity 2; and
- The Number Garden prepared for Activity 3.

ARRIVAL ———————— Sorting Seeds ————————————

All the children should have been asked to bring in different kinds of seeds today. As they arrive, have them sort their seeds into egg cartons.

OPENING ———————— Seed Talk ————————————

In the spring, people plant vegetable seeds and flower seeds in their gardens. After the rain falls and the sun shines, the seeds sprout. Soon, pretty flowers and yummy vegetables are growing.

We eat the seeds of some foods such as peas, peanuts, beans, cucumbers, and corn. Strawberries have seeds on the outside, and we eat those, too. We do not eat the seeds in apples, melons, oranges, or peaches. What else can you think of that has seeds?

———————————— Creative Expression ————————————

Play "All I Really Need" as children pretend to be a seed that is planted in the ground. You pretend to be the sun and the rain as your little plants sprout and grow to full bloom. As a large group, enjoy "Oats, Peas, Beans, and Barley Grow." Both of these songs are from the album *Baby Beluga* (SL 0010), by Raffi and Ken Whiteley (Shoreline Records, 6307 Yonge Street, Willowdale, Ontario, Canada M2M 3X7).

"Amazin' "*
Plant a teeny tiny seed
Early in the spring.
When summer comes
Just watch the way
That seed will do its thing!

Reprinted with permission from Phyllis Halloran from I'd like to hear a flower grow and other poems by Phyllis C. Halloran 1985.

© 1990 by The Center for Applied Research in Education

CRAFT _____ Seed Squares _____

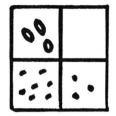

Materials Needed:

    sorted seeds from Arrival

    one square piece of cardboard per child

    two pieces of yarn per child

    glue

Explanation:
Children make lines to divide their cardboard into four equal sections, cover the lines with glue and lay the yarn over the glue. Now they can glue different kinds of seeds in each section.

FREEPLAY _____ Activity 1 _____

Plant Collage—Children cut pictures from seed catalogs to make a collage of things that grow from seeds.

_____ Activity 2 _____

Musical Chairs—Tape a seed package on the back of each chair. When the music stops say something such as, "People with carrot seeds on their chair stand up." Repeat, naming a different seed each time the music stops.

_____ Activity 3 _____

The Number Garden—Stick large adhesive dots on the sides of clay flower pots and fill the pots with sand. Make paper flowers on dowel rods, write a number in the center of each flower. Children are to choose a flower and place it in the pot which has the number of dots as the number on the flower. (This could be used as a bulletin board idea if the flower pots are made from paper.)

CLOSING _____ Story _____

Read one of the following stories: *Even That Moose Won't Listen to Me,* by Martha Alexandra (Dial Books for Young Readers, 1988). *The Tiny Seed,* by Eric Carle (Picture Book Studio, 1987). *A Garden For Miss Mouse,* by Michael Muntean (Parents Magazine Press, 1982).

Spring Day

PREPARATION _____ To the Teacher _____

Bring a bouquet of fresh flowers to your classroom because spring has sprung!
   You will need:

- matching colored bees and flowers (see p. 23) for Arrival;
- felt hats and animals (see pp. 23–24) for Opening;
- large cut-out flower for Activity 1;
- marigold seeds, soil, and egg cartons for Activity 2; and
- wallpaper flowers for Activity 3.

ARRIVAL _____ Flower Hunt _____

As the children arrive, tape a colored bee onto each child's shirt. Tell the children to pretend that they are bees looking for flowers (see p. 23). They must fly around the room until they find a hidden paper flower that is the same color as the bee that is taped on their shirt. When the matching colored flower is found, tape it onto the child's shirt, too.

OPENING _____ Spring Talk _____

Spring is a special time of year. It comes after winter. The days are warmer. It's sometimes rainy, sometimes windy, but the sun shines brightly, too. People are busy planting gardens and cleaning up their yards. Birds are building nests. The grass turns green, and flowers begin to bloom.

_____ Flannel Board Story _____

"Three Hats"—Make felt hats and animals to help you tell this story (see pp. 23–24).
   One nice spring day a bee, a butterfly, and a bunny were going for a walk. Along the way they found a hat.
   The bunny said, "It's mine because I'm the biggest." But the bee and the butterfly thought that was unfair. As the bunny placed the hat on his head, another hat fell out.
   The butterfly said to the bee, "It's mine because I am bigger than you." But the bee thought that was unfair.
   As the butterfly placed the hat on his head, another hat fell out, and the bee said, "It's mine because I'm big, too." And since his friends thought that was fair, they went happily on their way.

© 1990 by The Center for Applied Research in Education

CRAFT _____ Corncob Flower _____

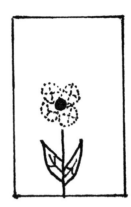

Materials Needed:

    corncobs sawed in half
    paint
    paper for circles
    scissors
    glue

Explanation:
Children cut out a small circle and glue it on a large piece of paper. Then they dip the end of the corncob in the paint and use it to make flower petals. They use crayons to make a stem and leaves.

FREEPLAY _____ Activity 1 _____

Mosaic Flowers—Cut out a large flower. The children can cut or tear colored shapes and glue them on the flower and leaves.

_____ Activity 2 _____

Planting Marigolds—Plant marigold seeds in egg cartons. Set them in the window so the children can watch them grow. They will need to be watered often since there is such a small amount of soil.

_____ Activity 3 _____

Sorting Flowers—Cut flowers from old wallpaper sample books. Children must sort them to find two flowers that are exactly the same.

CLOSING _____ Fingerplay _____

Teach the following poem (see p. 24):
Here is a beehive, where are the bees?   (Make a fist.)
Hiding away where nobody sees.
Watch them come creeping out of their hive   (Raise fingers one at a time as you count.)
1, 2, 3, 4, 5.

_____ Story _____

Read one of the following stories: *one bright Monday morning,* by Arline and Joseph Baum (Random House, 1962). *The Honeybee and the Robber,* by Eric Carle (Putman Pub. Group, 1986). *Bobby Bear in the Spring,* by Helmrath and Bartlett (Oddo Pub., 1986).

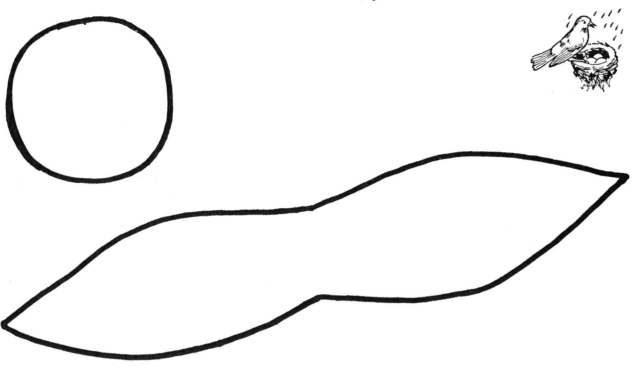

Rain Day—Arrival

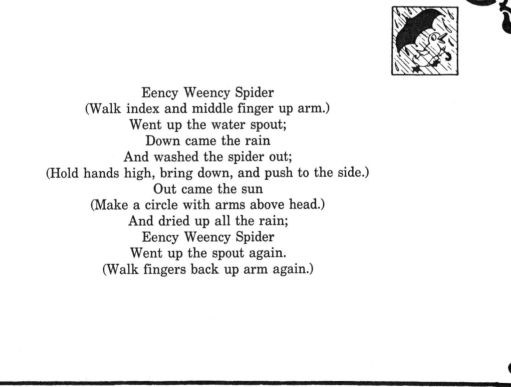

Eency Weency Spider
(Walk index and middle finger up arm.)
Went up the water spout;
Down came the rain
And washed the spider out;
(Hold hands high, bring down, and push to the side.)
Out came the sun
(Make a circle with arms above head.)
And dried up all the rain;
Eency Weency Spider
Went up the spout again.
(Walk fingers back up arm again.)

Here is a bunny with ears so funny
(Hold up index and middle fingers of left hand.)
And here is a hole in the ground
(Make circle with thumb and index finger of right hand.)
When a noise he hears, he pricks up his ears
(Wiggle fingers of left hand.)
And hops into his hole.
(Put fingers into hole made with right-hand fingers.)

Dear Parent(s),

We need your child to bring some seeds to class on _____.
                                                      (Date)
We will be sorting the seeds and using them for a craft project, so any kind will
be useful.

                                        Thanks!

Make three hats.

Spring Day—Closing

Dear Parent(s),

The children really had fun with the actions of this fingerplay!

Here is a beehive, where are the bees?
(Make a fist.)
Hiding away where nobody sees.

Watch them come creeping out of their hive
(Raise fingers one at a time as you count.)
1, 2, 3, 4, 5.

unit 2

ALL ABOUT ME

The five senses—sight, touch, taste, hearing, and smell—bring children information about the world around them. Children are born explorers. They do not need to be told to touch, taste, smell, look at, or listen to any given thing. Let them experience all the senses. . .within reason! That is how children learn best.

While using their senses, children should learn to distinguish between things that are the same and things that are different. (*Example:* Seeing colors and telling which are the same/different; feeling textures, etc.) In so doing, children will learn how things look, sound, taste, feel, and smell. Grass is green, lemon is sour, cows make a mooing sound, sandpaper is rough, and a rose smells sweet.

Our goal is to have each child become aware of the five senses and use them to learn more about the world.

The daily activity plans in Unit 2 include:

- Me, My Friends, and I Day
- Head and Neck Day
- Eye Day
- Ear Day
- Nose Day
- Hand and Finger Day
- Foot Day
- Mouth Day

Me, My Friends, and I Day

© 1990 by The Center for Applied Research in Education

PREPARATION _____ **To the Teacher** _____

You may want to ask a parent to come in and help with Activity 2, as you will need someone to wash and dry hands. Cookies for Arrival need to be made ahead of time.

You will need:

- cookies, frosting, and raisins for Arrival;
- yarn or string and 3″ × 5″ cards for Activity 1;
- mural paper and paint for Activity 2; and
- photocopied pictures (see p. 64) for Activity 3.

ARRIVAL _____ **Happy Face Cookies** _____

Give one round cookie to each child on arrival. The children frost the cookie with a thin layer of yellow icing and use raisins to make eyes and a big happy face. Enjoy at snack time.

_____ **Fingerplay** _____

Teach the following poem:

Cookies to share, 1, 2, 3.	(Hold up fingers.)
One for you, two for me.	(Point.)
Oh, no, no! That won't do!	(Shake head.)
Let's break the extra one in two!	

OPENING _____ **My Friend and I Talk** _____

Begin Opening by making a paper chain of children (see p. 42). This is done by using a piece of paper 8″ by 4″ and accordion folding. Draw a picture of a boy or girl on the folded paper, with hands and feet reaching to the folded edges. Cut out the figure except at the end of the feet and hand. When you open the folded paper, you will have a line of children holding hands.

Explain that this is like our class—we are each individual people, but all together we are friends! A friend is someone to have fun with, to play with, to laugh with, to sing with, and to share with. A friend is a buddy, a pal—a friend! Who are your friends? What special things do you like to do with your friends? What things do you like to do by yourself?

_____ **Record** _____

The children will be touching parts of their own body as well as the fingers of a friend as they respond to instructions on the song "Touch" from the album _Getting to Know Myself_ (AR543), by Hap and Martha Palmer (Educational Activities, Inc., Box 392, Freeport, N.Y. 11520).

CRAFT _____ Happy Face _____

Materials Needed:

    paper, circle patterns
    crayons, scissors
    yarn

Explanation:
Provide the children with circle patterns to trace and cut out. They can then use their crayons to make the eyes, nose, and mouth. Glue small pieces of yarn to make the hair.

FREEPLAY _____ Activity 1 _____

Comparing Heights—Using yarn or string, measure each child's height. After the string is cut to the correct height, the child tapes one end to a three-by-five card that has his or her name and "This is how tall I am" written on it. Children can compare their height to that of their friends.

_____ Activity 2 _____

Handprint Rainbow—On a sheet of mural paper, have the children create a beautiful rainbow. Use the colors in the rainbow starting with red, then orange, yellow, green, blue, and purple. Begin by printing the first pair of red handprints at the top center of the paper. Work your way down and to the right until half the arch is made. Go back up to the top and finish the arch to the left side. Repeat this with each successive color. Since each arch will become smaller, not every child will make his or her handprints in every color.

    To make clean-up easy, use an old magazine for the paint. Open the magazine and put a small amount of tempera on both pages. Roll the paint with a brayer (roller) until it is smooth. The child puts one hand on each page simultaneously and then onto the mural. (Ask the child which is the left/right hand.) When the magazine can no longer be used, throw it away and start with another one.

_____ Activity 3 _____

Friend Concentration—You will need two photocopied pictures (see p. 64) of each child. Mount each on a three-by-five card. Use the cards as you would for any concentration game. Place all cards face down on the table or floor. One child turns two cards over. If they both have the same picture on them, the child keeps the pair and takes another turn. If they do not match, he or she turns them over again, and play passes to the next child. Continue until all pairs have been matched. This is a good way for the children to get to know the names of their friends at school.

CLOSING _____ Story _____

Read one of the following stories: *Best Friends,* by Myra Berry Brown (Golden Gate, 1975). *Dandelion,* by Don Freeman (Penguin Publishing Co., 1977). *The Three Friends,* by Robert Kraus (Dutton, 1975).

Head and Neck Day

PREPARATION —————— To the Teacher ——————————————

The clown bulletin board begins with a clown suit today. Each consecutive day you will be adding a body part to the clown. A giraffe cookie cutter is necessary for the cookies in Arrival.
   You will need:

- giraffe cookies, peanut butter, and Cherrios® for Arrival;
- shoebox giraffe for Opening;
- clown suit, head, and neck for bulletin board for Opening; and
- die prepared for Activity 1.

ARRIVAL ——————————— Cookie Decorating ——————————————

Using a giraffe cookie cutter, prepare cookies prior to class (see p. 44). As the children arrive, have them frost a cookie with peanut butter. Decorate with Cheerios® and serve for snack time.

3/4 cup oleo
1/2 cup brown sugar
1 tsp. vanilla
1/2 tsp. soda
1 1/2 cups rolled oats
(quick or old-fashioned)
1/2 cup sugar
1 egg
1 2/3 cups flour
dash salt

Beat oleo until creamy; gradually beat in sugars. Add egg and vanilla to creamed mixture and mix well. Add flour and soda. Stir in oats. Chill several hours or overnight. Roll out to 1/8″ thickness using powdered sugar. Place cut cookies on ungreased cookie sheet. Bake at 350 degrees for five to eight minutes or until brown.

OPENING ——————————— Recording ——————————————

Play the song "Joshua Giraffe" from the album *Baby Beluga* (SL 0010), by Raffi with Ken Whiteley (Shoreline Records, 6307 Yonge Street, Willowdale, Ontario, Canada M2M 3X7).

——————————————— Bulletin Board ——————————————

Begin the bulletin board, which will eventually be a big clown. Each day, add a body part to the clown suit that you have already put up. On this day, add the head and neck.

——————————————— Head and Neck Talk ——————————————

Discuss with the children the actions of the head and neck, such as turning, nodding, etc. For this discussion, make a shoebox giraffe.*
Materials Needed:

shoebox
yellow and brown paint

paper
paper towel tube

Reprinted with permission from Puppetry In Early Childhood Education *by Tamara Hunt and Nancy Renfro (Nancy Renfro Studio, 1982).*

Explanation:
Draw the face of a giraffe on stiff paper and cut it out. Paint the box, tube, and face yellow. Paint brown spots on the box and tube. Set the shoebox on end and cut a round hole in the end just big enough for the tube to fit in and slide up and down. Place the tube in the hole with the face glued to the front, and you have a giraffe with a manipulable neck. You can make the neck long or short, make it turn, etc.

CRAFT _____ Shape Giraffe _____

Materials Needed:

> drawing of a giraffe for each child (see p. 43)
> scissors, glue, crayons
> small shape patterns
> brown paper

Explanation:
Each child colors a picture of a giraffe, then traces and cuts out several brown shapes and glues them to the giraffe.

FREEPLAY _____ Activity 1 _____

Picture Die—Make a square block from a small milk carton. Glue a picture of something that can be worn on your head or neck on each side. (*Examples:* necklace, necktie, ear muffs, baseball cap) Cover with clear self-sticking vinyl. Have a child roll the block like a die and identify the picture that comes up on top. Who would wear it? Is there a special time or condition for which it would be worn?

_____ Activity 2 _____

Missing Feature—Draw a person's head, neck, and face on a chalkboard. Ask the children to close their eyes while you erase one feature. Have them tell you what is missing and the function of that body part.

_____ Activity 3 _____

Simon Says—Play Simon Says using only things you can do with your head or neck. (*Examples:* nod yes or no, turn left or right, put your head on your knee)

CLOSING _____ Story _____

Read one of the following stories: *Mop Top,* by Don Freeman (Puffin Books, 1978). *Who Took the Farmer's Hat?*, by Joan Nodset (Harper & Row, 1963). *I Know a Giraffe,* by David Omar White (Alfred A. Knopf, 1965).

Eye Day

PREPARATION _____ To the Teacher _____

Check over the plans for this day, and if you do not have enough adults in your program to conduct all three of the Freeplay activities, you can switch the Arrival with Activity 3.
You will need:

- magnifying glasses and objects for Arrival;
- clown eyes for the bulletin board for Opening;
- several familiar objects for Activity 1;
- pictures for Activity 2; and
- milk, liquid detergent, food coloring, and 8″ round cake pan for Activity 3.

ARRIVAL _____ Science Table _____

Set up a table with magnifying glasses and several small objects for the children to examine. Include a potato with eyes. Make up a riddle—"What has eyes but cannot see?" Don't forget, a needle has an eye, too.

OPENING _____ Eye Talk _____

When you wake up in the morning, you can run to a window and see what kind of day it is—cloudy, rainy, or sunny. What helps you to see? Your eyes do! Your eyes see a picture and send a message to your brain, and then you are able to see. What else can you do with your eyes? (blink, wink, shut them, open them, look up, look down, rub them)
With your eyes, show me you are angry, sad, surprised, tired.
Some people have to wear glasses or contact lenses because their eyes do not see clearly.
Categorize children according to their eye color.

_____ Music _____

Make up a song about eyes. To the tune of "Here We Go 'Round the Mulberry Bush," sing:

This is the way I blink my eyes,
blink my eyes,
blink my eyes.
This is the way I blink my eyes,
early in the morning.

Continue with wink my eyes, shut my eyes, open my eyes, etc.

_____ Bulletin Board _____

Add two eyes to the clown today.

© 1990 by The Center for Applied Research in Education

CRAFT ——————— Color My World ———————

Materials Needed:

    glue, scissors   colored cellophane
    brads   lens pattern (see p. 44)

Explanation:
Have the children cut three lenses using the pattern you made. Cut a small circle out of the large end of each lens. Glue a different colored piece of cellophane over each circular opening. Punch a hole and brad the three together. Look at the world through different colors!

FREEPLAY ——————— Activity 1 ———————

What's Missing Tray—Arrange several familiar objects on a small tray and ask the children to look carefully at each object. Then ask them to close their eyes while you remove one object. When they open their eyes, ask them to guess which object you took off the tray.

——————— Activity 2 ———————

Matching Pictures—Show the children three pictures that look similar. Ask them to find the two that match.

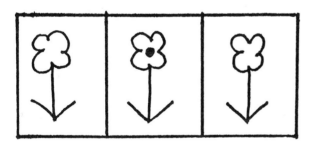 

——————— Activity 3 ———————

Marvelous, Moving Colors—Pour milk into an 8″ round pan so it is half full. Squeeze a few drops of food coloring (different colors) on top of the milk. Carefully add a drop of liquid detergent so it runs down the side of the pan. Almost instantly, the colors will move away and blend. Repeat on the opposite side of the pan. The colors will change again right before your eyes!

CLOSING ——————— Story ———————

Read one of the following stories: *Arthur's Eyes,* by Marc Brown (Little, Brown & Co., 1979). *Lucky Glasses,* by Jane Carruth (Modern Promotions/Publishers, 1982). *Goggles,* by Ezra Jack Keats (Macmillan, 1969).

Ear Day

PREPARATION _____ **To the Teacher** _____

Start the day by whispering, "Good morning." _Everyone_ has to be a good listener today.
   You will need:

- objects for listening game for Arrival;
- clown ears for the bulletin board for Opening;
- tape recording of sounds for Activity 1;
- clock for Activity 2; and
- mural paper and old magazines for Activity 3.

ARRIVAL _____ **Listen and Do** _____

Put an assortment of objects on a table (book, paper, marker, crayon, etc.). Give specific directions regarding the different objects. The children must follow the exact directions they hear. (_Example:_ Put the eraser _under_ the table.)

OPENING _____ **Ear Talk** _____

We are able to hear different sounds with our ears. We learn to know what different sounds mean because our ears and our brains work together.
   Sounds are made by movements called sound waves. When sound waves enter your ear, they hit the eardrum. Then you can hear.
   Think of sounds that make you feel happy, sad, angry, or excited. Some things are so quiet we cannot hear them. . .snowflakes falling, eyes blinking, or butterflies flying. These are things we can see, but cannot hear.
   Brainstorm: Ask the children to describe sounds that are "as soft as _____ ," "as loud as _____ ," and "as noisy as _____ ."

_____ **Following Directions** _____

Play "Listen and Move" from the album _We All Live Together,_ volume 2 (YR-002R), by Greg Scelsa and Steve Millang (Youngheart Records, Box 27784, Los Angeles, Calif. 90027).

_____ **Bulletin Board** _____

Place ears on the clown.

_____ **Fingerplay** _____

Teach the following rhyme.

This is my eye.
This is my ear.
This is to see.
This is to hear.

© 1990 by The Center for Applied Research in Education

CRAFT _____ Rabbit Shaker _____

Materials Needed:

    precut rabbit ears   glue, crayons, stapler

    small, white paper plates   beans

Explanation:
Children color ears and draw eyes, nose, mouth, and whiskers on the bottom of one paper plate. Glue the ears on behind the face. Put several dried beans on top of the plate, and staple two plates together. Listen to the sounds the rabbit can make!

FREEPLAY _____ Activity 1 _____

Identifying Sounds—Make a tape recording of different sounds, such as brushing teeth, using the trash compactor, running water, ringing the doorbell, starting the car, etc. Play the tape for the children and ask them to identify the sounds. Older children can draw a picture of each sound they hear.

_____ Activity 2 _____

Find the Clock—Hide a loud ticking clock and have the children take turns finding it.

_____ Activity 3 _____

Sound Mural—Divide a sheet of mural paper into several sections. Each section will illustrate one type of sound we hear. (*Examples:* music, animals, cooking, vehicles) Cut pictures out of magazines that show the different sounds.

CLOSING _____ Whisper Game _____

When everyone is sitting quietly in a circle, whisper a brief sentence in one child's ear. Each child whispers what he or she heard to the next person. What did the last person hear? Hopefully it was the same sentence as the first child heard!

_____ Story _____

Read one of the following stories: *The Runaway Bunny,* by Margaret W. Brown (Harper & Row, 1972). *Little Frog Learns to Sing,* by Lucille LeBlanc (Oddo Publishers, 1967). *Geraldine, the Music Mouse,* by Leo Lionni (Pantheon, 1979).

Nose Day

PREPARATION _____ To the Teacher _____

If your cooking facilities are not within smelling distance of your classroom, bring a toaster oven to bake the pizzas. The children need to *smell* the aroma!
   You will need:

- ingredients for pizza for Arrival;
- coding dots for Opening;
- shiny nose for the clown bulletin board for Opening;
- smelling tray for Activity 1;
- large plywood clown and beanbags for Activity 2; and
- powdered gelatin, drink mixes, salt shakers, cards, and glue for Activity 3.

ARRIVAL _____ Pizza Party _____

Have each child make an individual pizza. Spread pizza sauce on top of an English muffin half. Have on hand several spices such as oregano, basil, Italian seasoning, and garlic powder that the children can smell. They can choose which spices they want on their pizzas. Make sure the children smell the pizzas as they bake.

OPENING _____ Nose Talk _____

We smell with our noses. You can smell different things because your nose sends a message to your brain that tells you how some things smell. Some things smell good to you, and some do not. Something that *you* think smells good may not smell good to your friend. Can you think of different kinds of smells? (sweet, new, fishy, clean, delicious) There are indoor smells, and there are outdoor smells. What is one thing we can smell only outdoors or only indoors? There are all kinds of food smells. What is your favorite?

_____ Bulletin Board _____

Add a big, shiny nose to the clown today. Have the children choose their favorite colors of coding dots and stick them on their noses—instant clowns!

_____ Record _____

Do the action song "Simon Says" from the album *We All Live Together,* volume 3 (YMES-0003), by Greg Scelsa and Steve Millang (Youngheart Records, Box 27784, Los Angeles, Calif. 90027).

© 1990 by The Center for Applied Research in Education

CRAFT _____ Scented Flowers _____

Materials Needed:

> cupcake liners
> paper, crayons
> cotton balls
> perfume, glue

Explanation:
Children paste a cupcake liner on a sheet of paper. Next they draw a stem and leaves and glue a cotton ball that has been sprayed with perfume to the center of the flower. Smell!

FREEPLAY _____ Activity 1 _____

Smelling Tray—Prepare a smelling tray using film cases. Peanut butter, orange slices, liquid smoke, and vinegar or perfume on a cotton ball are some examples of smells you might put in the cases. Poke a hole in the lid of the case and leave on the lid. The children try to guess what they are smelling. Prepare two containers of each smell and have the children find the matching smells.

_____ Activity 2 _____

Beanbag Toss—Cut a clown out of a piece of thin plywood. Paint the clown bright colors, and cut a hole where the nose should be. Throw beanbags through the hole.

_____ Activity 3 _____

Smelly Cards—Children make their own smelly cards. Put different flavors of gelatin and powdered drink mixes in salt shakers. Children brush a small amount of glue in the center of a three-by-five card and sprinkle the powder on the glue. They can smell the difference between strawberry, raspberry, orange, etc. What makes each card smell different? Which smell do they like best?

CLOSING _____ Story _____

Read one of the following stories: *Arthur's Nose,* by Marc Brown (Little, Brown & Co., 1976). *Boris Bad Enough,* by Robert Kraus (Harper & Row, 1978). *The Nose Book,* by Al Perkins (Random House, 1970). *Whose Nose Is This?,* by Dr. Richard van Gelder (Walke & Co., 1974).

Hand and Finger Day

PREPARATION _____ To the Teacher _____

The rule today is *TOUCH*! The children will learn what the word *texture* means by doing just that. There are a lot of different items needed for this day.

You will need:

- plastic tubs and items of different textures for Arrival;
- two big hands for bulletin board for Opening;
- paper and scissors for Activity 1;
- feely box prepared for Activity 2; and
- sandpaper and textured materials for Activity 3.

ARRIVAL _____ Texture Tubs _____

Fill several plastic tubs with different textured items. (*Examples:* rice, cornmeal, macaroni, bark, cotton, velvet, shaving cream) As the children move from tub to tub, ask them to tell you how each item feels. Do any of them feel the same? Why are you able to feel the different textures?

OPENING _____ Hand and Finger Talk _____

You can see the size, shape, and color of a teddy bear. But do you know what the teddy bear feels like by looking at it? No! If you touch it with your hands and fingers, you will feel the texture. The texture tells you how something feels—soft, hard, sticky, rough, etc. Can you think of things that feel hot or cold? How else can things feel? There is something very special about your fingers. It's your fingerprints. No one else in the world has the same fingerprints as you. They are your very own!

_____ Record _____

"Count My Fingers" on the album *Songs About Me* (KIM 70223), by William C. Janiak (Kimbo Educational, Box 477, Long Branch, N.J. 07740) is a wonderful song to sing with young children.

_____ Bulletin Board _____

Add two big hands to the clown today.

_____ Story _____

Read to the children *Where Is Willy the Worm?*, by Demi (Random House, Follow-Me-Books, 1981). Have the children use their fingers as a worm and make it crawl along their arm as you tell the story.

CRAFT _____ Fingerprint Worms _____

Materials Needed:

    paper, crayons
    fingerpaint

Explanation:
Give each child a piece of paper and have him or her draw
several squiggly lines on it to represent worms. Have the
children dip their fingers in paint and press their fingerprints on the lines to complete the worms.

FREEPLAY _____ Activity 1 _____

Paper Cutting—Tape on the wall the top of a piece of paper (18″ by 3′) with vertical lines drawn
on it. The lines should be straight at first and then wavy or curvy. Children practice cutting
on the lines from the bottom of the paper to the top. Cutting this way doesn't allow them to
turn their hands. They keep their hands straight with their thumbs on top of the scissors.

_____ Activity 2 _____

Feely Box—Cut a hole just big enough for a child's hand to fit through in the top of a large shoebox.
Place several items in the box and see how many the children can identify. Or, put one item
at a time in the box, and ask the children to feel it and try to guess what it is. Ask them to
describe the texture.

_____ Activity 3 _____

Texture Art—Cut several different lengths and colors of
yarn, ribbon, ricrac, and Velcro®. Cut felt, corduroy, and
velvet into different shapes. Give the children 8 1/2″ by 11″
sheets of medium grade sandpaper. They are to create a picture by gluing the materials provided on the sandpaper.
They will be able to feel their picture.

CLOSING _____ Story _____

Read one of the following stories: _My Hands Can,_ by Jean Holzenthaler (E. P. Dutton, 1978).
Inch by Inch, by Leo Lionni (Scholastic, Inc., 1960). _Hand, Hand, Fingers, Thumb,_ by Al Perkins
(Random House, 1969).

Foot Day

PREPARATION _____ To the Teacher _____

Collect every imaginable pair of footwear you can find! Tell each child to wear his or her favorite shoes, and you wear yours, too!
    You will need:

- paper footprints, foot cookie cutter, and cheese slices for Arrival;
- examples of footwear for Opening;
- clown feet for bulletin board for Opening;
- a bed sheet and familiar objects for Activity 1; and
- shoes and shoe outlines for Activity 3.

ARRIVAL _____ Follow the Footprints _____

Lay out paper footprints on the floor for the children to follow to a table as they arrive. Have a foot cookie cutter and thin slices of cheese on the table so each child may cut footprints to eat at snack time.

OPENING _____ Foot Talk _____

We use our feet to move from one place to another. We put different footwear on depending on the weather and what we are doing.
    Have several pairs of footwear displayed and ask children who might wear them, where, when, and why. (*Examples:* snow boots, ski boots, roller skates, nurse's shoes, ballet slippers, tap shoes, cowboy boots)
    We can move our feet and toes in different ways. Ask the children to use their feet to stomp loudly, softly, wiggle your toes, walk, run, hop, gallop, jump, skip, etc.

_____ Footplay _____

Teach the following fingerplay:

> Feet can walk.
> Feet can run.
> Feet can jump.
> Feet have such fun!

_____ Records _____

"Turn Around" from the album *Getting to Know Myself* (AR 543), by Hap Palmer (Educational Activities, Inc., Box 392, Freeport, N.Y. 11520) and "Boogie Walk" from the album *We All Live Together,* volume 2 (YR-002R), by Greg Scelsa and Steve Millang (Youngheart Records, Box 27784, Los Angeles, Calif. 90027) are great songs for following directions as well as for using the feet.

_____ Bulletin Board _____

Add big, floppy feet to the clown today.

CRAFT _____ Dirty Feet _____

Materials Needed:

> foot cookie cutter
> potato
> brown tempera paint
> paper

Explanation:
Use the foot cookie cutter to make a potato print. Dip the potato in brown paint and make dirty footprints across a large sheet of paper. Ideate: What would your mom or dad say if you made tracks across the kitchen floor? Who has been walking across your paper? Where has he or she been?

FREEPLAY _____ Activity 1 _____

Feeling with the Feet—Lay several familiar objects on the floor. Cover them with a sheet. Have children take off one shoe and sock. Using their bare feet, children try to identify the objects. Is it easier or harder than using fingers?

_____ Activity 2 _____

Finding Shoes—Have children take off one shoe. Put all the shoes into the middle of a circle. When you say "Go," all children find their shoe; _or,_ when you describe a shoe to a child, he or she finds it in the pile.

_____ Activity 3 _____

Matching Shoes with Outlines—On heavy paper, trace around several pairs of different sized shoes. Have children match the correct sized shoes to each outline. Be sure the left shoe is on the left outline, and vice versa. Line up the shoes from smallest to largest.

CLOSING _____ Story _____

Read one of the following stories: _The Foot Book,_ by Dr. Seuss (Random House, 1968). _Dirty Feet,_ by Steven Kroll (Parents Magazine Press, 1981). _Shoes,_ by Elizabeth Winthrop (Harper & Row, 1986).

Mouth Day

© 1990 by The Center for Applied Research in Education

PREPARATION _____ **To the Teacher** _____

This is a day to taste lots of different foods and to learn about healthy eating habits. *Eating the Alphabet,* by Lois Elhert (Harcourt Brace Jovanovich, 1989) would be a good book to share with the children in Opening.

You will need:

- food to make a clown snack for Arrival;
- clown's smile for bulletin board for Opening;
- food for a tasting party for Activity 1;
- food wrappers and containers for Activity 2; and
- examples for all five senses for Activity 3.

ARRIVAL _____ **Create a Clown** _____

As the children arrive, they create a tasty clown for snack time. They will frost a large round cracker with peanut butter. Use two small marshmallows for eyes, a thin carrot slice for the nose, raisins for the mouth, and two small pretzels for ears.

OPENING _____ **Mouth Talk** _____

You know what foods you like to eat or don't like to eat because you can taste. The tip, sides, and back of your tongue are covered with bumps called taste buds. Your taste buds tell your brain how different foods taste. What foods taste good to you? Your teeth are in your mouth, too. They help you chew your food. What should you do to keep your teeth clean?

Briefly discuss the four basic food groups and what is included in each. They are: (1) milk and milk products, (2) cereals and grains or breads, (3) meat, fish, and poultry, (4) fruits and vegetables. Why is it important to eat healthy foods? What are some foods you like to eat that aren't in any of these groups? It's all right to eat sweets sometimes, but not too often.

_____ **Fingerplay** _____

Teach the following rhyme:

> Point to each facial feature as it is mentioned.
> Two little eyes to look around,
> Two little ears to hear each sound.
> One little nose to smell what's sweet,
> One little mouth that likes to eat.

_____ **Bulletin Board** _____

Add a big smile to complete the clown

CRAFT _____ My Healthy Meal _____

Materials Needed:

>   large paper plates
>   glue, scissors
>   old magazines

Explanation:
Children create a healthy meal by cutting pictures of foods
out of magazines and gluing them onto the paper plates.
Be sure to review the four food groups discussed in Opening as a reminder of what makes a healthy meal.

FREEPLAY _____ Activity 1 _____

Health Food Tasting—Have small samples of different kinds of food for the children to taste.
(*Examples:* raw coconut, avocado, rice cakes, kiwi, cucumber, broccoli, pea pods, cheeses) Encourage the children to tell you how each food tastes. Make a list of adjectives the children have
used to describe the foods. When each child decides what his or her favorite is, make a graph
to see which food is rated the best tasting.

_____ Activity 2 _____

Food Groups—Glue pictures of the basic food groups on four separate cardboard boxes. Display
wrappers and containers of foods that belong to each group. Have the children sort the empty
containers and wrappers into the appropriate boxes.

_____ Activity 3 _____

Five Senses Olympics—Set up five stations around the room to review the senses. Remove body
parts of the clown from the bulletin board and place them at the appropriate stations. Each station should provide an opportunity to use one of the five senses. The following are some
suggestions:

(1) Taste—This activity and Activity 1 can overlap. Use Activity 1 as your tasting station.

(2) Feel—Bring in the different textured items from Hand and Finger Day on page 36. The children
    can categorize these items as rough or smooth.

(3) Smell—Provide several scratch and sniff books.

(4) Sight—Seeing is very important when working on puzzles, so provide a few puzzles for the
    children to put together.

(5) Hear—Use or make the Sound Eggs from Bunny Day on page 13. The children are to find
    the two that sound alike.

CLOSING _____ Story _____

Read one of the following stories: *The Very Hungry Caterpillar,* by Eric Carle (Putman Publishing
Group, 1981). *Jam and Bread for Frances,* by Russell Hoban (Harper & Row, 1964). *Gregory,
the Terrible Eater,* by Mitchell Sharmat (Four Winds Press, 1980).

pattern
for paper chain
of children

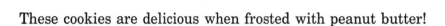

These cookies are delicious when frosted with peanut butter!

3/4 cup oleo
1/2 cup brown sugar
1 tsp. vanilla
1/2 tsp. soda
1 1/2 cups rolled oats
(quick or old-fashioned)
1/2 cup sugar
1 egg
1 2/3 cups flour
salt

Beat oleo until creamy; gradually beat in sugars. Add egg and vanilla to creamed mixture and mix well. Add flour and soda; stir in oats. Chill several hours or over-night. Roll out to 1/8″ thickness using powdered sugar. Place cut cookies on ungreased cookie sheet. Bake in 350-degree oven 5–8 minutes or until brown.

EYE DAY—CRAFT

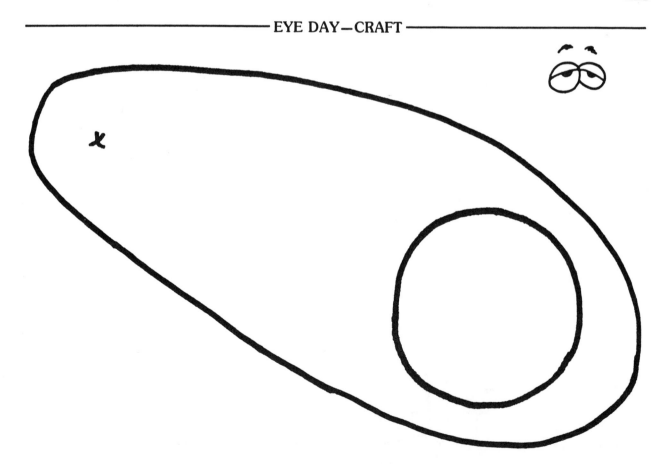

unit 3

FALL FANTASY

Fall is here. Days are getting shorter. The weather is cooler. Leaves are turning color and falling off the trees. Animals are busily getting ready for winter. These changes can be seen and felt on a nature walk.

Halloween will arrive soon, too! Thoughts of ghosts and witches fill the air. These thoughts can be a little unsettling for a young child. Take this opportunity to show the children it's all fun—nothing to fear.

The daily activity plans in Unit 3 include:

- Three Billy Goats Gruff Day
- Tree Day
- Ladybug Day
- Scarecrow Day
- Monster Day
- Pumpkin Day
- Witch Day
- Ghost Day

Three Billy Goats Gruff Day

PREPARATION _____ To the Teacher _____

This day is planned as a field trip. You and the children can walk to a nearby park or go outside to your play area at school. One of the activities planned for this day is to act out the story *The Three Billy Goats Gruff.* If the park or play area does not have anything you can use for a bridge, you will need to take along some boxes to build a bridge.

When you arrive at the park or play area, divide the children into three groups. You will have prepared a yarn necklace with a picture of a billy goat on it for each child. Group 1 will have white goats. Group 2 will have brown goats, and Group 3 will have gray goats. For durability, these pictures should be laminated or have gummed reinforcements on the back.

The children will do the three activities planned with their group and will move on to the next activity only when their entire group is ready to do so.

You will need:

- goat necklaces for each child (see p. 63);
- field trip permission slips (see p. 62);
- boxes to build a bridge if there is none for Activity 1;
- apples and Peanut Butter Spread for Activity 2 (see p. 64);
- yardstick for Activity 3; and
- nature items for Closing.

ARRIVAL _____ Recording _____

Collect field trip permission slips (see p. 62).

Use a balance beam or masking tape to make a bridge on the floor to use with the song "Crossing the Bridge" on the album *We All Live Together,* volume 4 (YMES-0004), by Greg Scelsa and Steve Mellang (Youngheart Records, Box 27784, Los Angeles, Calif. 90027).

OPENING _____ Story _____

Read to the children *The Three Billy Goats Gruff,* by Nova Nestrick (Platt & Munk, 1962).

CRAFT _____ Feely Boards* _____

Materials Needed:

    one cardboard square per child

    glue

Explanation:
Children should be instructed to look around the park for nature items:

something fuzzy	something smooth
something rough	something soft
something that floats	They can glue these objects on their feely boards.

© 1990 by The Center for Applied Research in Education

FREEPLAY _____ **Activity 1** _____

Acting Out the Story—Act out the story of *The Three Billy Goats Gruff,* using an existing bridge or one you've made.

_____ **Activity 2** _____

Peanut Butter Spread Snack—The children can help prepare a snack at the park or play area, such as apple wedges and Peanut Butter Spread.

Peanut Butter Spread

1 1/4 cup peanut butter

2/3 cup oatmeal

1/2 cup honey

1/2 cup mini chocolate chips

Variation: 1/2 cup raisins

Combine all ingredients. Mix well. Store in refrigerator. This makes about 1 1/2 cups and is delicious on apples, pears, and celery.

_____ **Activity 3** _____

Measuring Shadows—While at the park or play area, teach the children to measure by comparing the lengths of sticks, leaves, and shadows. Which one is longer? Which one is shorter? Push sticks of different lengths into the ground so that they stand up straight. Measure the lengths of the shadows. Measure again thirty minutes later. Have the lengths changed? Measure again a little while later if time allows. Place a marker on the ground each time the lengths of the shadows are checked so the children can see the changes.

CLOSING _____ **Categorizing Natural Objects** _____

Have three sizes of leaves, nuts, pine cones, rocks, and so forth available. Let the children arrange them from smallest to largest. They can also be arranged according to colors and textures.

_____ **Listening to Sounds in Nature** _____

Ask the children to think about sounds that they heard at the park or play area today. Identify sounds that were noisy (car horns), peaceful (birds chirping), happy (children laughing), frightening (troll stomping), and sounds that are heard only outside (motorcycles).

Tree Day

PREPARATION _____ To the Teacher _____

Trees are an important part of our world. You will be painting a fall tree, making a friendship tree, and constructing a tree beside Scarecrow's Garden—a bulletin board that the children will contribute to each day of this unit.

You will need:

- photocopied picture of each child (see p. 64) and friendship tree for Arrival;
- pressed leaves for Arrival and Activity 1;
- objects made of wood, glass, plastic, and cloth for Activity 2; and
- rectangle patterns and paper for Activity 3.

ARRIVAL _____ Friendship Tree _____

In a note to each child's parents, you will have asked each child to bring a picture of himself or herself and will have had it photocopied (see p. 64). You will also have collected leaves and pressed them. Place a branch in a coffee can filled with sand. As the children arrive, they find their photocopied picture and tape it to a leaf. Then they attach it to a branch on the friendship tree.

OPENING _____ Tree Talk _____

If possible, have your discussion under a tree. Identify the different parts of a tree: bark, branches, leaves, trunk, sap, and roots. Which parts are rough? Which are smooth? What do trees do for us? They (1) give us shade, (2) provide a home for the birds, (3) give us fruit to eat, (4) provide a place to hang a swing or build a tree house, (5) give us leaves to play in, and (6) can be made into lumber, paper, etc.

_____ Creative Movement _____

Have the children pretend to be trees, swaying in the wind. Talk them through different situations, such as a hot, sunny day, a tornado, and a snowstorm. Would they rather be a tree than a child? What are the advantages or disadvantages of being a tree? Use the song "Round in a Circle" on the album *We All Live Together,* volume 1, (YMES-0001), by Greg Scelsa, and Steve Millang (Youngheart Records, Box 27784, Los Angeles, Calif. 90027).

© 1990 by The Center for Applied Research in Education

CRAFT _____ Reverse Stencil of Tree _____

Materials Needed:

> brown paper
> several cut-out shapes of trees (see p. 65)
> orange, yellow, and red tempera paints
> sponges cut in small pieces

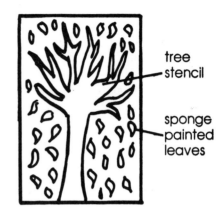

tree stencil

sponge painted leaves

Explanation:
Lay one of the tree cutouts on each child's brown paper. Have the children use the sponges to sponge paint colored leaves on the tree, falling, and on the ground. Tell children to cover the whole paper with leaves. When they have finished, lift off the tree cutout. A brown tree will be there with many colored leaves.

FREEPLAY _____ Activity 1 _____

Leaf Person—Children glue a leaf in the center of a piece of paper to be the body of a person. With crayons they can draw a head and add arms and legs.

_____ Activity 2 _____

Categorizing—Place objects made of wood, glass, plastic, and cloth on a table. The children will group them according to what they are made of. Suggestions for objects are: a wooden spoon, pencil, drinking glass, jar, toothbrush, shower cap, sock, and a handkerchief.

_____ Activity 3 _____

Scarecrow's Garden Bulletin Board—This month the children will add things to a bulletin board called Scarecrow's Garden. Today, have them trace and cut out brown rectangles. Use these rectangles to make the branches and trunks of several trees to be placed at the edge of the garden. Later in the month, they will add ladybugs, scarecrows, and pumpkins. At the end of the month, witches and ghosts will invade the garden.

CLOSING _____ Story _____

Read one of the following stories: *A Tree is Nice,* by Janice May Udry (Harper & Row, 1956). *The Giving Tree,* by Shel Silverstein (Harper & Row, 1964). *A Tree with a Thousand Uses,* by Aileen Fisher (Bowmar, 1977).

Ladybug Day

© 1990 by The Center for Applied Research in Education

PREPARATION _____ To the Teacher _____

All children like ladybugs and will enjoy learning more about them. The facts you teach in Opening are to be reinforced by the game Ladybug Spots in Activity 2. Make a special effort to get the book *The Grouchy Ladybug* by Eric Carle because several of the activities refer to that book.
   You will need:

- notes to parents requesting that children bring in flat rocks for Arrival (see p. 66);
- Ladybug Race prepared for Activity 1;
- magazines or the game Ladybug Spots prepared for Activity 2 (see p. 67); and
- corks, red paint, and black markers for Activity 3.

ARRIVAL _____ Painted Rocks _____

In advance, each child should have been asked to bring a small, flat, oval rock (see p. 66). As children arrive, they can put on a smock and paint their entire rock with red tempera paint.

OPENING _____ Ladybug Talk _____

Ladybugs are insects that are helpful to farmers and gardeners because they eat aphids, which are insects that eat healthy plants. Ladybugs are orangey red with black spots. They are very tiny. Never, never hurt a ladybug. Let it fly away, and it will bring you good luck.

_____ Story _____

Read to the children *The Grouchy Ladybug,* by Eric Carle (Harper & Row, 1986). If you cannot find this book, you may want to change Activity 2 and the closing for this day. Two other books that you can use are: *Ladybug and Dog and the Night Walk,* by Polly Berrien Berends (Random House, 1980), and *Lady Bug,* by Carl Kock (Harper & Row, 1986).

CRAFT _____ Ladybug Paperweight _____

Materials Needed:

   Q-tips®
   black and red tempera paint
   oval rocks painted in Arrival

Explanation:
Children use the Q-tips® to paint black spots on the rock they painted in Arrival.

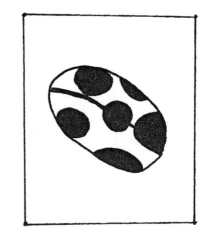

FREEPLAY _____ **Activity 1** _____

Ladybug Race*—Place a marble inside a walnut shell painted to resemble a ladybug. Hold two ladybugs on the raised end of an inclined board. Release. The marbles will roll, moving ladybugs down the board.

_____ **Activity 2** _____

Class Book—Have the children cut pictures from magazines to make a class book showing what the Grouchy Ladybug would eat. If you were unable to locate the book *The Grouchy Ladybug*, then play the following game, Ladybug Spots.

    Ladybug Spots—Using the patterns on page 67, make four to six ladybugs and enough black circles to cover the spots on the ladybugs. Also make cards containing questions about ladybug facts learned in Opening. To begin, give each child a ladybug and six spots. Children take turns drawing cards, and if they answer the question correctly, they put a spot on their ladybug. The first child to put on all the spots says, "Ladybug." *Sample questions:* What do ladybugs eat? Why do farmers like ladybugs? Is a ladybug an insect? *Variation:* Question cards can be a review of shapes, colors, numerals, or simple addition and subtraction facts.

_____ **Activity 3** _____

Bulletin Board Ladybugs—The children can dip the end of a cork in red tempera paint and print ladybugs on the ground and flying through the air in Scarecrow's Garden. Use black felt-tip pens to give the ladybugs their spots when the paint is dry.

CLOSING _____ **Class Book** _____

Using the Class Book made in Activity 2, discuss why the children chose the things they added to the book. Let each child tell about the things he or she thinks the Grouchy Ladybug would eat. Could a ladybug really eat those things?

    Recite the following poem with the children as they move around the room with you.

> Ladybugs, Ladybugs, Come *fly* with me
> Watch what I do, and do it with me.
> (Change the word *fly* to *skip, jump, hop*, etc.)

Scarecrow Day

© 1990 by The Center for Applied Research in Education

PREPARATION _____ To the Teacher _____

Many children may not have seen or heard of scarecrows, but before this day is over they should be well acquainted with the appearance and purpose of them.
    You will need:

- shapes and straw for Arrival;
- pictures of characters in story (see p. 69) for Opening;
- beanbag, hat, and broom for Activity 1;
- newspaper, yardstick, and clothes for Opening;
- 4″ × 8″ paper for each child for Activity 2;
- materials to make crowns for Activity 3; and
- shirts and straw hats for Closing.

ARRIVAL _____ Bulletin Board _____

The children will be building two or three scarecrows to add to the bulletin board today. Have circles, triangles, rectangles, and straw available. On arrival, hand each child a part of a scarecrow body. The child can put it on the bulletin board, adding it to the other scarecrow parts.

OPENING _____ Scarecrow Talk _____

A scarecrow is made to look like a person standing in a garden. The gardener wants the scarecrow to scare away the crows so they won't eat the plants. Shiny objects, such as pie tins, are hung from the scarecrow. These reflect the sun and scare crows, other birds, rabbits, raccoons, etc.

_____ Story _____

Read to the children *A Scarecrow Without a Name,* found on page 68.
    Let the children make a scarecrow for your classroom using newspaper to stuff an old shirt and pants. A yardstick can be pushed into the shirt and a hat placed on top for a head.

CRAFT _____ Scarecrow _____

Materials Needed:

    One plastic milk carton lid per child
    pretraced rectangles
    straw
    peanut-shaped styrofoam pieces
    one large piece of paper per child
    glue, scissors

Explanation:
Children cut out traced rectangles for the body of their scarecrow. They glue the rectangles on large pieces of paper and add the lids for the scarecrow's head and straw for arms and legs. The styrofoam pieces can be glued on for a hat.

FREEPLAY _____ Activity 1 _____

Beanbag Fun—Tape a broom securely to a chair and place a hat on top of the broom to resemble a crude scarecrow. Children throw a beanbag at the hat trying to knock it off the broom.

_____ Activity 2 _____

Story Review—Each child folds a 4″ by 18″ piece of paper into five sections. In each section, on one side the child draws a character from the story. On the other side, the child draws five things to scare out of a garden if he or she were a scarecrow.

_____ Activity 3 _____

Crowns—Have cornhusks, straw, paper, and glue available so the children can make crowns for themselves like the animals made for Sylvester, King of the Garden, in the story.

CLOSING _____ Scarecrow Scramble _____

Have all the children sit on the floor and face in one direction. Choose five children to put on five large shirts and five straw hats. Put these five scarecrows in a line and have the rest of the children look carefully at the order in which they are standing. Ask the children to close their eyes as the scarecrows change places. Then ask them to open their eyes. Choose one child to put the scarecrows back in their original order.

Monster Day

PREPARATION _____ To the Teacher _____

Cookie Monster and Harry Monster of "Sesame Street" have helped children to be less frightened by monsters. All the monsters in the stories suggested today also appeal to children.

You will need:

- utensils, ingredients, and recipe to make Monster Cookie;
- items to construct an obstacle course for Activity 1;
- tape recording for Activity 2; and
- play dough (see p. 55) for Activity 3.
- guessing game for Closing

ARRIVAL _____ Monster Cookie _____

As the children arrive, they can help make one large monster cookie. Early arrivals can help mix the dough. Later arrivals can help spread the dough on one large cookie sheet. The following is a recipe for monster cookies that you might want to try.

Monster Cookies

3 eggs	1 tsp. corn syrup	Combine all ingredients. For smaller cookies, bake at 350 degrees for ten minutes. It may take a little longer to bake one large monster cookie.
1 1/2 cup peanut butter	1 tsp. vanilla	
1 stick oleo	4 1/2 cups oatmeal	
1 cup white sugar	1/2 cup chocolate chips	
1 cup brown sugar	1/2 cup raisins	
1 tsp. soda		

OPENING _____ Story _____

Discuss that monsters are not real and exist only in our imaginations. Today's story is about a monster who is friendly. Read one of the following stories: _Lamont the Lonely Monster_, by Dean Walley (Hallmark book). _Where the Wild Things Are_, by Maurice Sendak (Harper & Row, 1963). _There's a Monster Eating My House_, by Art Cummings (Parents Magazine Press, 1981).

_____ Music _____

The album _Monsters and Monstrous Things_ (upbeat BASICS, P.O. Box 120516, Acklen Station, Nashville, Ind. 37212) has several enjoyable songs for preschoolers. "Monster Color Game" emphasizes listening and colors. "Monsters in My Room" reinforces counting skills.

CRAFT _____ Fingerpaint Monster _____

Materials Needed:

fingerpaint

small moving eyes, sold in craft stores
  (two per child)

glue

one rectangular piece of paper that has
  been folded in half and has a door
  cut in it for each child

Explanation:
Lay the paper flat and have each child fingerpaint a monster on the uncut half of the paper. Glue on the moving eyes. When the paint is dry, fold the paper in half and glue the edges. The children can open the door to see their monster.

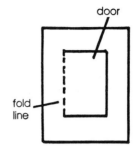

FREEPLAY ———————— Activity 1 ————————

Obstacle Course—Construct an obstacle course that the children can go through in search of a monster. At the end of the course, place a stuffed toy or picture of Cookie Monster or Harry Monster. Talk about spatial relationships as the children crawl under a row of chairs, climb over a stack of pillows, or step into shoeboxes.

———————— Activity 2 ————————

Listening Center—If the book is available to you, record in advance the story *There's a Monster at the End of This Book,* by Jon Stone (a Sesame Street book, 1971). Let the children listen to the recording as they look at the book. Use earphones if you wish.

———————— Activity 3 ————————

Play Dough—Have Pla-doh® or your own homemade modeling compound available for the children to create monsters.
    This recipe for play dough is inexpensive and keeps for months.

1/4 cup salt	Combine dry ingredients. Heat water and food coloring to boiling and add dry ingredients. Stir until well blended. Remove from pan and knead on lightly floured surface. Let cool. Store in an airtight container in the refrigerator.
2 tbsp. cream of tartar	
1 cup flour	
1 cup water	
2 tsp. food coloring	

CLOSING ———————— Monster Talk ————————

It was fun talking about monsters today. What monsters have you seen? (Halloween, "Sesame Street," stories or cartoons) Sometimes we make up monster stories just for fun or to tell a good story. Some monster stories are about fun monsters (Cookie Monster). Do monsters frighten you? Why? Some things look frightening but really aren't.

———————— Guessing Game ————————

In advance, locate pictures of people looking frightened or surprised. Tape each picture inside a Manila folder. Close the folder and cut a peephole to show only the person. Let the children look through the peephole and try to guess what is happening. When they are finished guessing, open the folder to reveal what is scaring or surprising the person in the picture.

Pumpkin Day

PREPARATION _____ To the Teacher _____

Painting, carving, tossing, and singing about pumpkins are all part of today's fun. The children learn what the difference is between a pumpkin and a jack-o-lantern.

You will need:

- items to prepare snack for Arrival;
- glove prepared for Opening;
- large pumpkin and knife for Activity 1;
- visual discrimination jack-o-lanterns for Activity 2;
- yarn pumpkins and patch for Activity 3; and
- visuals to use with record in Closing.

ARRIVAL _____ Pumpkin Snack _____

As the children arrive, have them frost round crackers with spreadable cheese. These can be served for snacks today. Raisins can be added for facial features as you discuss how pumpkins become jack-o-lanterns.

OPENING _____ Story _____

Read one of the following stories: *The Halloween Pumpkin,* by Pamela Oldfield (Children's Press, 1976). *A Halloween Happening,* by Adrienne Adams (Macmillan, 1981). *Mousekin's Golden House,* by Edna Miller (Prentice Hall, 1964).

_____ Pumpkin Talk _____

The pumpkin is an orange vegetable that grows on a long green vine. Pumpkins can be cooked and used to make muffins, pies, or breads. Even the seeds are a tasty treat when they are baked. You can turn a pumpkin into a jack-o-lantern by carving a face on it. Every pumpkin wants to be a jack-o-lantern on Halloween.

Teach the children the following poem:

> See the pumpkins fat and round
> Lying on the cold, wet ground.
> Now look up in the moonlit sky
> And you will see the bats that fly.
> Look oh so careful—ghosts can be seen
> Because this night is Halloween!

A visual can be made to wear while reciting this poem. Glue two to three orange pom-pom pumpkins close to the ribbing of an old glove (a dark brown work glove helps the children picture a nighttime scene). On the fingers, glue several ghosts and bats flying in front of the moon. As you begin the poem, fold over your fingers so that just the pumpkins are visible. Lift your fingers as the bats and ghosts are mentioned.

CRAFT _____ Orange Printing _____

Materials Needed:

several oranges cut in half horizontally
orange paint

pumpkin vine drawn on a piece of paper
(You can draw it for younger children, and older children can draw their own.)

Explanation:
Children dip the orange half in orange paint and print pumpkins on their vine.

© 1990 by The Center for Applied Research in Education

_____ Bulletin Board _____

Children can use oranges to print pumpkins in Scarecrow's Garden. Remember to draw the vines. After printing, invite the children to help wash and hollow out the used oranges. Frost inside with peanut butter, and sprinkle with bird seed. Now these feeders can be hung in trees for the birds.

FREEPLAY _____ Activity 1 _____

Acting Out the Story—The Halloween Pumpkin, by Pamela Oldfield, lends itself well to dramatization.

 Carving a Jack-o-Lantern—Children can help plan what kind of face they want to carve on the pumpkin. They can also help clean out the inside of the pumpkin. The seeds should be washed and saved for Witch Day, Activity 1 (see p. 59). After the children have decided what shape each facial feature should be, begin to carve. While carving, recite the following poem together, filling in the blanks with the chosen shape.

> Carve, Carve, the pumpkin with me
> Tell me what shape the *eyes* should be.
> A _____ , a _____ is that what you say?
> We're making a jack-o-lantern for Halloween Day!

Repeat two more times, substituting the words *nose* and *mouth.*

_____ Activity 2 _____

Visual Discrimination—Cut out and laminate eight to ten paper jack-o-lanterns using various colored shapes to make faces. Also cut out eight to ten plain paper pumpkins and many small shapes. Children try to create a jack-o-lantern that matches one of those that you have made by laying small shapes on their pumpkin.

_____ Activity 3 _____

Throwing Pumpkins into the Pumpkin Patch—Make a pumpkin patch by drawing vines on the side of a cardboard box. Make yarn pumpkins or use orange nerf balls to play this game. To make yarn pumpkins, wrap orange yarn around a cardboard rectangle. Slip yarn off the cardboard and hold in the middle. Tie the middle securely with yarn and then clip loops at the end. Fluff out the yarn to make an orange ball. To play the game, the children stand behind a line and try to throw the pumpkins into the patch.

CLOSING _____ Recording _____

"Five Little Pumpkins" on the album *Singable Songs for the Very Young* (SL-002), by Raffi with Ken Whitelay (Shoreline Records, 6307 Yonge Street, Willowdale, Ontario, Canada) is perfect to use today. You can make a visual to use with this record. Draw a gate on the side of a shoebox. Make five small paper pumpkins and glue each one to a clip-type clothespin. Clip the pumpkins on the shoebox. Take off each pumpkin as you mention it in the song.

Witch Day

© 1990 by The Center for Applied Research in Education

PREPARATION _____ To the Teacher _____

Halloween is a favorite holiday of children, so excitement will be palpable in your classroom. The fairy tale _Hansel and Gretel_ highlights this day of witches' activities.
    You will need:

- triangle and circle patterns for Arrival;
- props for story (see p. 70) in Opening;
- pumpkin seeds with holes in them for Activity 1 (saved from Pumpkin Day—see p. 57);
- paper punches, paper, and telephone wire for Activity 1;
- materials to decorate a witch's house for Activity 2;
- items to use with record in Activity 3; and
- colored leaves for Closing.

ARRIVAL _____ Cutting Shapes _____

Have available several cardboard patterns of circles and triangles. Children trace one triangle and one circle, cut them out, print their name on them, and save for Craft.

OPENING _____ Story _____

Read to the children _Hansel and Gretel,_ a Grimm fairy tale. To make the story more interesting, make a forest by putting artificial greens in a flat box. Make puppet figures (see p. 70) to walk through the forest as you tell the story. Have small pieces of bread to drop. Make a bird and glue it to a clip-type clothespin. The bird can fly through the forest and pick up the pieces of bread!

CRAFT _____ Egg Carton Witch _____

Materials Needed:

    circle and triangle cut in Arrival
    yarn
    markers
    egg carton nose and eyes

Slice through the bottom of a cardboard egg carton between each set of two egg holders. You will get six nose and eye sections from each carton. Two side-by-side egg holders will be the witch's eyes, and the protruding egg cup divider will be the witch's nose.

Explanation:
Children glue the circle they cut in Arrival onto a large piece of paper. Yarn can be added for the hair, and the triangle cut in Arrival can be added for the hat. The markers should be used to color the egg carton eyes, and the eyes should then be glued onto the witch's face. Finally, use the markers to add a crooked smile.

FREEPLAY _____ Activity 1 _____

Witch Jewelry—Prior to class, poke holes in the pumpkin seeds saved from Pumpkin Day. Use a darning needle so the holes will be large. Give the children small pieces of orange and black paper to cut into different shapes. Use a paper punch to punch holes in the cut paper. String the paper and pumpkin seeds on switchboard cable; twist ends together to make necklaces. (See the explanation about using this wire on p. 63.)

_____ Activity 2 _____

Witch's House—Scarecrow's Garden will now become a place for a witch's house in the forest. If your bulletin board is becoming too crowded, take down the scarecrows before you put up the house. Cut a house out of a large sheet of paper. Children can decorate it to look like the witch's house in the story *Hansel and Gretel,* and then it can be added to the bulletin board. Have the children cut out shapes of different colors to glue on the house. Colored marshmallows and cereal may also be used.

_____ Activity 3 _____

Witches' Brew—Children can help make witches' brew by adding all the things mentioned on the song "Witches' Brew" on the album *Witches' Brew* (AR576), by Hap and Martha Palmer (Educational Activities, Inc., Box 392, Freeport, N.Y. 11520). If possible, have a witch hat and a cape for the children to wear as they pretend to be a witch making her brew. You will also need a large kettle, a stir stick, and "dead leaves, spider webs, and moldy bread." Even without the record, you can pretend to make a witch's concoction.

CLOSING _____ Recording _____

Have leaves of different colors cut out and displayed on the floor. Children can walk around them as directed on the song "Move Around the Color" on the album *Easy Does It* (AR 581), by Hap Palmer (Educational Activities, Inc., Box 392, Freeport, N.Y. 11520). When it is time to go home, have each child hand you his or her leaf and tell you what color it is.

Ghost Day

PREPARATION _____ To the Teacher _____

A Book of Ghosts will delight the children, as it points out that our imaginations often mislead us into being frightened by things that are familiar. You will complete the bulletin board today by fingerprint painting some ghosts.

   You will need:

- pictures and riddles (see pp. 71–72) for Activity 1;
- materials to paint ghosts for Activity 2; and
- ghost stencils, erasers, and chalk for Activity 3.

ARRIVAL _____ Where is Thumbkin? _____

Have children join your circle and learn to sing and do the actions of this song.

Where is Thumbkin? Where is Thumbkin?
(Hide thumbs of both hands behind back.)
Here I am, Here I am.
(Bring out thumbs one at a time.)
How are you today, sir?
(Wiggle thumb on left hand.)
Very well, I thank you.
(Wiggle thumb on right hand.)
Run away, run away.
(First hide left thumb behind back and then right thumb.)
Verse 2—Where is Pointer?
(Repeat entire song using index fingers.)
Verse 3—Where is Tall Man?
Verse 4—Where is Ring Man?
Verse 5—Where is Pinky?
Verse 6—Where is the whole family?
(Bring out all fingers at once.)

OPENING _____ Ghost Talk _____

People often think of ghosts at Halloween, perhaps because it's a time when we think of scary things! Lead the children in a discussion about ghosts by asking questions. Do you think there are really ghosts? What would a ghost feel like if you could touch it? What do they eat? How does a ghost move? Where would you like to go if you were a ghost? It is fun to think about imaginary things such as ghosts.

_____ A Book of Ghosts _____

Share with the children *A Book of Ghosts,* published by Child's Play Ltd. (1974), a Child's Play Imagination Book. It is illustrated by Pam Adams and Ceri Jones and does a great job of showing that ghosts that frighten us often turn out to be familiar, unfrightening objects.

© 1990 by The Center for Applied Research in Education

CRAFT _____ Fingerprint Ghosts _____

Materials Needed:

> black paper
> white paint
> fine-tip black markers

Explanation:
Children use their fingertips to make white ghosts on black paper. Just a little blowing dries the ghosts so that the children can use markers to make eyes on their ghosts.

FREEPLAY _____ Activity 1 _____

Halloween Riddles—Have available pictures of different things we think of at Halloween to go on the flannel board. You can make up riddles about the items, and the children choose the picture that goes with each riddle. (See pp. 71–72.)

Examples:

I have four paws.	I wear a black hat.
I am black and furry.	I ride a broom.
I say meowww.	I fly in the sky.
Who am I?	Who am I?
I am white.	I am round.
I say booo!	I am orange.
I scare you.	I have a crooked smile.
Who am I?	Who am I?

_____ Activity 2 _____

Bulletin Board—Cut several windows in the witch house on the bulletin board. (See Witch Day, Activity 2, p. 59.) After the children finish their craft, they can fingerprint some ghosts in the windows and flying around the house. (Older children can tear paper ghosts instead of making fingerprint ghosts.)

_____ Activity 3 _____

Chalk Dust Ghosts—Children rub chalk on a chalkboard eraser. Place several ghost stencils on the board or a large piece of black paper. Pat the eraser over the ghosts. Remove the stencils.

CLOSING _____ Story _____

Read one of the following stories: *The Ghost with Halloween Hiccups,* by Stephen Mooser (Avon, 1981). *The Ghost Said BOO,* by John McInnes (Garrard, 1974). *The Ghost in Dobbs Diner,* by Robert Alley (Parents Magazine Press, 1981).

_____
(Name of Facility)

_____
(Address)

_____

FIELD TRIP AUTHORIZATION

I do/do not (circle one) give my permission for _____
(Child's Name)

to leave the above-named facility for a trip to _____
(Destination)

on _____ .
(Date)

Please return this form by _____ .
(Date)

_____
(Signature of Parent)

_____
(Date)

No More Needles!
No More Yarn!

Your local telephone company is the place to find a scrap piece of switchboard cable. Three or four feet will last you a LONG time! After removing the outer covering, you'll find hundreds of colorful pieces of thin plastic wire. The wire is perfect for pretend rings and bracelets just the way it is. Stringing decorative pieces of paper or ribbon on the wire will make a beautiful necklace. It is perfect for stringing Cheerios®, cranberries, or popcorn for the birds.

No needles are necessary! Use it for any craft. . .it's easy to cut, it's clean, and it's usually free!

Dear Parent(s),

We prepared and enjoyed this recipe for Peanut Butter Spread at the park today. We want to share this recipe with you.

Peanut Butter Spread

1 1/4 cup peanut butter
2/3 cup oatmeal
1/2 cup honey

1/2 cup mini chocolate chips
Variation: add 1/2 c. raisins

Combine all ingredients. Mix well. Store in refrigerator. Makes about 1 1/2 cups. Delicious on apples, pears, and celery.

——— TREE DAY—ARRIVAL ———

Dear Parent(s),

We need you to send a snapshot or a small photo of your child to school by

_____ . We will make several photocopies of it, and then we
      (Date)
will return it to you. These photocopies will be used in crafts and on bulletin boards throughout the year.

Thanks!

Dear Parent(s),

We need your child to bring a small, flat

rock to school by _____ .
                           (Date)

It should be fairly smooth, oval-shaped, and
approximately 3 inches by 4 inches.

                                      Thanks!

Dear Parent(s),

We learned the song "Where Is Thumbkin"
sung to the tune of "Frère Jacque." We
send the words home so you and your child can have fun
singing the song together. Be sure to have your child show
you the actions.

Where is Thumbkin, where is Thumbkin?
Here I am, here I am.
How are you today, sir?
Very well, I thank you.
Run away, run away.

Verse 2—Where is Pointer?
Verse 3—Where is Tall Man?
Verse 4—Where is Ring Man?
Verse 5—Where is Pinky?
Verse 6—Where is the whole family?

A SCARECROW WITHOUT A NAME

by Judy Galloway, Lynette Ivey, and Gloria Valster

Robby Rabbit hopped down the path and came to a beautiful garden. Robby loved to eat carrot tops, but as he began to eat he heard a voice shout, "Get out of my garden!" Robby Rabbit turned, and there he saw a scarecrow!

Robby asked, "Who are you?" and the voice answered, "I'm the scarecrow who takes care of this garden."

But Robby wanted to know his name. Scarecrow replied, "I have no name."

Robby then said, "I'm not afraid of a scarecrow who has no name," and he continued to eat the carrot tops.

Soon Rory Raccoon came along and wanted a snack. The corn looked delicious, so he began to eat. Again the scarecrow shouted, "Get out of my garden!" Rory was terribly frightened; however, Robby Rabbit stopped munching carrot tops long enough to tell Rory not to be scared.

Robby said, "That scarecrow doesn't even have a name." Both Rory Raccoon and Robby Rabbit continued to nibble.

As Connie Crow was flying around, she spotted very red, ripe tomatoes in the garden. Robby Rabbit and Rory Raccoon were enjoying their snack so much that she decided to join them. Just as she began to eat that first tomato, she heard a loud voice shout, "Get out of my garden!"

Connie began to tremble and was almost ready to cry when her friends said, "Don't be afraid of that scarecrow. . .he doesn't even have a name."

Betty Bug and Sherry Squirrel were having a great game of chase and tag when, to their surprise, they found themselves in the middle of a garden! "Oh what yummy food!" Betty Bug exclaimed.

Betty Bug began eating beans, and Sherry Squirrel was nibbling lettuce, when all of a sudden they heard that voice shout, "Get out of my garden!"

Sherry Squirrel squealed, "Let's run!"

The other animals laughed and cried out, "Stay and eat. That's just a silly scarecrow with no name."

All the animals were having a great picnic when they saw how very sad the scarecrow felt. The animals weren't sure why, but they felt sad, too. Robby Rabbit suggested, "Let's go to my house. We need to talk." At Robby's house, the animals decided to think of a name for the scarecrow.

Betty Bug said, "Let's name him Patches. He has patches on his jacket." The other animals thought Patches was a name for a puppy.

Rory Raccoon said, "Let's name him Jingles. He has pie pans hanging on his jacket that jingle when the wind blows." The other animals thought Jingles was a name for a clown. They had to think of a name that was perfect.

Suddenly Robby Rabbit said, "I have an idea. Come with me."

The animals began to work very hard on Robby Rabbit's idea, and then altogether they went back to the garden. Robby Rabbit announced, "Scarecrow, we have a name for you. We name you Sylvester— King of the Garden!" At that moment, Connie Crow flew to the scarecrow and placed their gift upon his head. . .a crown of corn shucks and straw. From that time on, the animals never ate the vegetables in King Sylvester's garden.

Robby Rabbit

Sherry Squirrel

Rory Raccoon

Scarecrow

Connie Crow

Sylvester—King of the Garden

Betty Bug

unit 4

FOOD AND FUN

Everyone likes to eat, but it can also be fun to prepare food. Children enjoy mixing, pouring, stirring, and measuring. The learning experiences with food in this unit provide a means for expanding concepts of numbers, measuring, size, texture, taste, time, and color. There are supervised opportunities for the children to use an egg beater, a mixer, and a rolling pin as well as measuring spoons and cups.

Sharing is important, both in preparation and in eating. Encourage the children to share in both.

The daily activity plans in Unit 4 include:

- Let's Celebrate Day
- Cookie Monster's Birthday
- Apple Day
- Fruit Day
- Popcorn Day
- Pie Day
- Cornbread Day
- Turkey Day

Let's Celebrate!

© 1990 by The Center for Applied Research in Education

PREPARATION _____ To the Teacher _____

This is a day on which you can celebrate the birthdays of all the children in your class. In preschools that meet only two times per week, it is sometimes difficult to recognize each child on his or her special day. This day allows you to have one big party for everyone in your class!
   You will need:

- notes to parents requesting that children bring in baby photos (see p. 90) for Arrival;
- large paper birthday cake for Arrival;
- recipe (see p. 90), ingredients, and utensils for Arrival;
- a parent to bring in a baby for Opening;
- candlestick for Activity 1;
- art supplies and old greeting cards for Activity 2; and
- growth chart for Activity 3.

ARRIVAL _____ Class Birthday Cake _____

Send notes home prior to this day asking each child to bring a baby picture of himself or herself to class (see p. 90). Make a large paper birthday cake to put on an easel or bulletin board. As the children arrive, they tape their baby picture on the birthday cake.

_____ Muffin Cupcakes _____

After putting their picture on the class cake, the children can help make applesauce muffins to eat for a snack (see p. 90). Make this a special snack time. You might want to decorate with balloons or have the children wear party hats. Be sure to sing "Happy Birthday" before the children eat their muffin birthday cakes.

Applesauce Muffins

2 cups flour
4 tsp. baking powder
1/2 tsp. cinnamon
1/4 cup sugar
1 egg (beaten)
1/3 cup vegetable oil
1/2 cup milk
2/3 cup applesauce

Combine all ingredients. Sprinkle top of each muffin with cinnamon and sugar. Bake fifteen to twenty minutes at 350 degrees.

OPENING _____ Let's Celebrate _____

Birthdays mean we are getting older and are growing. Look at the baby pictures the children have brought and discuss how they have grown. Ask a parent to bring a baby to visit, and let the children discuss things that they do now but could not do when they were a baby. What are some special ways to celebrate birthdays? Who do you like to have celebrate with you? What can you do for someone else who is having a birthday?

_____ Where, Oh Where Is Todd? _____

Conclude by singing "Where, Oh Where Is Todd?" to a simple tune (such as "Muffin Man"). Substitute each child's name. Have each child come up and point to his or her baby picture when you sing this phrase.

CRAFT _____ Birthday Cake _____

Materials Needed:

    picture of birthday cake for each child (see p. 91)
    paper for candles
    crayons, scissors, paste

Explanation:
Children cut out rectangular strips for candles to paste on top of their cakes. Then they use crayons to color the flames on the candles and to decorate their cakes.

FREEPLAY _____ Activity 1 _____

Jack Be Nimble—Bring in a candlestick so that the children can recite and act out this nursery rhyme. Discuss that candles are a fun part of birthdays, but they can be dangerous. It is fun to substitute each child's name for *Jack* as he or she jumps over the candlestick.

    Jack be nimble
    Jack be quick
    Jack jump over the candlestick.

_____ Activity 2 _____

Birthday Cards—Since you will be celebrating Cookie Monster's birthday on your next day of class, the children might enjoy making birthday cards for him. Have available scissors, crayons, paper, old stickers, old greeting cards, etc., so the children can design their own cards. Put all the cards in an envelope and mail them to Cookie Monster, care of Children's Television Workshop, One Lincoln Plaza, New York, N.Y. 10023.

_____ Activity 3 _____

Growth Chart—Make a growth chart that looks like one large candle. Mark the height and record the weight of each child on this growth chart.

CLOSING _____ Story _____

Read one of the following stories: *Ask Mr. Bear,* by Marjorie Flack (Macmillan, 1986). *Happy Birthday, Henrietta,* by Syd Hoff (Garrard, 1983). *Benny Bakes a Cake,* by Eve Rice (Greenwillow Books, 1981).

Cookie Monster's Birthday

PREPARATION _____ To the Teacher _____

Did you know that November 10 is Cookie Monster's Birthday? He is a special character with so much mystery about him. Celebrate with cookies, of course, and speculate about what Cookie Monster is really like.

You will neeed:

- edible play dough (see below), rolling pins, and cookie cutters for Arrival;
- large picture of Cookie Monster, paper cookies, and blindfold for Activity 1;
- large paper *C* and blue tissue paper for Activity 2; and
- patterns of circles and generic raisins, peanuts, and chocolate chips for Activity 3.

ARRIVAL _____ Make Cookies _____

As the children arrive, they can make cookies with this recipe for edible play dough. Have rolling pins and cookie cutters available for them to use. Allow them to play with their play dough until they make that special cookie they want to save for snack time.

Edible Play Dough

1 cup peanut butter

1/2 cup powdered sugar

approximately 1/4 cup honey

Combine ingredients and mix well.

OPENING _____ Cookie Monster Talk _____

How old do you think Cookie Monster is? Has he grown like you have? How big was he when he was born? What would happen if Cookie Monster only ate cookies? Does Cookie Monster have good manners when he eats?

_____ Records _____

Sing the song "C is for Cookie" on the album *Bert and Ernie Sing Along* (CTN-22068), or dance to "Cookie Disco" on the album *Aren't You Glad You're You?* (CTW 22083), both from Sesame Street Records, Children's Television Workshop, One Lincoln Plaza, New York, N.Y. 10023.

CRAFT _____ Cookie Monster _____

Materials Needed:

precut shape of Cookie Monster (preferably cut out of blue paper (see p. 93)

dyed blue spaghetti or blue yarn

glue

miniature marshmallows

small brown coding dots

© 1990 by The Center for Applied Research in Education

Explanation:
Give each child a precut Cookie Monster. The children will glue two miniature marshmallows where the eyes should be and attach a small coding dot to the end of each marshmallow. You should have made the blue spaghetti by cooking spaghetti in boiling water to which you added blue food coloring. Drain the spaghetti slightly before the children put short pieces of it on Cookie Monster's body. The wet spaghetti should be sticky enough that you won't need to use glue. Short pieces of blue yarn may be glued on if you prefer not to use the spaghetti.

FREEPLAY _____ **Activity 1** _____

Blindfold Game—In advance, make a large picture of Cookie Monster with his mouth wide open. Tape it to the wall. Also make some small paper cookies to feed him. Put tape on the back of each cookie. One at a time blindfold the children and have them try to get the cookie in Cookie Monster's mouth.

_____ **Activity 2** _____

Bulletin Board—Cut a large *C* out of heavy paper. Children twist small pieces of blue tissue paper around the end of a pencil and glue them on the *C*. This *C* can be placed in the middle of a bulletin board, and the cookies the children make in Activity 3 can be placed around it. Older children can also cut out pictures of things that begin with the letter *C*.

_____ **Activity 3** _____

Paper Cookies—Have available patterns for the children to trace circles. Children should cut out the circles and glue on generic raisins, peanuts, or chocolate chips to make the kind of cookie they think Cookie Monster would like best.

CLOSING _____ **Story** _____

Read one of the following stories: *Happy Birthday, Cookie Monster!*, by Felice Haus (Random House, 1986). *Monster Birthday Party*, by Sally Freedman (Whitman, 1983).

Apple Day

PREPARATION _____ **To the Teacher** _____

To make apple dumplings with a class of preschoolers, you will need to be well organized. For many children, both preparing and eating the dumplings is a new experience. The pastry is very easy to handle, and we have altered the recipe so the dumplings are small.

You will need:

- pastry dough and sauce (see below) for Arrival;
- apples, rolling pins, and other supplies for Arrival;
- several kinds of apples for Opening;
- possibly an orchard worker for Opening;
- Apple/Worm Match prepared for Activity 1;
- flannel apples and worms for Activity 2; and
- different colored paper apples and tree for Activity 3.

ARRIVAL _____ **Apple Dumplings** _____

Have the children roll out the pastry for the apple dumpling they will eat for snack today. Prepare the dough and sauce before class.

You can make areas for the children to roll out the pastry by taping 12″ by 12″ pieces of wax paper on the table. Use masking tape and tape the complete perimeter of the paper.

Apple Dumplings

1 1/2 cups sugar

1 1/2 cups water

1/4 tsp. cinnamon

6–10 drops red food coloring

3 tbsp. margarine

2 cups flour

2 tsp. baking powder

1 tsp. salt

2/3 cup shortening

1/2 cup milk

apples, pared and quartered

Combine sugar, water, spices, and food coloring; bring to a boil. Remove from heat; add butter. Sift together dry ingredients; cut in shortening until mixture resembles coarse crumbs. Add milk all at once and stir just until flour is moistened. Roll small pieces into 4″ squares. Place 1/4 apple on dough and sprinkle with sugar and cinnamon. Moisten edges and fold corners to center. Bake at 375 degrees for thirty-five minutes. Spoon syrup over dumpling and serve warm.

OPENING _____ **Apple Talk** _____

Apples are a fruit which grows in different sizes and colors. Bring in several kinds of apples, such as Jonathans, Red and Yellow Delicious, and Granny Smith, to show the children the differences. Apples are a great snack whether eaten alone or used to make cider, muffins, dumplings, pie, or applesauce. If possible, have someone who works in an orchard visit your class and talk about growing apples.

© 1990 by The Center for Applied Research in Education

_____ **Poem** _____

Teach the children this poem about apples as found in *Everyday Circle Times,* by Dick Wilmes
(A Building Blocks Publication, 1983).

OUCH

by Dick Wilmes

Apple green, apple red
Apple fell upon my head!

CRAFT _____ **Apple Prints** _____

Materials Needed:

> pretraced apple shape on red, yellow, or green paper (see p. 92)
> scissors
> several apples sliced in half vertically
> white tempera paint

Explanation:
Have each child cut out a paper apple. The child then dips
one of the apple halves in the white paint and makes prints
on the paper apple. Have children wash the apples and put
them out for the birds to eat.

FREEPLAY _____ **Activity 1** _____

Apple/Worm Match—Cut out several apples and punch a varying number
of holes in them using a paper punch. (You might want to laminate or
cover the apples with clear self-stick vinyl.) Make worms by gluing small
craft pom-pom balls together and onto a piece of paper. Add coding dots
for eyes. Trim the paper with scissors so you don't see it. (It is for support only.) Make the worms of different sizes by varying the number of
pom-pom balls you use. The children are to match the number of holes
in the apple with the number of pom-pom balls used to make the worm.

_____ **Activity 2** _____

Flannel Board Apples and Worm—Make one red, one yellow, and one green felt apple and one
brown worm. Have the children follow your instructions as to where to put the worm. *Examples:*
"Place the worm behind the red apple. . .above the yellow apple. . .next to the green apple."

_____ **Activity 3** _____

Apple Match—Draw a large apple tree on heavy paper. Color apples of different sizes and colors
on the tree. Cut out apples of those same sizes and colors. The children match the apples to those
drawn on the tree.

CLOSING _____ **Story** _____

Read one of the following stories: *Fresh Cider and Apple Pie,* by Franz Brandenberg (Macmillan,
1973). *Rain Makes Applesauce,* by Julian Scheer (Holiday, 1964). *Who's Got the Apple?,* by Jan
Loof (Random House, 1975).

Fruit Day

© 1990 by The Center for Applied Research in Education

PREPARATION _____ To the Teacher _____

You will be teaching all about fruits today. Bring in lots of different types so the children can actually see, touch, taste, and smell each one as you talk about it.
     You will need:

* cranberries, Cheerios®, and telephone wire (see p. 63) for Arrival;
* basket or cornucopia and many samples of fruit for Opening;
* pictures of fruit (see p. 94) and a banana for Opening;
* ingredients and recipe for Activity 1;
* large paper fruits and magazines or catalogs for Activity 2; and
* Fruit Concentration (see p. 96) for Activity 3.

ARRIVAL _____ Bird Feeding _____

String cranberries and Cheerios®. Hang them in a tree or bush where you can watch the birds eat!

OPENING _____ Fruit Talk _____

Show the children a basket or cornucopia filled with fruits such as pineapple, kiwi, apples, mangos, oranges, grapefruit, blueberries, bananas, and grapes. Use the visuals as you and the children verbally describe each fruit. Cut them in half to discover which ones have seeds and what the "meat" of the fruit looks like.
     Questions for discussion are as follows: Which fruits do you like to eat? Do we ever eat the seeds of the fruit? Which fruits do we eat the skins of? Where does fruit grow? (on trees, vines, bushes)
     If you use a cornucopia, tell the children that it represents a symbol of abundance and is sometimes called a "horn of plenty."

_____ Hot Banana _____

Have all the children sit in a circle to play this game, which is the fruity version of Hot Potato. Place pictures of different kinds of fruit on the floor in the middle of the circle (see p. 94). Children pass the banana around the circle until the music stops. The child holding the banana must point to and name his or her favorite fruit. Encourage the children to respond with a complete sentence.
Example: "My favorite fruit is _____ ."

CRAFT _____ Fruit Painting _____

Materials Needed:

> picture of cornucopia or basket for each child (see p. 95)
> brown crayons
> red, orange, and yellow paint
> several apples, lemons, and oranges

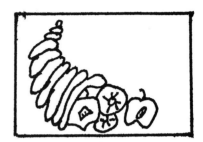

Explanation:
The children color the cornucopia brown. Cut the apples in wedges and the lemons and oranges in half. The children dip these in the paint and print fruit in the cornucopia. Have children wash the fruit and put it out for the birds to eat.

FREEPLAY _____ **Activity 1** _____

Mini Fruit Kabobs—Let the children make mini fruit kabobs by putting pineapple, bananas, mandarin oranges, and pieces of apple on a toothpick. The fruit snack will be more special if you also make a dip. This recipe is quick and easy to prepare.

3 oz. soft cream cheese

1 tsp. cinnamon

1 tbsp. milk

8 oz. whipped topping

Mix the first three ingredients until smooth. Fold in the whipped topping.

_____ **Activity 2** _____

Fruit Collage—In advance, cut a large orange out of orange paper, an apple out of red paper, and a banana out of yellow paper. Make as many of these fruits as you like. The children cut pictures of the fruits from magazines and glue them on the large paper fruits. Seed catalogs are an excellent source of illustrations for this activity.

_____ **Activity 3** _____

Fruit Concentration—You can make this game using the patterns on page 96. Put the pictures on small cards and make sure you have two cards for each kind of fruit. For example, have two cards with pictures of apples, two cards with kiwi, and so forth. To play the game, scatter all cards face down on the table. The first player chooses two cards and turns them face up. If the two cards show the same fruit, the player keeps the cards and continues to play. If they do not match, the player turns them face down. The next player turns two cards face up, remembering the two cards that the previous player turned over. Play continues until all cards are gone. The winner is the player who matches the most cards.

CLOSING _____ **Story** _____

Read one of the following stories: *Cranberry Thanksgiving*, by Wende and Harry Devlin (Macmillan, 1980). *An Apple Is Red*, by Nancy Curry (Bowman Publication Corp., 1967). *Jam*, by Margaret Mahy (The Atlantic Monthly Press, 1985).

Popcorn Day

PREPARATION _____ **To the Teacher** _____

Watching and listening to popcorn popping can be fun, but _do_ be careful. When popping the corn during Arrival, be sure that the children sit along the edge of the sheet or blanket, but not _on_ it. This will assure that no one gets hit by hot popcorn. Warn the children to stay back so that everyone will have a good time and no one gets hurt.

You will need:

- an electric popper and sheet or blanket for Arrival;
- several kinds of popcorn poppers for Opening;
- ingredients and recipe for Activity 1;
- Popcorn Number Game prepared for Activity 2; and
- Color Bingo and markers for Activity 3.

ARRIVAL _____ **Make Popcorn** _____

Place an electric popcorn popper in the middle of a blanket or sheet on the floor. Do not put on the lid. Let the children watch the popcorn pop. (Save the popcorn for use in Activity 1.)

OPENING _____ **Popcorn Talk** _____

Ears of popcorn grow on stalks in fields. Popcorn is a type of corn with very small, hard kernels. When heated, the kernels burst into a white, fluffy snack that is very popular with young and old people. As the children observed in Arrival, popcorn makes a popping sound when it bursts. Show the children different kinds of popcorn poppers—electric, over the flame, and microwave poppers.

_____ **Record** _____

Listen to the song "Popcorn" on the album _We All Live Together,_ volume 2 (YR-002R), by Greg Scelsa and Steve Millang (Youngheart Records, Box 27784, Los Angeles, Calif. 90027), as the children pretend to make and eat popcorn.

CRAFT _____ **Smoke Circles** _____

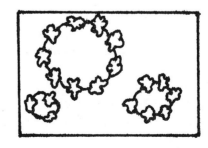

Materials Needed:

sheet of paper for each child
    with three circles of different
    sizes drawn on it
three colors of crayons
three colors of popcorn
glue

© 1990 by The Center for Applied Research in Education

Explanation:
(Popcorn can be colored by popping it in an air popper and then shaking it in a brown bag with dry tempera paint. Add as much paint as needed to achieve your desired color.) If you read *Popcorn Dragon* for your story today, call the circles on the paper the puffs of smoke that come out of the dragon's mouth. Instruct the children to color the biggest circle one color, the smallest circle another color, and the middle-sized circle still another color. Then the children glue popcorn of the same color around the edge of each circle. Caution the children that the popcorn is no longer good to eat.

FREEPLAY _____ Activity 1 _____

Edible Popcorn Circles—Using the popcorn saved from Arrival, make these circles for your snack (see p. 82). Children can shape this mixture into circles and then count the chocolate chips as they place them on top.

Popcorn Circles

1/4 cup margarine 1/2 cup peanut butter 1 package miniature marshmallows 10 cups unsalted popcorn 1/2 cup chocolate chips	Melt margarine in a heavy skillet. Stir in peanut butter and marshmallows. Heat very slowly, stirring constantly until mixture is melted and smooth. Remove from heat. Stir in popcorn; toss until evenly coated.

_____ Activity 2 _____

Popcorn Number Game—In advance, make cards to use in this game. Each card will have a numeral on it in one of three colors. Have colored popcorn available in those same colors. (See Craft for how to color popcorn.) Hold the cards as each child chooses one card and lays it on the table. The child is to place on the card the number and color of popcorn that the numeral indicates.

_____ Activity 3 _____

Color Bingo—Play Color Bingo using popcorn for markers. Make cards by drawing circles in several different colors where the numerals on a Bingo card usually are. Make small cards with one colored circle on each, including all the colors you have used on the playing cards. Each child has a playing card and popcorn. Children take turns drawing a small card, and everyone places a popcorn on that color on their playing card. The first player to cover one row says, "Bingo."

CLOSING _____ Poppin' Popcorn _____

Teach the children to sing this song to the tune of "Muffin Man":

Do you know how to pop popcorn,
pop popcorn, pop popcorn?
Do you know how to pop popcorn?
Pop-Pop-Pop

Make it hot and watch it pop,
watch it pop, watch it pop.
Make it hot and watch it pop.
Pop-Pop-Pop

Pour in a bowl and share with a friend,
share with a friend, share with a friend.
Pour in a bowl and share with a friend.
Mmmm-Mmmm-Mmmm

_____ Story _____

Read one of the following stories: *The Popcorn Dragon,* by Jane Thayer (Morrow, 1953). *Popcorn,* by Frank Asch (Parents Magazine Press, 1979). *Popcorn Book,* by Tomie de Paola (Scholastic Books, Inc., 1978).

Pie Day

© 1990 by The Center for Applied Research in Education

PREPARATION _____ To the Teacher _____

Cooking has been a major activity of this unit, but you do not need a recipe for today's adventure. You will prepare a very simple pie and continue working with numbers and fractions through water play.

You will need:

- pastry dough, pie filling, and mini-muffin pans for Arrival;
- picture of a pie and triangles for Opening;
- play dough, pie tins, and rolling pins for Activity 1;
- different sized containers for Activity 2; and
- Number Matching Game for Activity 3.

ARRIVAL _____ Blueberry Pie _____

As the children arrive, have them make a small blueberry pie for their snack today. Buy pie crust mix and a can of blueberry pie filling. Pat a small amount of crust in a mini-muffin pan. Fill with pie filling. Bake at 350 degrees for fifteen to twenty minutes.

OPENING _____ Pie Talk _____

Pie is a favorite dessert of many people. It is a pastry with fruit or cream filling. Fruit pies usually have two crusts. The top crust can either be one solid piece or several strips of pastry dough woven together across the filling. Cream pies have one crust on the bottom and whipping cream or meringue on top. Meringue is made by whipping the white part of an egg with sugar. Encourage discussion by asking the following questions: Have you ever eaten pie? What is your favorite kind of pie? Have you ever eaten ice cream with pie?

_____ Bulletin Board _____

Make a large picture of a pie to put on the bulletin board. Divide the pie into as many slices as you have children in your class. Cut colored triangles to fit onto these slices. Hand one triangle to each child and say: "A great big pie I made you see; Tell your favorite kind to me." As children pin their slice onto the class pie, write the name of the kind of pie they like on their triangle.

CRAFT _____ Blueberry Pie _____

Materials Needed:

one small paper plate per child

brown construction paper

scissors, glue, crayons

shell macaroni, dyed blue, or blue play dough

Explanation:
In advance, dye the macaroni blue by putting it in water with blue food coloring for a few minutes. Dry thoroughly on paper towels. If you choose to use play dough, have the children roll it into small balls. The children color their paper plate brown to resemble pie crust. Then they glue the "blueberries" onto the plate. Finally, they cut brown strips and glue the ends to the edge of the paper plate to make a lattice top for their pie.

FREEPLAY _____ Activity 1 _____

Play Dough Pies—Place play dough, pie tins, and rolling pins on a table so the children can pretend to make pies. Frozen meat pie tins make nice small pies.

_____ Activity 2 _____

Water Play—Let the children experiment with water in different sized containers. Have tall, thin containers, wide, flat containers, and measuring cups and spoons available for the experiments. Talk about whole and half cups and how the shape of a container can make you think it has more water in it than it really does.

_____ Activity 3 _____

Number Matching Game—Divide a pizza board into six equal parts by drawing lines on it. In each part, draw one of the following: one brown raisin, two purple plums, three red cherries, four blueberries, five yellow peaches, and six green limes. Also, make six pie-shaped pieces which have a colored numeral to correspond to the color of the fruit on the pie, for example, a green six. The children are to match the color and number on their slice to the fruit on the pie.

CLOSING _____ Story _____

Read one of the following stories: *The Mouse Family's Blueberry Pie,* by Alice P. Miller (Elsevier-Dutton Co., 1981). *Apple Pie,* by Anne Wellington (Prentice-Hall, 1978). *Pancake Pie,* by Sven Norquist (William Morrow & Co., 1984).

Cornbread Day

PREPARATION _____ To the Teacher _____

While cooking with the children, take every opportunity to count with them and refer to the numbers in the recipe. Point out that a fraction of a cup is less than a whole cup.

You will need:

- ingredients and recipe (see below) for Arrival;
- cornbread and white bread for Opening;
- whipping cream and a jar for Opening;
- ears of corn and paper plates for Activity 1;
- cornmeal and dry tempera for Activity 2; and
- muffin tins and kernels of corn for Activity 3.

ARRIVAL _____ Cornbread Muffins _____

As the children arrive, have them make cornbread muffins to be eaten at snack time. Write the recipe in picture form on a large chart so the children can see what is needed to make their muffins.

Cornbread Muffins

1 1/4 cups flour
1/3 cup sugar
1/2 teaspoon salt
1/4 cup vegetable oil
3/4 cup cornmeal
2 tsp. baking powder
1 cup milk
1 egg (beaten)

Combine dry ingredients. Beat egg; add milk and oil. Stir into dry ingredients. Mix just until moistened. Fill muffin cups two-thirds full and bake at 375 degrees for fifteen minutes. Yield: twelve

OPENING _____ Cornbread Talk _____

Bring cornbread and a loaf of white bread for the children to see and taste and compare the differences. Explain that cornbread has cornmeal in it, which is made from corn that has been ground very fine. This is unlike most breads that have flour in them, which is made from ground wheat. Point out that cornbread is yellow and crumbly. As children taste the two breads, discuss the two textures.

_____ Make Butter _____

The children will enjoy making butter to spread on their muffins. Pour a half pint of whipping cream into a jar with a tight lid. Let the children take turns shaking it until it turns into butter, while enjoying "Muffin Man" on the album _We All Live Together,_ volume 2 (YR-00ZR), by Greg Scelsa and Steve Millang (Youngheart Records, Box 27784, Los Angeles, Calif. 90027).

© 1990 by The Center for Applied Research in Education

CRAFT _____ The Muffin Man _____

Materials Needed:

> 2″ × 4″ rectangle patterns
> muffin papers (smallest size available)
> paper
> scissors, glue, crayons

Explanation:
Have children trace a rectangular pattern and cut it out.
Glue it on a larger piece of paper. This will be the muffin
man's cart. Glue two mini-muffin papers under the cart
for the wheels, and glue one mini-muffin paper beside the
cart for the muffin man's head. Children use crayons to
draw the muffin man's body and the handle of the cart.

FREEPLAY _____ Activity 1 _____

Paper Plate Shakers—Bring ears of corn to class. As the children are shelling the corn, review
what they learned about cornmeal in Arrival and Opening. Use the kernels of corn to make
paper plate shakers. Give each child two paper plates, some kernels of corn, and crayons to decorate
the shaker. Staple the plates together, leaving an opening to add the corn.

_____ Activity 2 _____

Cornmeal Designs—In margarine tubs, mix 1/2 cup cornmeal with dry tempera. Children draw
a design with glue on paper and then sprinkle the cornmeal mixture over the glue. Pour off the
extra cornmeal to reveal the colored design.

_____ Activity 3 _____

Counting Kernels—Cut small circles to fit in the bottom of muffin tins. Write a numeral on each
circle. The child is to count that many kernels of corn into that section of the muffin tin.

CLOSING _____ Story _____

Read one of the following stories: *Benny's Magic Baking Pan,* by Kenneth Truse (Garrard, 1974).
Bread and Jam for Frances, by Russell Hoban (Harper & Row, 1964). *When Batistine Made Bread,*
by Treska Lindsey (Macmillan, 1985).

Turkey Day

PREPARATION _____ To the Teacher _____

Unit 4 has concentrated heavily on math, which is difficult for many children. Turkey Day is a little more relaxed, with activities encouraging creativity and color identification reinforcement.
     You will need:

- paint and pie tins for Arrival;
- pictures of a turkey for Opening;
- fingerplay glove for Opening;
- feather pattern for Activity 1;
- turkey body, feathers, and magnet for Activity 2 (see p. 97);
- feathers for Activity 3; and
- turkey on the bulletin board and feathers for Closing.

ARRIVAL _____ Handprint _____

Have the children lay one hand in a pie tin containing tempera paint and then make a handprint on their craft paper for today. Have them spread their fingers apart to resemble feathers in a turkey's tail.

OPENING _____ Turkey Talk _____

A turkey is a bird that has feathers over its body except on its head and neck. Identify the parts of a turkey's body using pictures—feathers, tail, wings, feet, etc. The pouch-like area in front of the throat is called a gullet. The female turkey is called a hen, and the male turkey is called a tom. Turkeys have rather large beaks that must be clipped so they cannot eat dirty things that are not good for them. With a clipped beak, they can only eat out of a turkey feeder. The turkeys' wing feathers also must be clipped; otherwise, the turkeys fly over the fence.

_____ Fingerplay _____

Teach the children the following poem. You can make a visual with an old white dress glove, five turkey stickers, and Velcro®. Place the stickers on light cardboard and cut them out. Glue Velcro® on the end of each finger of the glove and on the back of each sticker. Now, stick each turkey on a finger of the glove and you have five little turkeys to show the children during the poem. Because you used Velcro®, the glove can be used again and again with different pictures or stickers.

Five Little Turkeys (traditional)
Five little turkeys are we.
We slept all night in a tree.
When cook came around,
We couldn't be found.
That's why we're here, you see.

© 1990 by The Center for Applied Research in Education

_____ Story _____

Read one of the following stories: *Sometimes It's Turkey, Sometimes It's Feathers,* by Lorna Balian (Abingdon, 1986). *How Spider Saved Turkey,* by Robert Kraus (Windmill Books, 1973). *Farmer Goff and His Turkey Sam,* by Brian Schatell (Harper & Row, 1982).

CRAFT _____ Handprint Turkey _____

Materials Needed:

    handprint painted in Arrival
    brown construction paper
    circle and oval patterns
    scissors, crayons, glue

Explanation:
Children trace and cut out a circle and an oval. The children will paste the shapes on top of the handprint leaving the fingers to show above the circle. Children then use crayons to draw legs and a beak.

FREEPLAY _____ Activity 1 _____

Fringing Feathers—Have the children trace a feather pattern, cut it out, and fringe the edges. Provide a variety of colors from which to choose. (Save these feathers to be put on the bulletin board in Closing.)

_____ Activity 2 _____

Fun with Magnets—Draw the head and body of a turkey on heavy paper (see p. 97). Cut several feathers for the turkey's tail and attach a paper clip to each one. Lay the feathers on top of the turkey picture. The children hold a magnet under the paper and use it to move the turkey's tail feathers into the proper place.

_____ Activity 3 _____

Painting with Feathers—Allow the children to use feathers to paint pictures. Use the rest of the paint you mixed for the handprints made in Arrival.

CLOSING _____ Bulletin Board _____

Prior to class, draw a large turkey (omitting the tail) and place it on the bulletin board. Pass out the feathers cut in Freeplay Activity 1. As you say the following verse with the children, have them bring their feathers to the bulletin board to add to the turkey's tail.

Use your eyes, use your eyes
Quickly look and see,
If your feather is the color of mine,
Bring it here to me.

Dear Parent(s),

We will be having a day to celebrate all the children's birthdays. This will stimulate discussion of growing and getting older, so we would like you to send to school

a baby picture of your child. We need the picture on _____,
(Date)

and it will be returned to you. Please write your child's name on the back of the picture.

Thanks!

Dear Parent(s),

What a day of celebration! Our muffin birthday cakes were delicious. Plan an evening when you can make them with your child while he or she explains what having a birthday means.

Applesauce Muffins

2 cups flour   1 egg (beaten)
1/2 tsp. cinnamon   1/3 cup vegetable oil
4 tsp. baking powder   1/2 cup milk
1/4 cup sugar   2/3 cup applesauce

Combine all ingredients and pour into muffin cups. Fill 2/3 full and sprinkle sugar and cinnamon on top of each muffin. Bake 15–20 minutes at 350°.

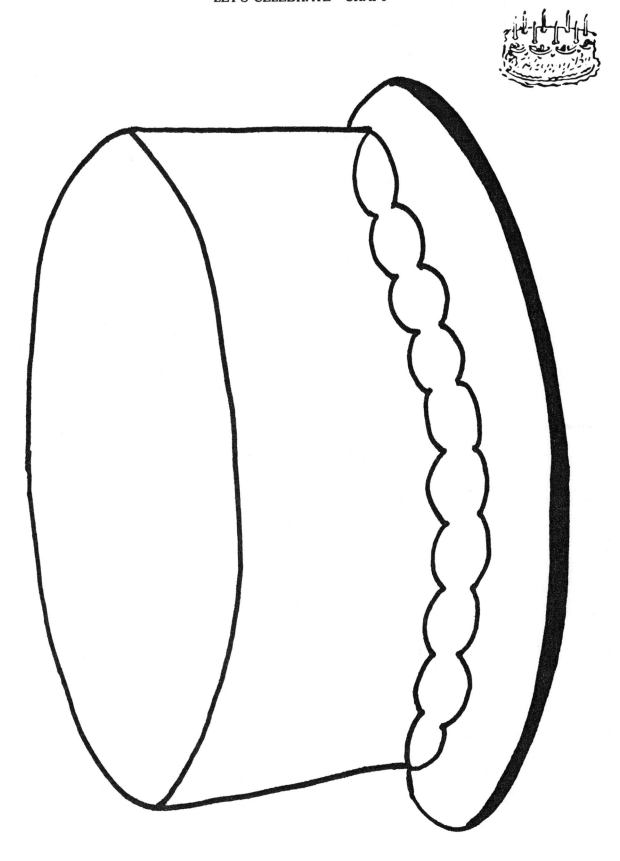

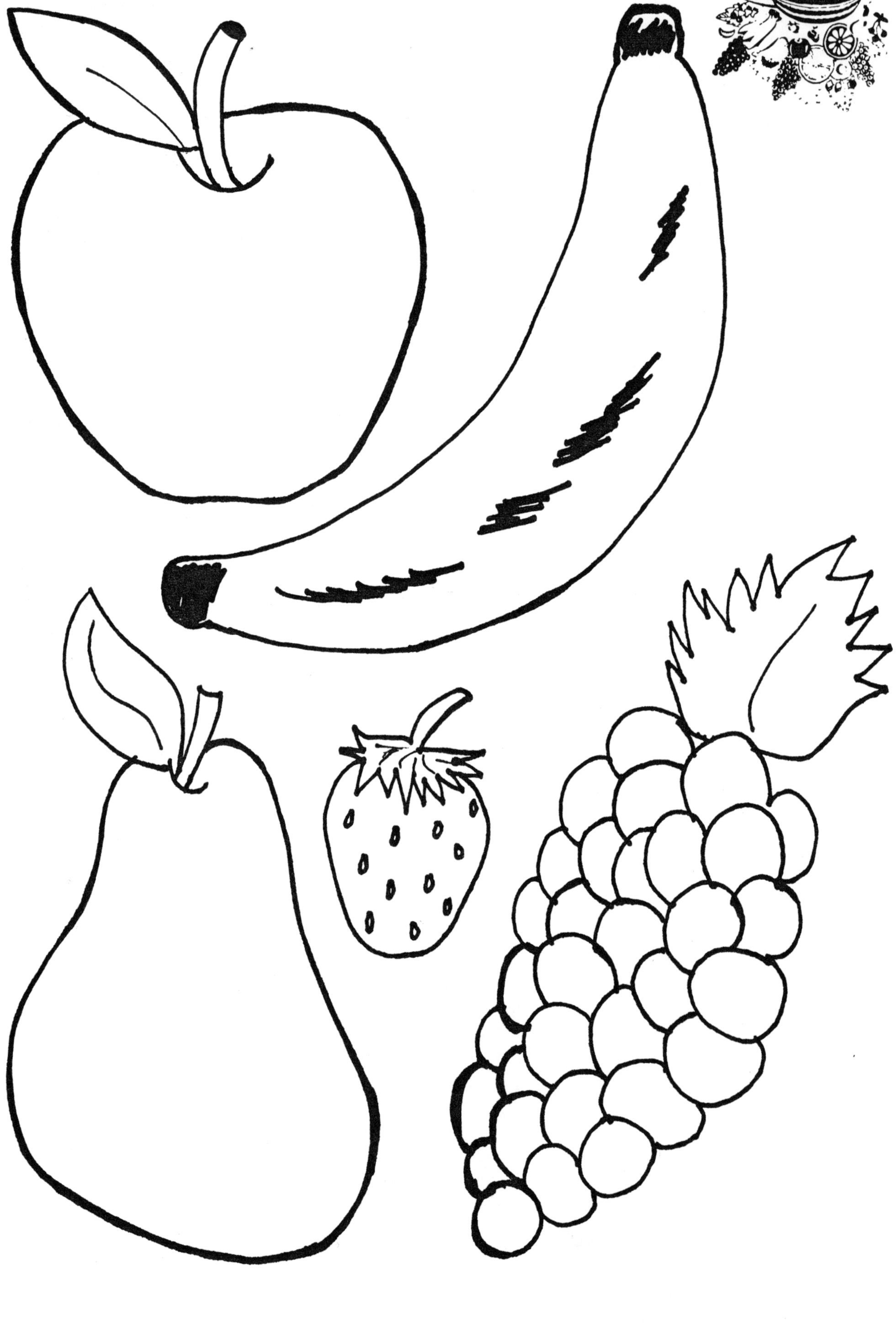

Make two of each card.

unit 5

HAPPY HOLIDAYS

December is a season of holidays. It's a time when everyone can have fun together. Although it's a festive time, it can also be a time when children and adults feel pressured. There is too much to do! Try to keep your classroom as calm as possible with an emphasis on giving and sharing.

Please note that these days lead toward giving something the children make to someone who is special to them. Spend time discussing the gifts they will be giving rather than what they might like to receive.

The daily activity plans in Unit 5 include:

- Cookie Jar Day
- Cookie Day
- Mouse Day
- Star Day
- Box Day
- Wrapping Paper Day
- Ribbon and Bow Day
- Giving and Sharing Day

Cookie Jar Day

© 1990 by The Center for Applied Research in Education

PREPARATION _____ **To the Teacher** _____

When thinking of Christmas, special goodies we eat come to mind. That is the reason for the theme of this day and the following one—Cookie Day.
   You will need:

- notes to parents requesting that children bring in a small oatmeal box (see p. 118);
- felt characters for Story in Opening (see p. 116);
- fabric circles for Arrival;
- cookie jars for Opening and Activity 1;
- cards for Activity 1;
- Cookie Monster and catalogs for Activity 2;
- materials to design a cookie jar for Activity 3; and
- circles for Closing.

ARRIVAL _____ **Design a Lid** _____

As the children arrive, have them color a design on a circle of cotton fabric, which will be glued on the lid of the cookie jar they will make in Craft today. Iron these circles to set the crayon (this can be done after class because they are not glued on until the next day). To set the crayon, cover the design with four to five sheets of paper towels. Press with an iron on medium heat setting until the crayon design no longer prints onto the paper towels. (The paper towel on top of the drawing will need to be changed several times.)

OPENING _____ **Cookie Jar Talk** _____

Where do you keep cookies at your house? Why do we need to keep cookies in a container? Why is the cookie jar sometimes placed too high for you to reach? Have available cookie jars of different shapes and sizes to show the children and talk about.

_____ **Story** _____

Share the story *Our Cookie Jar Friends* with the children today. It's a good idea to make flannel board pieces to aid in telling the story (see p. 116). Another story you may want to share today is *The Sweet Smell of Christmas,* by Patricia Scarry (Western Publishing Co., 1970).

Our Cookie Jar Friends

Our cookie jar friends jumped out one night
When the cookie jar lid was not on tight.
The gingerbread boy blinked his eyes
And looked around with much surprise.
The frosted duck shook the sugar off his back
As he flapped his wings and said, "quack quack."
The little lamb kicked his heels and began to run.
He knew this night was going to be fun.
The big, heavy elephant raised his long, gray trunk
And down went the cookie jar lid—ker plunk!
The cookies danced and played but didn't stray far
And one by one hopped back to the cookie jar.

CRAFT _____ Decorate a Cookie Jar _____

Materials Needed:

one small oatmeal box per child (Ask each child to bring his or her own. See p. 118.)

paper to cover the outside of the oatmeal box

tempera paint in two colors

wide paintbrushes

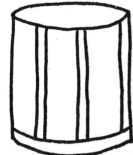

Explanation:
Either strip the paper off the outside of the oatmeal boxes, or cover them by taping or gluing paper around the outside. The children use the paint and brushes to make stripes on the outside of their cookie jars. The children will complete these cookie jars on Cookie Day.

FREEPLAY _____ Activity 1 _____

Cookie Jar Lid Game—To play this game, use the cookie jars from Opening, or make some cookie jars like the ones the children made in Craft. Make word cards that say *on, off, behind, beside, in front of, left,* and *right.* The children draw a card and place the lid where the card tells them.

_____ Activity 2 _____

Bulletin Board—On the bulletin board, place a large picture of Cookie Monster. Discuss with the children how much Cookie Monster likes to eat cookies and how excited he would be to be surrounded with cookie jars. Let the children cut pictures of cookie jars out of catalogs or draw pictures of cookie jars to place on the bulletin board with Cookie Monster.

_____ Activity 3 _____

Design a Cookie Jar—Have the children cut out a cookie jar (see p. 117). Provide different ways for them to decorate their cookie jar, such as cutting shapes, lacing the edges with yarn, cutting pictures from magazines, or using crayons or stickers.

CLOSING _____ Music _____

"Circle Game," on the album *Getting to Know Myself* (AR 543), by Hap Palmer (Educational Activities, Inc., Box 392, Freeport, N.Y. 11520), will reinforce the concepts worked on in Activity 1. Give each child a plastic or cardboard circle approximately 12″ in diameter. Children respond to the directions to stand inside the circle or to put the circle between their legs.

Cookie Day

© 1990 by The Center for Applied Research in Education

PREPARATION _____ **To the Teacher** _____

You will finish the cookie jar today and concentrate on cookies—all kinds of cookies. You will need:

- cookie dough for Arrival (see p. 118);
- measuring cups and spoons for Opening;
- prepared cloths for cookie jar lids for Activity 1;
- poems for Activity 1 (see p. 103); and
- paper cookie and cookie jar for Activity 3.

ARRIVAL _____ **Make Cookies** _____

Using the following recipe, prepare cookie dough prior to class. As the children arrive, have them roll out a small piece of dough and cut out two round cookies. Talk about the shape of their cookies and have them name other things they eat that are round. Decorate the cookies with sprinkles or chocolate chips, if you wish. Each child can eat one cookie at snack time and take one home in his or her cookie jar. (See Activity 1 and p. 118.)

Roll-out Cookies

1 pkg. instant vanilla pudding
1 egg
1/2 cup sugar
1/2 cup margarine
1 1/2 cups flour
1 tsp. cinnamon
1/2 tsp. soda
1 tsp. vanilla

Mix all ingredients. Chill dough. Roll out, cut, and bake at 350 degrees for ten to twelve minutes. Yield: one dozen

OPENING _____ **Cookie Talk** _____

What is your favorite kind of cookie? Where do you get your favorite cookie? Group the children according to the kind of cookie they like best or according to where they get their favorite cookie. Discuss how cookies are made and what kinds of ingredients are used when making cookies. Use measuring cups and spoons and a large tub of sand to demonstrate measuring ingredients. Talk about how many teaspoons there are in a tablespoon, how many half cups in a cup, etc. Measuring utensils can be left out for a Freeplay activity.

CRAFT _____ **Bulletin Board Cookies** _____

Materials Needed:

paper, pencils, glue, scissors
cookie cutters
colored sprinkles or glitter

Explanation:
Have the children trace around the cookie cutters and cut out their cookies. They may decorate them by gluing on sprinkles or glitter. Put these cookies on the bulletin board with Cookie Monster and his cookie jars. (See Cookie Jar Day, Activity 2.)

FREEPLAY _____ **Activity 1** _____

Finish Cookie Jar—Finish the cookie jar started in Craft on Cookie Jar Day by gluing the cloth circle on the oatmeal box lid. Insert the cookie made in Arrival and the following poem. The cookie jar is ready to take home!

> Cookies are my favorite treat.
> They are always good to eat.
> This one last cookie I give to you
> Because I know you like them, too.
> Together let us mix and bake
> More and more cookies we will make!

_____ **Activity 2** _____

Class Book—Have each child draw a picture of his or her favorite kind of cookie to go in a class book. Write the child's version of the recipe for making these cookies in the corner of his or her paper.

_____ **Activity 3** _____

"Who Took the Cookie?"—In advance, make a paper cookie and cookie jar (see p. 117). Place them on the floor in the middle of a circle of children. Choose one child to hide his or her eyes while another takes the cookie from the cookie jar. As the child hides the cookie behind his or her back, the rest of the children chant, "Who took the cookie from the cookie jar?" The first child then opens his or her eyes and tries to guess who took the cookie. He or she points to a child and says, "Did you?" If that child did not take the cookie, he or she says, "Not I. She [or he] took the cookie from the cookie jar," and points to the child who did take the cookie. If the child guesses correctly, the child with the cookie says, "I took the cookie from the cookie jar." You can then choose different children, and play continues.

CLOSING _____ **Story** _____

Read one of the following stories: *Christmas Cookie Sprinkle Snatcher,* by Robert Kraus (Windmill Books, 1969). *Arthur's Christmas Cookie,* by Lillian Hoban (Harper & Row, 1972). *If You Give a Mouse a Cookie,* by Laura Jaffe Numeroff (Harper & Row, 1985).

Mouse Day

© 1990 by The Center for Applied Research in Education

PREPARATION _____ To the Teacher _____

Many authors have chosen to depict the mouse as a cute, lovable character in Christmas stories. Including Mouse Day in this unit allows you to share one of these stories and to teach the nursery rhyme "Hickory Dickory Dock."

You will need:

- flannel board pieces for Opening (see p. 119);
- clock with movable hands and a bell for Activity 1;
- special lacing boards for Activity 2; and
- plastic cheese for Activity 3.

ARRIVAL _____ Cutting Shapes _____

Have each child cut out a rectangle (2″ by 4″) and a triangle (2″ equilateral) to be used in Craft.

OPENING _____ Mouse Talk _____

A mouse is grayish brown. It is small with a long tail, and it makes a noise that sounds like a very soft, high-pitched squeal. If you talk about more than one mouse, you need to say _mice._ When mice get into a house, they eat food and chew furniture and clothing. They scamper along very quickly and quietly. Have you ever heard someone say "quiet as a mouse"?

Have you ever seen a mouse? Why are people so afraid of such a little animal? Are you afraid of a mouse? Why, or why not?

_____ Hickory Dickory Dock _____

Teach the children this nursery rhyme. You might want to bring visuals or make flannel board pieces to use as the children recite the poem (see p. 119).

> Hickory dickory dock
> The mouse ran up the clock;
> The clock struck one,
> And down he run,
> Hickory dickory dock!

CRAFT _____ Shape Mouse _____

Materials Needed:

    rectangle and triangle cut in Arrival
    paper, glue, crayons
    yarn cut in different lengths

Explanation:
Have the children glue the rectangle and triangle on a large piece of paper in the position shown. Then give them pieces of yarn cut in different lengths and ask, "How would you use these pieces of yarn to make this look more like a mouse?" They can use the crayons to finish the mouse's features.

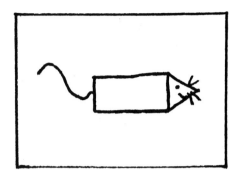

FREEPLAY _____ Activity 1 _____

Ringing the Chimes—You will need a large clock with movable hands. The children take turns moving the small hand to point to different numbers. Another child rings a chime that many times. The triangle or bell from your rhythm instruments could be used for the chime. *Example:* One child moves the small clock hand to point to the numeral 3. The child holding the chime rings it three times.

_____ Activity 2 _____

Lacing Boards—Use scraps of pegboard approximately 8″ by 10″ to make special lacing boards for this day. Begin by painting the boards white. Stencil or freehand a mouse in one corner and cheese in the corner diagonally across. (Paint or marker work equally well.) Attach a piece of plastic telephone wire close to the mouse (see p. 63). Children choose the path their mouse wants to take to the cheese by weaving the wire through the holes of the pegboard.

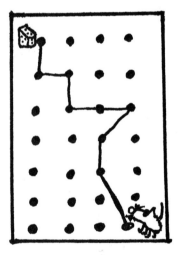

_____ Activity 3 _____

Circle Game—Children stand in a circle and say the poem "Hickory Dickory Dock." One child is chosen to be "it" and walks around the circle as the poem is recited. When children say "the clock strikes one," the child drops a piece of plastic cheese behind another child. As the group finishes the poem, the two race back to the vacated spot

CLOSING _____ Story _____

Read one of the following stories: *Santa Mouse,* by Michael Brown (Grosset & Dunlap, 1966). *How Brown Mouse Kept Christmas*, by Clyde Watson (Farrar, 1980). *The Christmas Mouse,* by Elisabeth Wenning (Holt, 1959).

Star Day

PREPARATION _____ To the Teacher _____

This is the first of five days that relate to each other. Today, the children make a gift, and then during each of the next four days, they continue to work on it.

You will need:

- spatter paint boxes, black paper, and white paint for Arrival;
- ingredients for baker's dough (see below);
- supplies for Activity 1;
- star necklaces for Activity 2; and
- cards with stars for Activity 3.

ARRIVAL _____ Spatter Paint _____

Using spatter paint boxes, have each child spatter white paint on black paper so that it appears to be a night sky full of twinkling stars.

Spatter paint boxes can be made by stretching and tacking mesh screen over a wooden frame approximately 9″ by 11″ by 1 1/2″. To use, cover a table with newspaper. The child then sets the box over the black paper, dips a toothbrush in white paint, and rubs the brush across the screen. The paint that sifts through the screen spatters onto the paper.

OPENING _____ Dough Ornaments _____

Have the children help you mix some baker's dough to be used in Activity 1 for making star ornaments. These ornaments will be taken home later this month as a gift for someone special. The children will also make wrapping paper and a card to take home with this gift on Giving and Sharing Day.

Baker's Dough

4 cups flour
1 cup salt
1 1/2 cups cold water
food coloring

Mix all ingredients. Knead until pliable. Shape as desired. Bake at 350 degrees for one hour or until evenly browned.

_____ Star Talk _____

Stars are suns. They are bigger and brighter than our sun but are much farther away, which is why they look so small. There are stars that are so far away that we are unable to see them. There are lots and lots of stars. In fact, there are more stars than there are people in the world!

Where are the stars when we look for them on a cloudy night? Where are they during the day?

Conclude your discussion by singing "Twinkle, Twinkle Little Star."

Twinkle, twinkle little star;
How I wonder what you are,
Up above the world so high,
Like a diamond in the sky!
Twinkle, twinkle little star,
How I wonder what you are.

CRAFT _____ Night Scene _____

Materials Needed:

> spatter painting from Arrival
> gummed stars
> stencils cut in the shape of a moon
> yellow paint
> sponges

Explanation:
Children stencil a moon and add stars to the night sky that
they spatter painted earlier.

FREEPLAY _____ Activity 1 _____

Dough Ornaments—Children roll out baker's dough, made in Opening, and use a star cookie
cutter to cut out a star ornament. The ornaments may be sprinkled with sequins or glitter before
baking. Poke a hole in the top of each ornament with a straw. (Bake the ornaments after class.)

_____ Activity 2 _____

The Big Dipper—In advance, cut out several large
stars and put them on a string so they can be
worn as a necklace. Show the children pictures
of different constellations, such as the Big Dipper. Have the children put on the star necklaces
and stand in the shape of the different constellations. (See p. 120.)

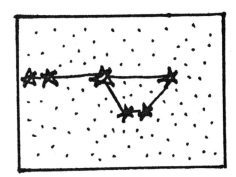

_____ Activity 3 _____

Star Game—In advance, make various colored cards with different numbers of yellow gummed
stars on them. Children sit in a circle and pass the cards until the music stops. When the music
stops, say, for example, "Children with three stars on your card stand up." Those children stand
and tell you the color of their card.

CLOSING _____ Story _____

Read one of the following stories: *Ottie and the Star,* by Laura Jean Allen (Harper & Row, 1979).
A Christmas Story, by Mary Chalmers (Harper & Row, 1956). *Little Christmas Star,* by Janet
Crais (Troll Associates, 1988).

Box Day

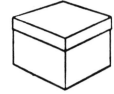

© 1990 by The Center for Applied Research in Education

PREPARATION _____ To the Teacher _____

Boxes are an appropriate topic at Christmas since lots of time is spent wrapping them. In addition to all the box activities, continue work on the gift which you made on Star Day.
   You will need:

- varnish and brushes for Arrival;
- note to parents requesting that each child bring in a box;
- dough art stars from Star Day for Arrival;
- props for story for Opening;
- two boxes for Activity 1; and
- a very large box for Activity 3.

ARRIVAL _____ Star Shine _____

Varnish the stars you baked on Star Day. Use a small sponge paintbrush. (This brush can be purchased for a minimal cost at most hardware or discount stores. No clean up. . .just throw it away!)

OPENING _____ Box Talk _____

What things do you eat that come in a box? What things do you wear that are in a box? Why is it easier to store large things in a box rather than a bag? Why do some boxes have lids? What different shapes can a box be?

_____ Story _____

The best story for today is one that you create as you tell it. You will need the following props:

   one rectangular box (child's shoebox)

   one square box (watch box)

   one circular box (metal candy box)

   one string of gold triangles (cut ten small triangles out of heavy, shiny paper—old greeting cards work well.)

   Glue five triangles to a piece of string. Then glue the remaining triangles to the back of the other triangles.

Place the string of triangles inside the circular box, which is inside the square box, which is inside the rectangular box.
   Hold these boxes on your lap as you begin to tell a story about a poor family—so poor that they have nothing in their cupboards to eat. The family goes out to the garden, hoping to find some potatoes. While digging, their shovel hits something—a box! They are very anxious to open it and see what is inside.
   Build up the suspense as you open each box only to find another box and, finally, the gold triangles. (Emphasize the shape of each box as it is discovered.)
   The conclusion, of course, is that the golden triangles solve the family's financial problems. Refer to this story when doing the craft today.

CRAFT _____ Clay Surprises! _____

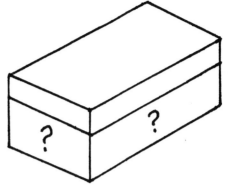

Materials Needed:

    one box per child (shoebox size or smaller) with a lid
    art clay

Explanation:
Ask each child to create whatever he or she would like
to find in a box if it contained a lucky surprise. Put
the completed surprise in the box. Perhaps you can
help the child make up a story about the clay
sculpture!

FREEPLAY _____ Activity 1 _____

Passing Boxes—Find two identical boxes. Fill one with clay, and wrap both boxes in plain brown
paper. Children sit in a circle and pass the boxes around while music plays. When the music
stops, the child holding the boxes tells which one is heavier.

_____ Activity 2 _____

Acting to a Song—Lead the children's actions to the song "Big Heavy Box," on the album *Pretend* (AR 563), by Hap and Martha Palmer (Educational Activities, Inc., Box 392, Freeport, N.Y.
11520).

_____ Activity 3 _____

Spatial Relationships—Bring a large box to class—large enough for a child to fit inside. (Save
this box to use during Arrival on Wrapping Paper Day.) Give the children verbal commands
specifying where they should be in relationship to the box. *Examples:* Climb into the box, sit
behind the box, stand beside the box, place your hand under the box.

CLOSING _____ Jack in the Box _____

Have the children sit in a circle. Place the box from Activity 3 in the center of the circle. Choose
one child to hide in the box. The class says:

> Jack in the box sits so still.
> Won't you come out?
> Yes, I will! (child pops out)

_____ Story _____

Read one of the following stories: *The Box Book,* by Cecilia Maloney (Western Publishing, 1978).
The Christmas Box, by Eve Merriam (William Morrow & Co., 1985). *Miss Dog's Christmas,* by
James Marshall (Houghton-Mifflin, 1973).

Wrapping Paper Day

PREPARATION _____ To the Teacher _____

The children will discover that wrapping paper can be found in all colors and designs to celebrate special days.

You will need:

- note to parents requesting that each child bring in wrapping paper (see p. 121);
- large box from Box Day;
- flannel board pieces to be used with the record in Opening (see pp. 122–23);
- many kinds of wrapping paper for Activity 1;
- wrapping paper worm for Activity 2; and
- lots of small boxes and wrapping paper for Activity 3.

ARRIVAL _____ My Favorite Paper _____

Ask the children to bring a small piece of their favorite wrapping paper to class today (see p. 121). As they arrive, glue the paper on the large box from Box Day.

OPENING _____ Wrapping Paper Talk _____

Different kinds of wrapping paper are used depending on the reason or occasion for gift giving. Show the children birthday, wedding, graduation, baby, and Christmas papers. Ask them to look carefully at the papers and tell when they would use each one. Use the following questions for discussion: Why do we wrap gifts? What do we need to hold the paper on the box? What kinds of special paper did we put on the box in Arrival? Do you save the paper when you open a present? What can you do with this paper?

_____ Book _____

Share with the children the book _Christmas!_, by Peter Spier (Doubleday, 1983). It is a picture book that illustrates lots of wrapping paper and every aspect of Christmas.

_____ Record _____

The children will enjoy the song "Pack Up the Sleigh" on the album _Witches' Brew_ (AR 576), by Hap and Martha Palmer (Educational Activities, Inc., Box 392, Freeport, N.Y. 11520). You might want to make some flannel board pieces to use with this record—such as a sleigh to hold the gifts, a wagon, a rabbit, etc. (see pp. 122–23). Give these pieces to the children, and as you sing about "something that is red and has four wheels," the child with the red wagon can bring it up and pack it in the sleigh. When you sing about "something that is soft and fuzzy and brown," the child with the rabbit can bring it up to the sleigh.

© 1990 by The Center for Applied Research in Education

CRAFT _____ Wrapping Paper _____

Materials Needed:

    large piece of newsprint for each child
    tempera paint
    cookie cutters

Explanation:
The children dip the cookie cutters in the paint and print on their paper. This makes lovely wrapping paper for the star ornaments that children made on Star Day. Gift wrapping will be done on Giving and Sharing Day.

FREEPLAY _____ Activity 1 _____

Categorizing Wrapping Paper—Use ribbon to divide a bulletin board into four sections and label them: Birthday, Christmas, Baby, and Children's Fun Paper. Cut small pieces of many kinds of wrapping paper for the children to put in the proper category.

_____ Activity 2 _____

Mr. Wrapping Paper Worm—Make each section of Mr. Worm from a different piece of wrapping paper. Give the children circles cut from the same papers and direct them to lay them on top of the identical circle in Mr. Worm.

_____ Activity 3 _____

Wrap a Box—Bring in small boxes of varying sizes, scrap pieces of wrapping paper, and tape. Let the children wrap presents. Encourage them to speculate about what might be inside the package and who it might be for.

CLOSING _____ Story _____

Read one of the following stories: _Claude the Dog,_ by Dick Gackenbach (Seabury Press, 1974). _Bialosky's Christmas,_ by Leslie McGuire (Western Publishing Co., 1984). _Henry and Mudge in the Sparkle Days,_ by Cynthia Rylant (Bradbury Press, 1988).

Ribbon and Bow Day

PREPARATION _____ To the Teacher _____

Today the children finish the star ornament by making a hanger from a piece of ribbon. Ribbons and bows are also the finishing touches for packages. Notice that this day provides a review of concepts introduced in this unit: shapes, colors, and numerals.

You will need:

- notes to parents requesting that children bring in ribbon (see p. 121);
- large box from Wrapping Paper Day;
- baked star ornaments from Star Day;
- box, wrapping paper, and ribbon for Opening;
- felt shapes for shape pictures in Opening;
- triangles (musical instruments) for Activity 1; and
- several large bows for Activity 2
- wrapped boxes from Activity 3 on Wrapping Paper Day (see p. 111).

ARRIVAL _____ Ribbon Fun _____

Ask the children to bring in pieces of their favorite color of ribbon (see p. 121). Put a piece of ribbon through their star ornament for a hanger. Use the remaining ribbon to decorate the large box the children wrapped on Wrapping Paper Day. Every nicely wrapped box looks prettier with ribbons on it!

OPENING _____ Ribbon and Bow Talk _____

Ribbons are used as trim on clothing, pillows, and packages. Little girls look very pretty with ribbons in their hair. Show the children how to curl ribbon to make a bow. People choose ribbon because of what color it is. It is always chosen to complement or go with something else. As you are talking with the children, wrap a box in very colorful paper. Point out all the different colors as the children identify them. Let the children know that any one of the colors could be chosen for the ribbon color. Tie ribbon around the package, and the children will agree how pretty it is!

_____ Shape Pictures _____

Cut squares, circles, rectangles, ovals, and triangles out of felt. Using the flannel board, ask each child what he or she could make out of two triangles. (A kite?) Use a circle and a triangle to create something. (An ice cream cone?) You might want to make up riddles to go along with the shape pictures. _Examples:_ "Flying high above the tree, I wish this kite belonged to me." "I like things that are cold and sweet; ice cream is my favorite treat."

CRAFT _____ Triangle Creations _____

Materials Needed:

    large sheet of newsprint for each child
    ribbon scraps
    crayons, glue

Explanation:
Have each child draw a triangle anywhere on the paper. Outline and fill in the triangle by gluing pieces of ribbon on it. Encourage the child to turn the paper any way he or she wishes. Use crayons to make the triangles into a person or object (a tree, your mom, an ice cream cone. . . anything). Use crayons to fill in the background of the picture.

FREEPLAY _____ Activity 1 _____

Triangle Rhythms—Play a rhythm on a triangle (the musical instrument). Each child who has a triangle takes turns echoing the rhythm. After a few turns, the children can do this in pairs.

_____ Activity 2 _____

Simon Says—Fold masking tape and put it on the back of several large bows. Give several children bows and say, "Simon Says, put the bow on your arm." "Simon Says, put the bow on your longest finger." Children follow commands. If you do not say "Simon Says," the bow should not be moved.

_____ Activity 3 _____

Counting Ribbon—Use the boxes the children wrapped in Freeplay on Wrapping Paper Day. Paste a numeral on each box. The children put that many pieces of ribbon on the box.

CLOSING _____ Story _____

Read one of the following stories: *Merry Christmas, Mom and Dad,* by Mercer Mayer (Western Publishing Co., 1982). *The Christmas Party,* by Adrienne Adams (Scribner's, 1978). *Wake Up, Bear. . .It's Christmas,* by Stephen Gammel (Lothrop, Lee & Shepard, 1981).

Giving and Sharing Day

PREPARATION _____ To the Teacher _____

Children wrap the star ornament so it is ready to give to someone special. This is just one of the ways the children will experience the wonderful feeling of friendship and sharing today.
  You will need:

- notes to parents requesting that children bring in something to share (see p. 124);
- puppets for Opening;
- wrapping supplies for Activity 1;
- photocopied photos and camera for Activity 2;
- beanbags for Activity 3; and
- pictures of things that go together for Closing (see pp. 125–26).

ARRIVAL _____ Music _____

Ask the children to bring something from home that they would like to share with their friends (see p. 124). After each child has shared what he or she has brought, sing "Sharing Song" from the album _Singable Songs for the Very Young_ (SL-002), Raffi with Ken Whiteley (Shoreline Records, 6307 Yonge Street, Willowdale, Ontario, Canada M2M 3X7). "The More We Get Together" is another song from the same album that the children will enjoy.

OPENING _____ Giving and Sharing Talk _____

Young children tend to be me-oriented. They are most concerned with whether they will be first in line or whether they will get to play with that new toy. Hopefully, their school experiences will teach them that it is fun to have a friend to share a book with or to converse with during snack time.
  Today children will think about things they can share with another child that will make that child feel happy. Puppets are an effective means to get children to think about their feelings and behavior. Use puppets that you have on hand to act out some of the following situations: (1) Lisa shared her crackers with her brother Tim. (2) Staci put her arm around Heather when she fell and skinned her knee. (3) Alan let Marc use the orange paint first while he watched and waited for his turn.
  You can use the following questions as discussion starters as you examine the different situations. Is it ALWAYS easy to share? Why, or why not? What are some things for you to share? Whom do you share with at your house? Can you think of something you could share with me?

_____ Story _____

Choose one of the following stories to read: _What Mary Jo Shared,_ by Janice May Udry (Scholastic Books, Inc., 1970). _Christmas Is a Time of Giving,_ by Joan Walsh Anglund (Harcourt Brace, 1961). _Cranberry Christmas,_ by Wende and Harry Devlin (Parents Magazine Press, 1976).

© 1990 by The Center for Applied Research in Education

CRAFT _____ Greeting Cards _____

Materials Needed:

> old greeting cards glue
> wrapping paper one piece of paper (8 1/2″ by 11″) per child

Explanation:
Fold the piece of paper in half to make a card. Then the children cut pictures from the greeting cards and wrapping paper to decorate their cards. You might want to use the following verse and a photocopied picture (see p. 64) of each child in addition to the decoration.

> *Outside the card:* Can you guess
> who loves you?

> *Inside card with photocopied picture:*
> Yes, it's true.
> I LOVE YOU!!

This card will accompany the star the child is giving to someone special.

FREEPLAY _____ Activity 1 _____

Wrap a Star—Children use the wrapping paper they made on Wrapping Paper Day to wrap their star for someone special. Boxes, ribbons, bows, and tape will all be necessities! Attach the card made in Craft when completed, and send the gift home today.

_____ Activity 2 _____

Take a Picture of a Friend—Make available photocopied pictures of everyone in the class (including the teachers!). Create a camera from a small box. Punch a hole in one side of the box to make a lens. Tape a picture of someone in the box on the side opposite the hole. (whoever is having their picture taken). Glue a button to the side of the box. The child can look through the lens at his or her friend, press the button and make a clicking sound, and instantly have a perfect picture! Be sure the child shows the friend how well the picture turned out.

_____ Activity 3 _____

Beanbag Friends—Give each child a beanbag with which to follow the instructions on the song "Make Friends with a Bean Bag" on the album *Bean Bag Activities and Coordination Skills* (KIM 7055), by Georgiana Liccone Stewart, (Kimbo Educational, Box 477, Long Branch, N.J. 07740).

CLOSING _____ A Pair of Friends _____

In advance, make cards with pictures of things we usually use in pairs (see p. 125). (*Examples:* shoes/socks, bat/ball, toothbrush/toothpaste.) Pass out the cards to the children. Ask one child to stand in front of the class and hold up his or her card. Then ask the child holding the card showing the "friend" of this object to come up front, too. Continue until all the pairs of friends have been matched.

Dear Parent(s),

Surprises are always exciting! We are going to make something that we want to share with you, but we need your child to bring a small oatmeal box to class

by _____ to help us with the surprise.
(Date)

Thanks!

© 1990 by The Center for Applied Research in Education

Cookies are my favorite treat.
They are always good to eat.

This one last cookie I give to you
Because I know you like them, too.

Together let us mix and bake,
More and more cookies we will make!

Here's a recipe we can use to make more cookies to fill my cookie jar.

1 pkg. instant vanilla pudding

1 egg

1/2 cup sugar

1/2 cup margarine

1 1/2 cups flour

1 tsp. cinnamon

1/2 tsp. soda

1 tsp. vanilla

Mix all ingredients. Chill dough. Roll out, cut, and bake at 350° for 10–12 minutes. Yield: one dozen

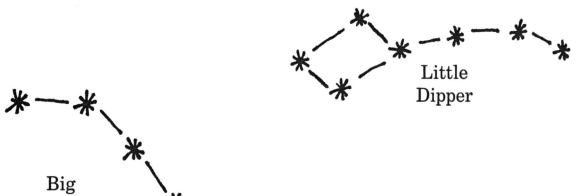

Little
Dipper

Big
Dipper

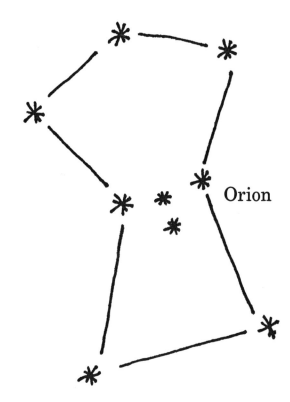

Great Square of
Pegasus

Orion

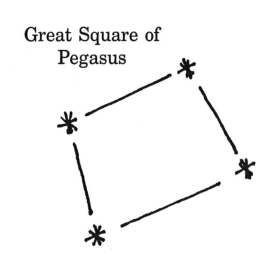

Dear Parent(s),

Christmas makes all children think about presents and what surprises await them inside the packages. They seldom pay much attention to how those packages are

wrapped. On _____ ,we want to examine the different wrapping
             (Date)

papers used on packages for various occasions. To aid us in our study, we are asking the children to bring a small piece of wrapping paper on that day.

                                     Thanks!

Dear Parent(s),

We have several projects planned for Ribbon and Bow Day that require different colors of ribbon. You can help us by sending several small pieces of ribbon with

your child on _____ .
               (Date)

                                     Thanks!

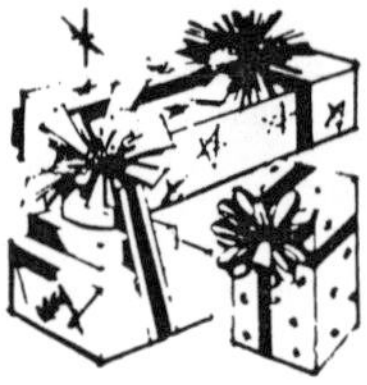

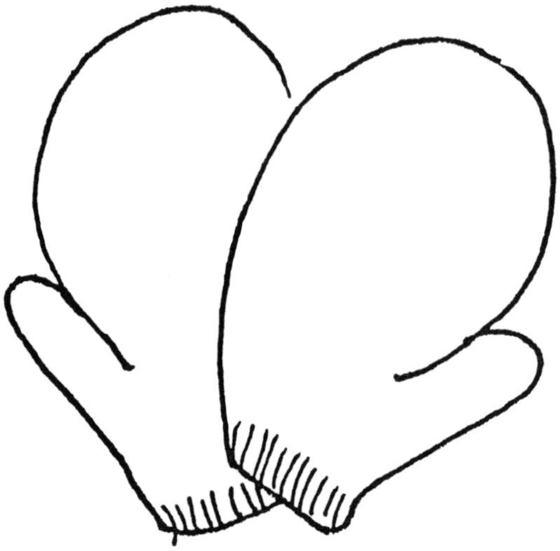

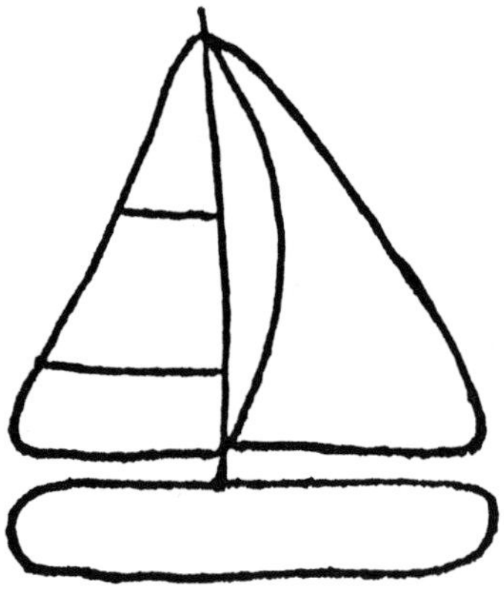

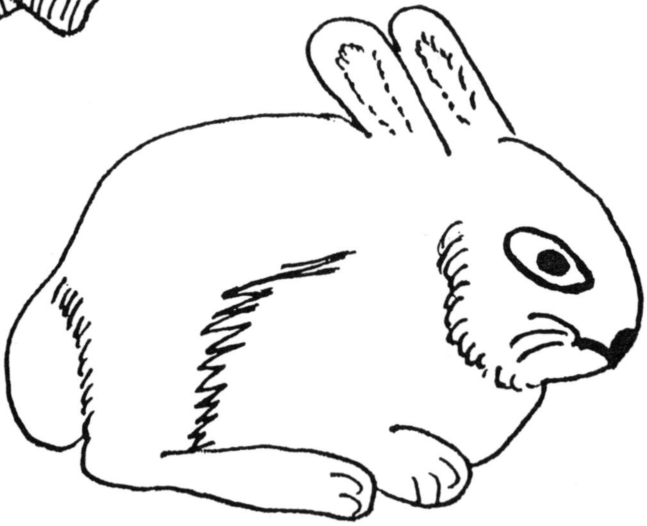

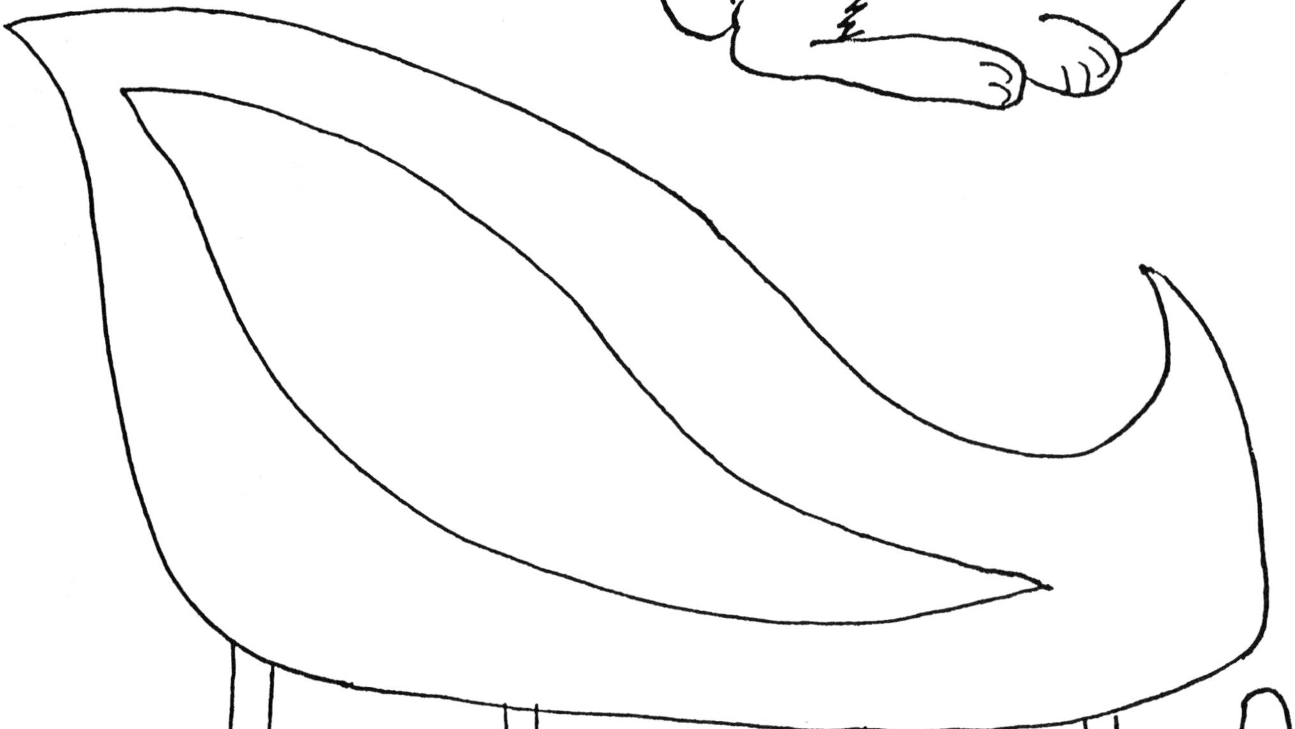

Dear Parent(s),

Children tend to be me-oriented. This is an exciting time of year for them as they anxiously await Christmas morning when they will open their gifts. On

_____ , we will be exploring another aspect of Christmas—
(Date)

the joy of giving or sharing with friends and family. On that day, we are asking each child to bring something special to share with the class. The following are some suggestions, but please be creative: a favorite book, a family picture, a song to sing for the class.

Dear Parent(s),

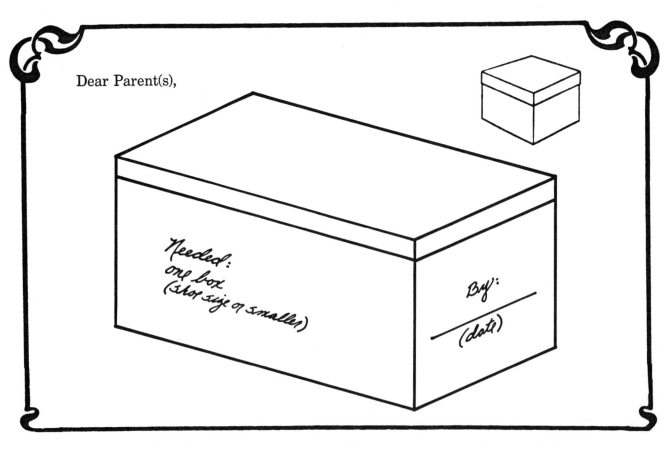

unit 6

FLAIR FOR FASHION

During the winter, in many parts of our country people must wear many clothes to keep warm. For that reason, January is a good month to develop a child's understanding of the different articles of clothing. This unit emphasizes teaching children to button, snap, and zip. Encourage the children to start dressing themselves at home. A child's self-esteem is nurtured by learning to do more things without an adult's help.

The daily activity plans in Unit 6 include:

- Pocket Day
- Cap Day
- Pants Day
- Shoes and Socks Day
- Coat Day
- Mitten Day
- Apron Day
- Closet Day

Pocket Day

PREPARATION _____ To the Teacher _____

This is the first of eight days focusing on clothing. A kangaroo named Kara helps you introduce a new article of clothing each day.

    You will need:

- clothing with pockets for Arrival;
- pita bread and an apron with a large pocket for Opening;
- a paper apron, pockets, and shapes for Activity 2; and
- a large kangaroo and pocket shapes with commands for Activity 3.

ARRIVAL _____ Pocket Count _____

Display articles of clothing with pockets. With the children, count the pockets in each article. Which one has the most, least, biggest, and smallest pockets?

OPENING _____ Pocket Talk _____

A pocket is a small pouch sewn into our clothes, a purse, or a bag. Wear clothing with many pockets today. Lead the children in a discussion about the things we keep in our pockets as you remove those items from your pockets. *Examples:* money, Kleenex®, keys, gum, or candy.

    Which articles of clothing usually have pockets; which seldom have pockets (socks, hats, shoes)? Point out that some tennis shoes (Kangaroos®) do have pockets and are named for the animal that has a "pocket." A kangaroo carries her joey in her pouch (a special name for her pocket).

    Can you think of a pocket that you can eat?!! Bring some pita bread and show the children how to fill it with meats and cheeses.

_____ Stretch Your Imagination _____

What Can You Do with a Pocket?, by Eve Merriam (Alfred A. Knopf, 1964), is a fun book that uses real and imaginative pockets to stretch the children's imaginations.

_____ Will It Fit? _____

You will need an apron with one large pocket which either you or a child can wear. (In this game, you wear the apron.) Display several familiar objects on a table. Show the children one object at a time and ask if this (e.g., comb) will fit in your apron pocket. If it will, children point thumbs up. If not, thumbs down. Be sure to show the children if it fits or not.

CRAFT _____ Shape Pockets _____

Materials Needed:

    construction paper   scissors, pencils
    cardboard shapes (patterns)   glue
    wallpaper scraps

© 1990 by The Center for Applied Research in Education

Explanation:
The children trace and cut as many shapes as desired. Glue all but one side of each shape and place it on the construction paper. Have the children tell you what shape each pocket is.

FREEPLAY _____ Activity 1 _____

Guess the Object—Use the same apron as in Opening. Put an object in the apron pocket. Have a child feel it and try to guess what it is. Ask the child to describe what he or she is feeling. . .something bumpy, small or large, etc., before taking a final guess. Allow children to wear the apron and be the teacher.

_____ Activity 2 _____

Apron Bulletin Board—Make a large paper apron. Cover it with wallpaper pockets. On the front of each pocket, glue a construction paper shape. Pass out matching shapes to the children. One at a time, they place their shape in the correct pocket as they tell you the name of the shape.

_____ Activity 3 _____

Kara the Kangaroo—Introduce Kara the kangaroo. (Kara will be in your classroom for the remainder of the month. To make Kara, cut out a large kangaroo from a scrap piece of paneling or heavy cardboard. Cover her with brown furry material, making a large pocket across her front. Use felt to make facial features.) Cut out pocket shapes for a Listen and Do game. On each pocket shape, write things for the children to do (shut the door, bring me a red book). Each child picks a pocket from Kara's pouch. Read the command, and the child follows the directions.

CLOSING _____ Story _____

Today's story is entitled *Where Is Joey?*, by Donna Lugg Pape (Garrard Publishing Co., 1978). It is about a mother kangaroo, Kara, and her baby, Joey, who are at the park playing when Joey gets lost. Kara hops all over looking for Joey and asks many people if they have seen him. Eventually, she finds Joey. . .but we don't want the children to know this yet, so don't read the end of the story. Kara will be in your classroom every day looking for Joey. Instead of finding Joey in Kara's pouch, the children find an article of clothing which will be your introduction each day. If you are unable to locate this book, make up a story about Kara using the foregoing information and read one of the following stories: *Katy No-Pocket,* by Emmy Payne (Houghton-Mifflin, 1944). *Peter's Pocket,* by Judi Barrett (Atheneum, 1974). *Joey,* by Jack Kent (Scholastic Books, Inc., 1984).

Cap Day

© 1990 by The Center for Applied Research in Education

PREPARATION _____ To the Teacher _____

Both you and the children will wear your favorite caps today! The humor in the story *Caps for Sale* is a delight to children, so it will be worth your effort to locate this book.

You will need:

- notes to parents requesting that children wear a cap (see p. 144);
- large kangaroo from Activity 3 of Pocket Day with cap in pocket;
- Reggie for bulletin board;
- games for Activity 1;
- recorded story and props for Activity 2; and
- caps, hats, and objects for Activity 3.

ARRIVAL _____ Cap Tricks! _____

Have the children wear their favorite cap or hat today (see p. 144). Ask the children to watch you and see if they can do what you do with your cap. (Yes, you have to wear your favorite cap today, too!) Some suggestions: Put your cap behind your back, on your knee, over your head, etc. The last command should be to drop the caps.

OPENING _____ Cap Talk _____

Caps differ from hats because they have a bill rather than a brim. This bill shades the wearer's eyes from the sun. Caps can be worn for many reasons—to keep the head warm, to shade the eyes from the sun, to identify members of a team, or just for fun. Many caps have pictures or wording on them to advertise places to visit or business establishments. Some people wear caps or hats to their job every day. *Examples:* police officer, chef, nurse, professional football player, butcher, military personnel, and the ringmaster at the circus.

Allow the children to show the class the cap or hat they brought as you ask some of the following questions: Where did you get your favorite cap? Why is it your favorite? When do you wear it? Can you name the colors in your cap?

_____ Kara's Pouch Check _____

Do you remember Kara the kangaroo? She is back today and is still looking for Joey. Ask the children to check Kara's pouch to see if Joey came back. (Have a cap in the pocket.) How do you think this cap got in the pocket? Point to a bulletin board where you have placed a picture of a boy approximately three feet tall wearing only a shirt and shorts. Explain that you met this little boy, named Reggie, who was playing with Kara and Joey and became so warm that he shed some of his clothing. And now his clothes are nowhere to be found. Every day we will have to look for Reggie's clothing and Kara's baby. I think this cap belongs to Reggie. Let's put it on his head.

_____ Story _____

Read to the children the story *Caps for Sale,* by Esphyr Slobodkina (Scholastic Books, Inc., 1976).

CRAFT _____ Lots of Caps! _____

Materials Needed:

> paper for each child
> gummed eraser cap stencils
> crayons
> sponges and paints

Explanation:
The child draws a stick person on the paper. Pour some paint in an aluminum pie plate and set a small piece of sponge in it so the sponge will soak up the paint. Lightly press the gummed eraser cap stencil on the sponge and stencil caps on the top of the stick person's head. (To make the stencil, simply draw a cap on the eraser and cut away the excess with an X-ACTO® knife, leaving the cap raised on the eraser.)

FREEPLAY _____ Activity 1 _____

Monkey Games—Make a tree, several monkeys, and several caps from construction paper. Laminate or cover with clear self-stick vinyl for durability. *Game 1:* Put numbers on some of the monkey's tummies. Choose one monkey to hang in the tree. The child puts as many caps in the tree as the monkey's tummy indicates. *Game 2:* Put colored dots on some of the monkeys. Hang one monkey in the tree and ask the child to put all caps that are the same color as the dot in the tree.

_____ Activity 2 _____

Dramatization—Children love dramatization, and *Caps for Sale* is an excellent story to act out. Tape record the story, bring the necessary props, and let the children enjoy.

_____ Activity 3 _____

Whose Hat?—Display caps and hats that are used in a particular profession. Hand the child something that represents the profession and ask him or her to match the hat to the object (rolling pin to baker's hat, baseball to baseball cap, etc.). A good book to use with this activity is *Whose Hat?*, by Margaret Miller (Greenwillow Books, 1988).

CLOSING _____ Music _____

Play the following selections from the album "We All Live Together," volume 4 (YMES-0004), by Greg Scelsa and Steve Millang (Youngheart Records, Box 27784, Los Angeles, Calif. 90027): "Hand Jive" and "Just Like Me." Both songs require the children to do as the leader does, just like the story for today!

Pants Day

© 1990 by The Center for Applied Research in Education

PREPARATION _____ To the Teacher _____

Much of this day is about the saying "ants in your pants." You must discuss the meaning of this saying in Opening so that the Craft and Activity 2 will make sense to the children.
   You will need:

- several pairs of pants and belts;
- small pair of pants to hide in Kara's pouch;
- pants and tops for Opening;
- old greeting cards for Activity 1;
- Ants on the Pants game for Activity 2; and
- large jogging pants for Activity 3.

ARRIVAL _____ Loop to Loop _____

Place many kinds of belts and pants on a table. Children choose a belt and pants and practice fastening the pants and putting the belt through the loops.

OPENING _____ Kara's Pouch Check _____

The children check Kara's pouch, in which you have hidden a small pair of pants. Of course they are not Joey's but they are pants exactly Reggie's size! Place them on the bulletin board on Reggie.

_____ Pants Talk _____

Pants come in many shapes and sizes and are worn by all people from babies to grandparents. All pants have some way to make them fit securely around the person's waist—elastic waistband, zippers or buttons, and belts. Bring to class six to eight different kinds of pants and the tops worn with them. (*Suggestions:* jogging pants, painter pants, bib overalls, football pants, baseball pants, ski or snow pants) Discuss the occasions when these pants are worn.
   Talk about the meaning of the phrases "Keep your pants on" (be patient) and "You have ants in your pants" (you can't sit still.)

_____ Pants Pantomime _____

Use the aforementioned pants and tops to play this game. Choose children to go to another room and put on these pants. When they return, they are to act out what they would do when wearing that kind of pants. Children remaining in the room are to guess what each child is pantomiming and match the tops with the pants.

CRAFT _____ Ants in the Pants _____

Materials Needed:

      paper, scissors, glue
      rectangle patterns, pencils
      black tempera paint
      black crayons or markers

Explanation:
Children trace and cut three rectangles and glue them on a large piece of paper in the shape of a pair of pants. Next, they dip their littlest finger into the paint and print some ant bodies on their pants. Finally, they use the black markers or crayons to give their little ants legs.

FREEPLAY _____ Activity 1 _____

Matching Top and Bottom—Collect greeting cards with pictures of people on them. Cut out the people and then cut them in half at the waist. Mix up the people and let the children find the tops and bottoms that go together.

_____ Activity 2 _____

Ants on the Pants Game—You might want to make this game on the inside of a Manila folder so that you can fold it up and store it easily. Prior to class, make a picture of a pair of pants on the inside of the Manila folder. On each pant leg draw six shapes, making both legs identical. Also, draw and cut out approximately twenty ants for each game you make. To make a spinner, poke a long brad in the middle of a small pizza board or cardboard circle. Attach a paper clip under the brad. Divide the circle into six pie-shaped pieces and draw one shape in each section. *Procedure:* Two children play at one game board. Each child has one pant leg to put ants on. The children take turns spinning, placing one ant per spin on the shape at which the spinner stops. If the spinner stops at a shape that already has an ant, the child may put on a second ant. The game is over when all shapes on one pant leg have at least one ant on them.

_____ Activity 3 _____

Pants Relay—Using two pairs of large jogging pants, let the children choose teams and have a relay in which they put on and take off the jogging pants.

CLOSING _____ Story _____

Read one of the following stories: *The Emperor's New Clothing,* by Hans Christian Andersen, retold by Nadine Bernard (Westcott, Little & Brown, 1984). *Harlequin and the Gift of Many Colors,* by Remy Charlip and Burton Supree (Parents Magazine Press, 1973). *Max's New Suit,* by Rosemary Wells (Dial Press, 1979).

Socks and Shoes Day

PREPARATION _____ To the Teacher _____

Be prepared for lots of activity on this day. Most of the learning centers suggest and encourage active participation by the children.
    You will need:

- sock and hoop for Arrival;
- small socks and canvas shoes for Kara's pouch;
- pictures and objects to use with songs in Opening (see pp. 145–46);
- different kinds of shoes and socks for Opening;
- pictures of people for Activity 1;
- socks, clothespins and rope for Activity 2; and
- special socks for Activity 3.

ARRIVAL _____ Sock It to Me _____

Roll up a sock and let the children take turns throwing it through a hoop or into a basket.

OPENING _____ Kara's Pouch Check _____

The children check Kara's pouch, in which you have hidden socks and a pair of canvas shoes. Of course they are not Joey, but these socks and shoes belong to Reggie! Place them on the bulletin board on Reggie.

_____ Music _____

Make pictures of the items mentioned in the song "Go Together" on the album _Witch's Brew_ (AR576), by Hap and Martha Palmer (Educational Activities, Inc., Box 392, Freeport, N.Y. 11520). Pass out the pictures to the children (see p. 145), and as they listen to the record, they go up to the front of the group when the picture they are holding is mentioned. Another fun song to do this day is "1, 2, Buckle My Shoe" on the album _We All Live Together,_ volume 3 (YMES-003), by Greg Scelsa and Steve Millang (Youngheart Records, Box 27784, Los Angeles, Calif. 90027). Collect actual objects sung about in the song. Find a shoe, a toy barn with a door, sticks, and a toy chicken. Choose five children to come to the front of the group and hold up the object when it is mentioned. (This includes a child to lay the sticks straight.)

_____ Socks and Shoes Talk _____

Bring lots of pairs of shoes to the classroom, such as baseball cleats, ski shoes, bicycling shoes, tennis shoes, high heels, shelling shoes, etc. Also bring a variety of socks, such as white athletic sock, ladies' knee-high sock, black sock, lacy knee sock, and a thermal sock. Discuss which socks go with which shoes.

CRAFT _____ Nail Painting _____

Materials Needed:

> paper
> paint
> large nails
> masking tape

Explanation:
Trace around each child's shoe. The child uses the nail head to paint dots around the drawn outline of the shoe. (Put masking tape on the sharp part of the nail.)

FREEPLAY _____ Activity 1 _____

Whose Shoes?—Use the shoes from Opening and mix them up. On the floor, display pictures of people involved in different activities. Children pair up the shoes and put them on their feet. Then they walk in those shoes to the picture of the person who would be wearing them.

_____ Activity 2 _____

The Great Sock Sort—Stretch a piece of rope between two chairs. Have available a basket of snap clothespins and a basket containing many different socks. Instruct the children to hang socks on the clothesline that meet your specifications. _Examples:_ all the lacy socks, only the white socks, four socks that are exactly the same, five socks arranged from shortest to longest.

_____ Activity 3 _____

Great Sock Relay—Using two pairs of really wild, crazy, men's socks, have a relay race. Divide the class into two teams. The first child of each team pulls the pair of socks on over his or her shoes, runs to a circle made of masking tape on the floor, removes socks, runs back, and gives the socks to the next child. (**For safety reasons this relay should be done on a carpeted floor.**)

CLOSING _____ Story _____

Read one of the following stories: _The Elves and the Shoemaker,_ by Jacob Grimm, adaptation of Wichtelmanner (Lothrop, Lee & Shepard, 1983). _Socks for Supper,_ by Jack Kent (Parents Magazine Press, 1978). _Funny Feet,_ by Leatie Weiss (Watts, 1978).

Coat Day

PREPARATION _____ To the Teacher _____

Learning to zip, button, and snap can be difficult for preschool children. Coats can provide practice in all three of these tasks. This day is also a great help in introducing and/or reviewing colors and the four seasons.

You will need:

- jackets;
- small coat for Kara's pouch;
- pictures of different seasons and appropriate clothing;
- game for Activity 1;
- puzzles for Activity 2; and
- buttons and egg cups for Activity 3.

ARRIVAL _____ Snap, Zip, Button _____

Make available jackets with zip-out sleeves and detachable hoods. Children match a coat to its sleeves and hood so they can then practice zipping, snapping, and buttoning.

OPENING _____ Kara's Pouch Check _____

The children check Kara's pouch, in which you have hidden a small coat. Of course it isn't baby Joey, but it is Reggie's coat! Place the coat on the bulletin board on Reggie.

_____ Coat Talk _____

Today is a good time to talk about the four seasons and how the weather changes in some parts of the country during each season. Show pictures depicting the weather and suitable clothing for each season. Note the difference between a lightweight jacket, which would be suitable for spring and fall, as opposed to a heavier coat, which is necessary in winter. Discuss the advantages of coats with zip-out linings and sleeves.

How do animals adjust to seasonal changes? Many animals, such as foxes, rabbits, and raccoons, grow thicker coats of fur to keep themselves warm as the weather gets colder. Birds, whales, and seals don't have that ability, so they move to warmer climates (migrate) for the winter months. Still other animals, such as bears, bats, and chipmunks, hibernate or sleep during the winter.

_____ Story _____

Read to the children one of the following stories: *The Purple Coat,* by Amy Hest (Four Winds Press, 1986). *No Roses for Harry,* by Gene Zion (Harper & Row, 1958). *Animals Should Definitely not Wear Clothing,* by Judi Barrett (Atheneum, 1970).

© 1990 by The Center for Applied Research in Education

CRAFT _____ Designer Coats _____

Materials Needed:

> several patterns of coats (see pp. 147–48)
> buttons
> small pieces of fabric
> small pieces of fake fur

Explanation:
Cut out of heavy paper several patterns for different styles of coats and jackets. The children trace around their choice of pattern and then choose buttons, small pieces of fabric for patches, and small pieces of fake fur for collars and cuffs. They are sure to create some very interesting fashions.

FREEPLAY _____ Activity 1 _____

Manila Folder Game—Make this game by gluing to the inside of a Manila folder pictures of clothing that are a solid color, such as a blue coat, red pants, etc. Cover with yarn small metal rings used in macrame. You should have one circle the same color as each clothing item pictured. The children place the colored circle on top of the picture of clothing that is the same color.

_____ Activity 2 _____

Coat Puzzles—This is a teacher-made game emphasizing colors and left and right. Choose four colors to teach today. Make four coats in those colors using the pattern on page 147. Laminate and then cut out all coats in identical puzzle pieces so they can be interchanged. Use markers to color picture cards designing one special coat on each card. Give the child a card showing how to make a coat from a pattern. For example, one card might show a coat with green sleeves, a red right side, blue left side, yellow buttons, and a green collar.

_____ Activity 3 _____

Button Sort—Paint a stripe around the top of each egg cup in a carton. All the cups in a carton are to be the same color. Give each child a carton with a different color. Place many buttons of all colors in the middle of a table. Children find buttons that are the same color as their carton. Next time, children trade cartons.

CLOSING _____ Music _____

Children wear their coats and sing (to the tune of "London Bridge"): "I see a girl/boy with a red coat on, red coat on, red coat on. I see a girl/boy with a red coat on, who are you?" Children wearing red coats stand up, and when you point to each one they say their name. Continue singing using other colors.

After the song, the children practice fastening their coats.

Mitten Day

© 1990 by The Center for Applied Research in Education

PREPARATION _____ To the Teacher _____

Point out differences between mittens and gloves and review the items of clothing from previous days. Be sure to continue discussion of the four seasons.
   You will need:

- paper mittens for Arrival, and Activity 3;
- mittens and gloves for Opening
- mittens for Kara's pouch;
- Hangman game for Activity 1;
- styrofoam balls and building blocks for Activity 2; and
- clothesline and clothespins for Activity 3.

ARRIVAL _____ The Three Little Kittens _____

Tell the story *The Three Little Kittens,* by Paul Galdone (Clarion, 1986). At the conclusion of the story, give each child one paper mitten you have cut out and put a design on. Tell the children you lost the other mitten, just like the kittens, and you need help finding it. Each child looks for the mitten that matches the one you have given him or her. Have the mittens hidden around the room.

OPENING _____ Mitten Talk _____

Review the information about the seasons discussed on Coat Day and include the following questions: When do you wear mittens? Why don't you wear mittens in the summer? What is the difference between mittens and gloves? (Have a pair of each to show the difference.) Does it matter which hand you put your mittens on (right and left hand)?
   Some people wear gloves or mittens when they work. Surgeons wear sterilized gloves to protect their patients from infection. Baseball players wear special gloves to help them catch the ball. Welders wear gloves to protect their hands from welding sparks. People who work with frozen foods wear gloves to keep their fingers from freezing.

_____ Kara's Pouch Check _____

The children look in Kara's pouch, in which you have put a pair of mittens. It isn't baby Joey, but the mittens belong to Reggie! Ask children how Reggie would keep his hands warm if he didn't have any mittens (hands in pocket, wear gloves). Place a mitten on each of Reggie's hands on the bulletin board.

_____ Ready for Preschool _____

Teach this song to help the children review the articles of clothing discussed this month (see p. 144).

(Tune: "Mulberry Bush")

This is the way we button our pants,
                   button our pants,
                   button our pants.
This is the way we button our pants when we dress
for preschool.

138

Verse 2: This is the way we pull on our socks.
Verse 3: This is the way we tie our shoes.
Verse 4: This is the way we zip our coats.
Verse 5: This is the way we put on our mittens.
Verse 6: Now we're ready for preschool,
for preschool,
for preschool.
Now we're ready for preschool,
So early in the morning.

CRAFT _____ My Own Mittens _____

Materials Needed:

mitten patterns (see p. 149)   yarn, crayons
colored paper   masking tape
paper punch, scissors, pencils

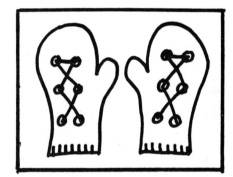

Explanation:
Children trace and cut out a pair of mittens. Punch six holes in each pair of mittens. Tape a long piece of yarn on the backside of the mitten. Wrap tape around the opposite end of the yarn to act as a needle. Each child sews a design on his or her pair of mittens. Use crayons to decorate.

FREEPLAY _____ Activity 1 _____

Clothing Game—Play this game as you would Hangman, but you will be adding items of clothing rather than body parts. Draw a cap, mittens, coat, shirt, pants, and shoes on a small heavy piece of paper. Glue one of these pictures on each side of a styrofoam square to make a die. Cut several of each of the clothing articles out of catalogs to use as playing pieces and place them in the center of a table. Give each child a playing card with a stick person drawn on it. Children take turns rolling the die and dressing their stick person. The object of the game is to dress the stick person completely.

_____ Activity 2 _____

Make Believe—Have children put on real mittens and play with snowballs (styrofoam balls) or build a snow fort (building blocks).

_____ Activity 3 _____

Pairing Mittens—Use the mittens from Arrival. Tie a clothesline between two chairs. Using snap clothespins, have the children find a pair of mittens and hang them on the line. Continue until all the mittens are in pairs and hung on the line to dry!

CLOSING _____ Story _____

Read one of the following stories: *The Mitten,* by Alvin Tresselt (Lothrop, Lee & Shepard, 1964). *The Mystery of the Red Mitten,* by Steven Kellogg (Dial Press, 1974). *One Mitten Lewis,* by Helen Kay (Lothrop, Lee & Shepard, 1955).

Apron Day

© 1990 by The Center for Applied Research in Education

PREPARATION _____ To the Teacher _____

For the activities during Freeplay, aprons with pockets are used to continue work with shapes, colors, and numerals. Keep in mind when drawing at the easel that the objective is teaching shapes, colors, and following directions rather than creativity.

You will neeed:

- puzzles for Arrival (see pp. 150–53);
- small tool apron for Kara's pouch;
- different kinds of aprons and objects for Opening;
- fish crackers for Opening;
- aprons with pockets for Opening, Activity 1, and Activity 3;
- apron from Pocket Day for Activity 2;
- play dough and shapes for Activity 1; and
- instruction cards and crayons for Activity 3.

ARRIVAL _____ This Is Puzzling! _____

As children arrive today, give each of them a puzzle piece which will go into one of four puzzles put together at this time. The puzzles are four aprons in four different colors—a white baker's apron, a brown carpenter's apron, a green cook's apron, and a red child's smock (see pp. 150–53). The children will know which puzzle their piece goes into by looking at its color.

OPENING _____ Kara's Pouch Check _____

The children check Kara's pouch, in which you have hidden a small tool apron. Of course it is not baby Joey, but Reggie has always wanted a tool apron. Place it on the bulletin board on Reggie.

_____ Apron Talk _____

We wear an apron to help keep our clothes clean while we do different kinds of work. Show the children the aprons worn by a carpenter, a baker, a waitress, and a welder as well as a child's paint apron and an apron worn while barbequing. On a table, display objects that the people wearing these aprons might use. Choose a child to wear each apron. The child selects the object necessary to do his or her work.

_____ Teacher's Apron _____

Wear an apron with a pocket today. (Hide some fish crackers in the pocket.) Tell the children why you wore an apron to school (to hold your pencil or Kleenex®, to hide a special surprise for someone who is feeling sad). Then say, "But today I wore this apron to play a special game with you. I want you to try to guess what is in the pocket of my apron. I will give you one clue— it is an animal. Can you think of any animals that might fit in this pocket?" As the children guess different animals, help them decide if they would be too large to fit. After awhile tell the children, "This animal is doing a very special trick today—usually it can only be in water." Let children guess what kind of animal that might be. When they mention fish, ask them what kind of fish could be in your apron that can be eaten as a snack. When they guess, pass out fish crackers for each child to eat.

CRAFT _____ Cook's Apron _____

Materials Needed:

    scissors, glue

    paper

    one round paper doily per child

    Kleenex® tissue

Explanation:
Children cut one long, rectangular strip for the
waistband and ties of the apron. Then they glue
the doily and the strip on their paper. Have them
cut a small pocket for the apron from scraps of
paper. Finally, they insert a small piece of tissue
paper in the pocket.

FREEPLAY _____ Activity 1 _____

Play Dough Shapes—Wear an apron. Have play dough (see p. 55) and laminated shapes in three
colors. Place the play dough in the center of a table and the laminated shapes in the pocket of
your apron. Children take turns reaching in the pocket and pulling out a shape. They use the
matching color of play dough to form the same shape.

_____ Activity 2 _____

Counting Shapes—Use the apron made for Activity 2 on Pocket Day. Add a numeral to the shape
on each pocket and have the children put that many of each shape in the pocket.

_____ Activity 3 _____

Easel Drawings—Wear an apron with instruction cards in the pocket. Children pull a card from
the apron pocket. At the easel, they draw what the card suggests. *Examples:* Draw a small yellow
triangle. Draw a blue circle inside a red circle.

CLOSING _____ Story _____

Read one of the following stories: *No Good in Art,* by Miriam Cohen (Greenwillow, 1980). *Katy
No-Pocket,* by Emmy Payne (Houghton-Mifflin, 1973). *Yellow, Yellow,* by Frank Asch (McGraw-
Hill, 1971).

Closet Day

PREPARATION _____ To the Teacher _____

Ending this unit means finding the baby kangaroo. For the Craft, be sure to obtain telephone wire. It works well for making hangers.

You will need:

- picture or stuffed toy for Opening;
- felt pieces for Activity 1 (see p. 155);
- very large box for Activity 2; and
- supplies for Activity 3

ARRIVAL _____ Clothing Count _____

As children arrive, help them count the number of articles of clothing they are wearing. Tape a piece of paper to their shirts with that number on it. During Opening, children should sit with other children who are wearing the same number of articles of clothing.

OPENING _____ Kara's Pouch Check _____

Surprise! Joey has come back. In advance, hide a small joey (picture or stuffed toy) in Kara's pouch. Discuss how happy the children's families would be when they returned after being lost.

_____ Joey Says _____

Children are to listen to Joey and do as he instructs. Joey tells the children to touch their articles of clothing. For example, Joey says, "Touch your shirt."

_____ Closet Talk _____

Do you have a closet? Is it dark in your closet? Do you hide things in your closet? What special things do you have in your closet? Do you share your closet with anyone?

CRAFT _____ Shoebox Closet _____

Materials Needed:

one small shoebox per child (see p. 154)

straws

telephone wire (see p. 63)

catalogs

tape

scissors

© 1990 by The Center for Applied Research in Education

Explanation:
Using a small shoebox and a straw, children make a closet. Stand the shoebox on end and poke holes in each side approximately one quarter of the way down. Slip a straw through to make a closet rod. Children bend telephone wire (see p. 63) to make hangers. Provide catalogs from which the children cut out pictures of clothing to tape on their hangers and then hang in their closet. Encourage them to include each item of clothing discussed this month.

FREEPLAY _____ Activity 1 _____

Flannel Board Closet—Make a big felt closet with a door that opens and closes with several articles of clothing in it made out of felt (see p. 155). Show a small group of children the clothes in the closet and then ask them to close their eyes. Take away one or two items of clothing and then ask the children to look and tell you what is missing.

_____ Activity 2 _____

Who's Missing?—Get a refrigerator box and make a door opening in it. Ask one child to sit behind the box, which is a closet, while another child hides in the closet. Ask the child to come from behind the closet and to tell you which classmate is missing.

_____ Activity 3 _____

Dress for the Weather—Cut two people figures 6–8 inches tall out of white paper. Use crayons to add facial features and hair, making a girl and a boy. Cut pictures of clothes out of catalogs suitable for all types of weather. Weather pictures are to be drawn on 3″ × 5″ cards. On each card draw one type of weather including snow, rain, clouds, wind, and sun.

Select one weather card and place it on the table in front of a child. The child chooses the appropriate clothing for that weather and lays them on the paper people figures. Be sure when cutting out the clothing from the catalogs to find hats, caps, long and short pants, coats, jackets, raincoats, gloves, etc.

Repeat activity placing a different weather card in front of child.

CLOSING _____ Story _____

Read one of the following stories: *There's a Nightmare in My Closet,* by Mercer Mayer (Dial Press, 1968). *A Noise in the Closet,* by Richard Hefter (Strawberry Books, 1974). *Molly's Moe,* by Kay Charao (Seabury Press, 1976).

_____ Record _____

As a conclusion to this unit, the children will enjoy the song "Point to my Clothes" on the album *Songs About Me* (KIM 70223), by William Janiak (Kimbo Educational, P.O. Box 477, Long Branch, N.J. 07740).

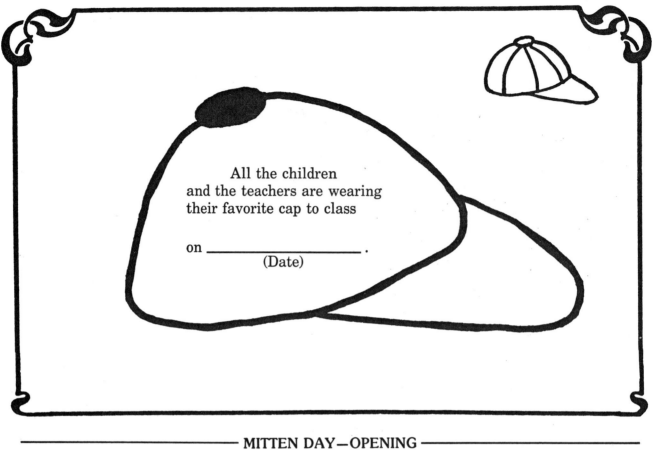

All the children
and the teachers are wearing
their favorite cap to class

on _____ .
　　　　(Date)

Dear Parent(s),

We learned this song to help us remember all the articles of clothing we have been discussing this month.

Ready for Preschool
(Tune: "Mulberry Bush")

This is the way we button our pants,
Button our pants, button our pants.
This is the way we button our pants
When we dress for preschool.

Verse 2—This is the way we pull on our socks.
Verse 3—This is the way we tie our shoes.
Verse 4—This is the way we zip our coats.
Verse 5—This is the way we put on our mittens.
Verse 6—Now we're ready for preschool,
　　　　　For preschool, for preschool.
　　　　　Now we're ready for preschool
　　　　　So early in the morning.

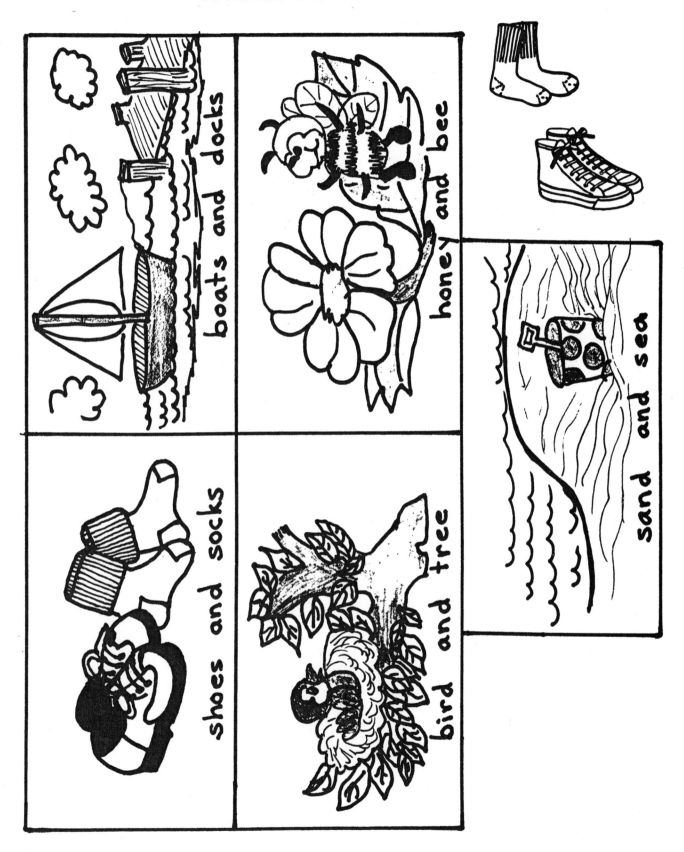

boats and docks

honey and bee

sand and sea

shoes and socks

bird and tree

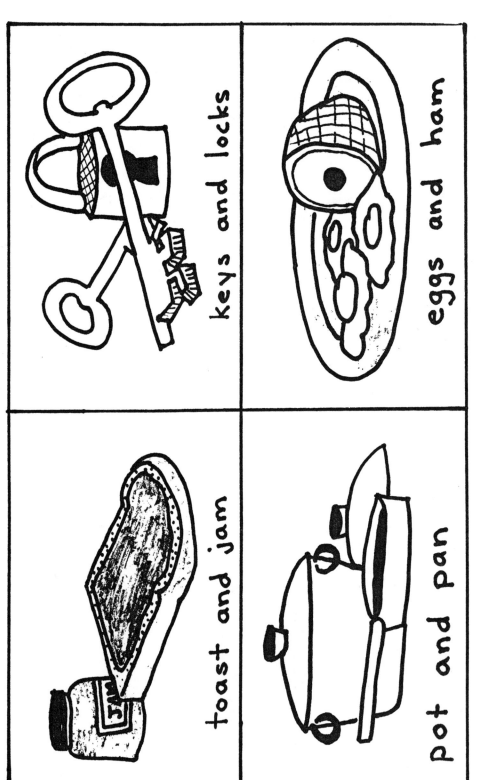

keys and locks

eggs and ham

toast and jam

pot and pan

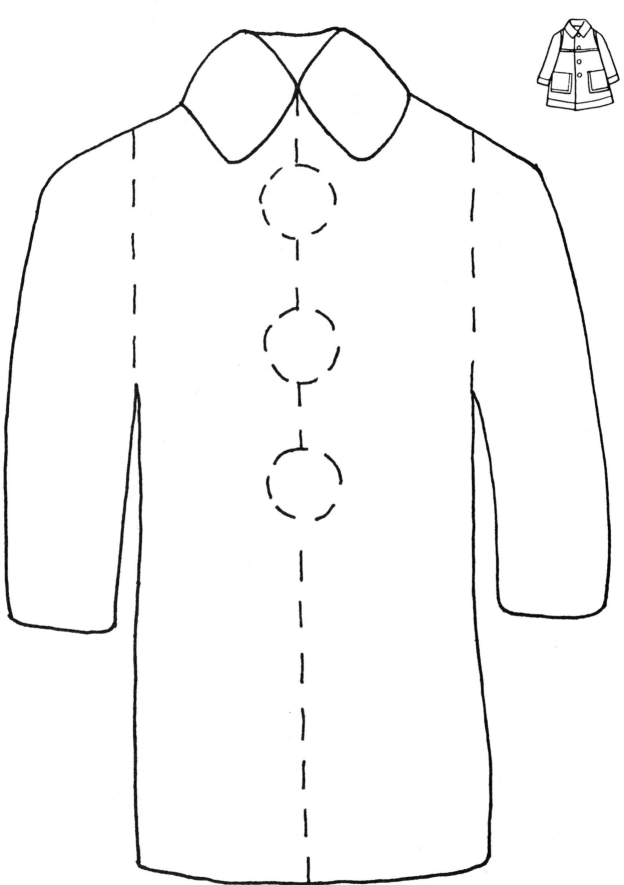

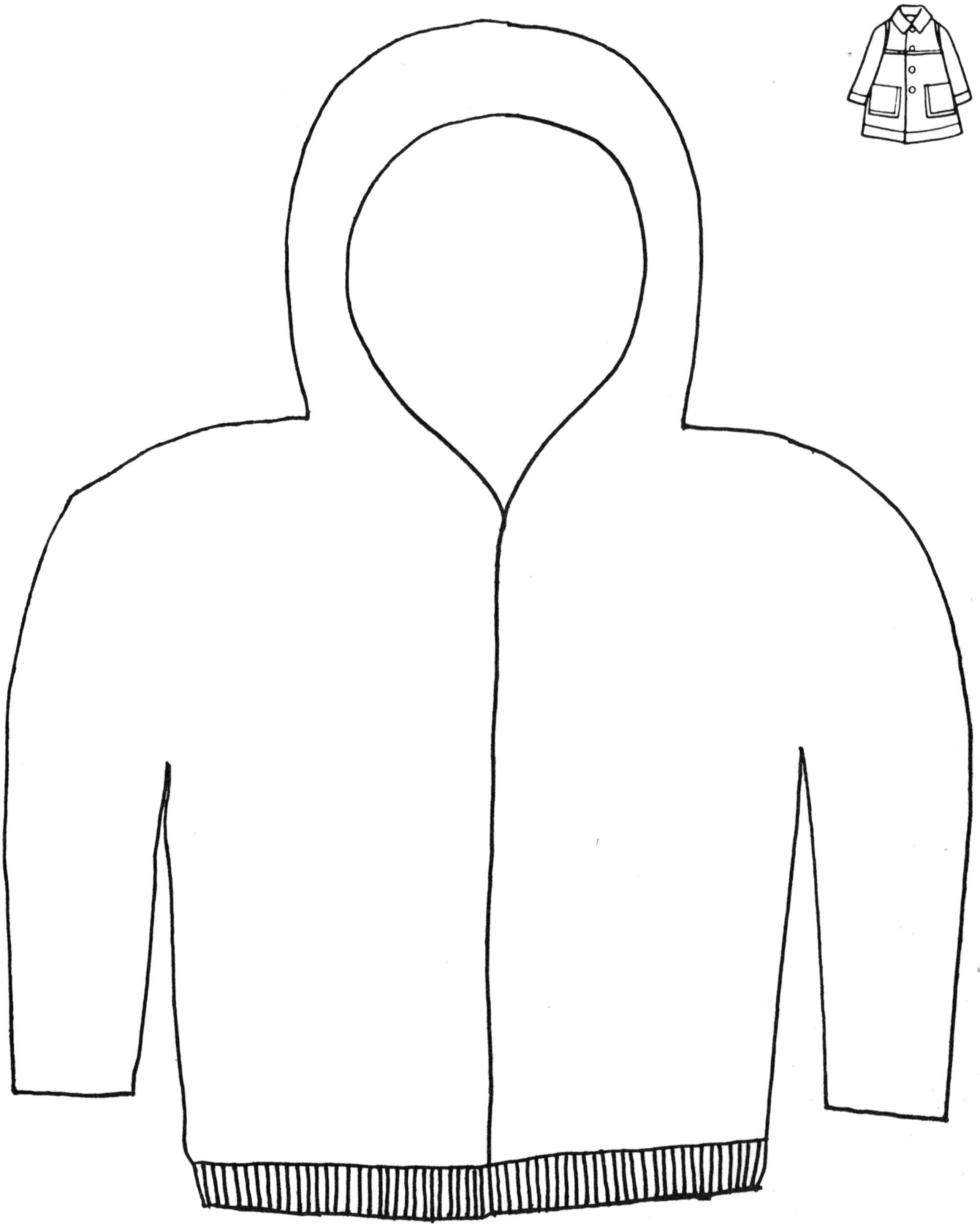

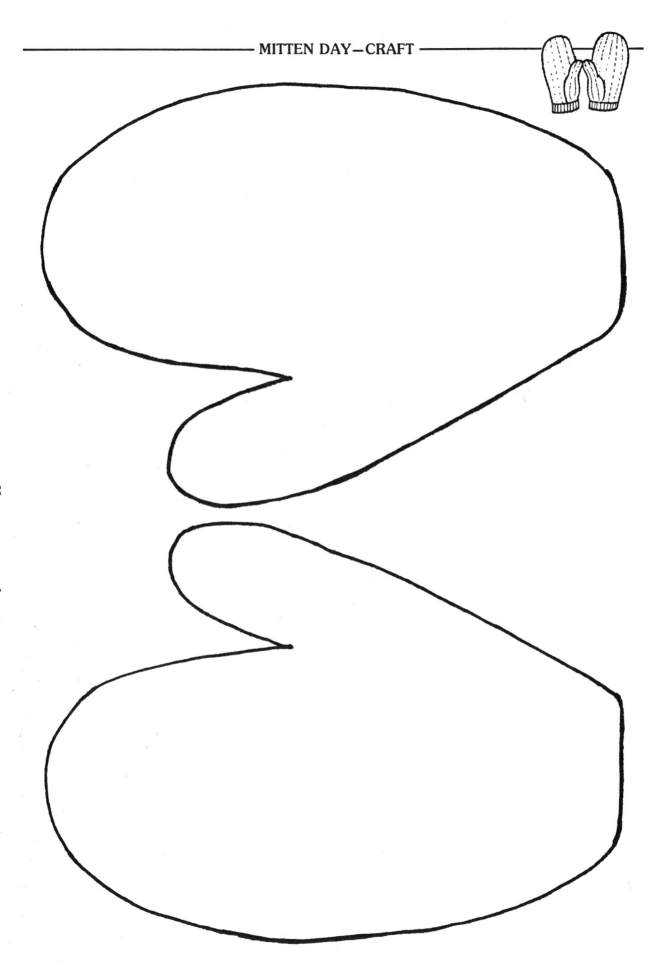

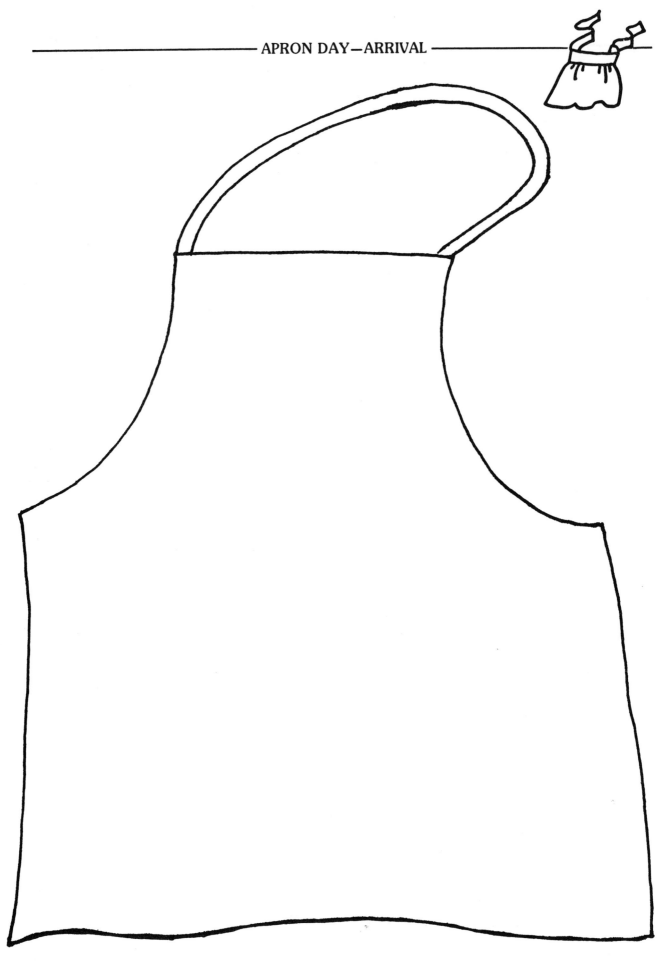

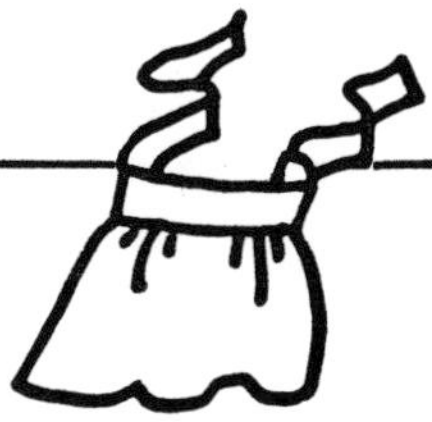

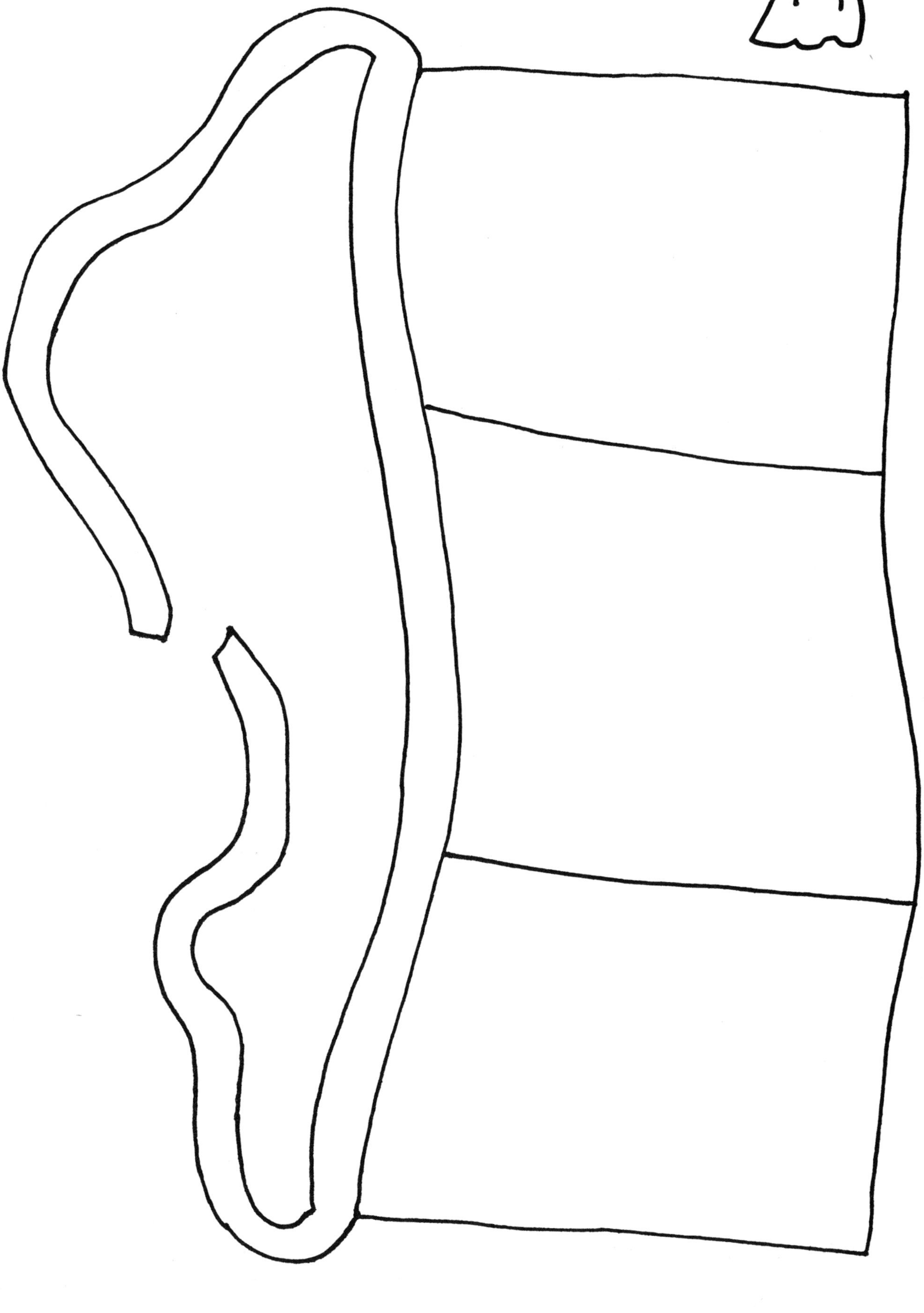

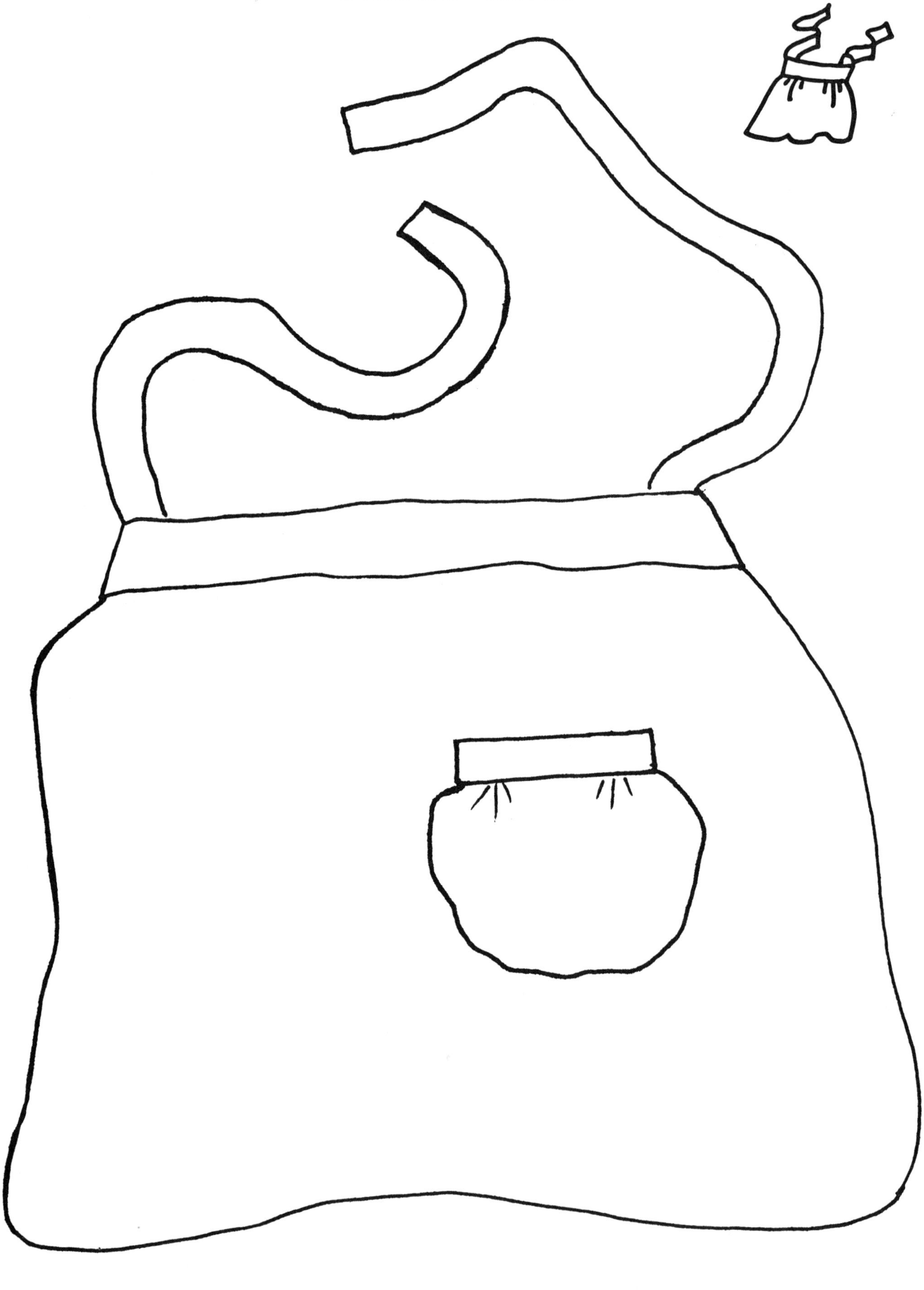

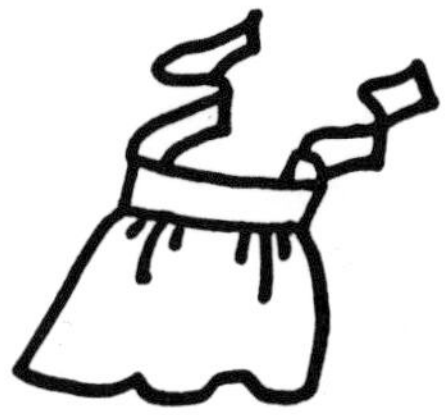

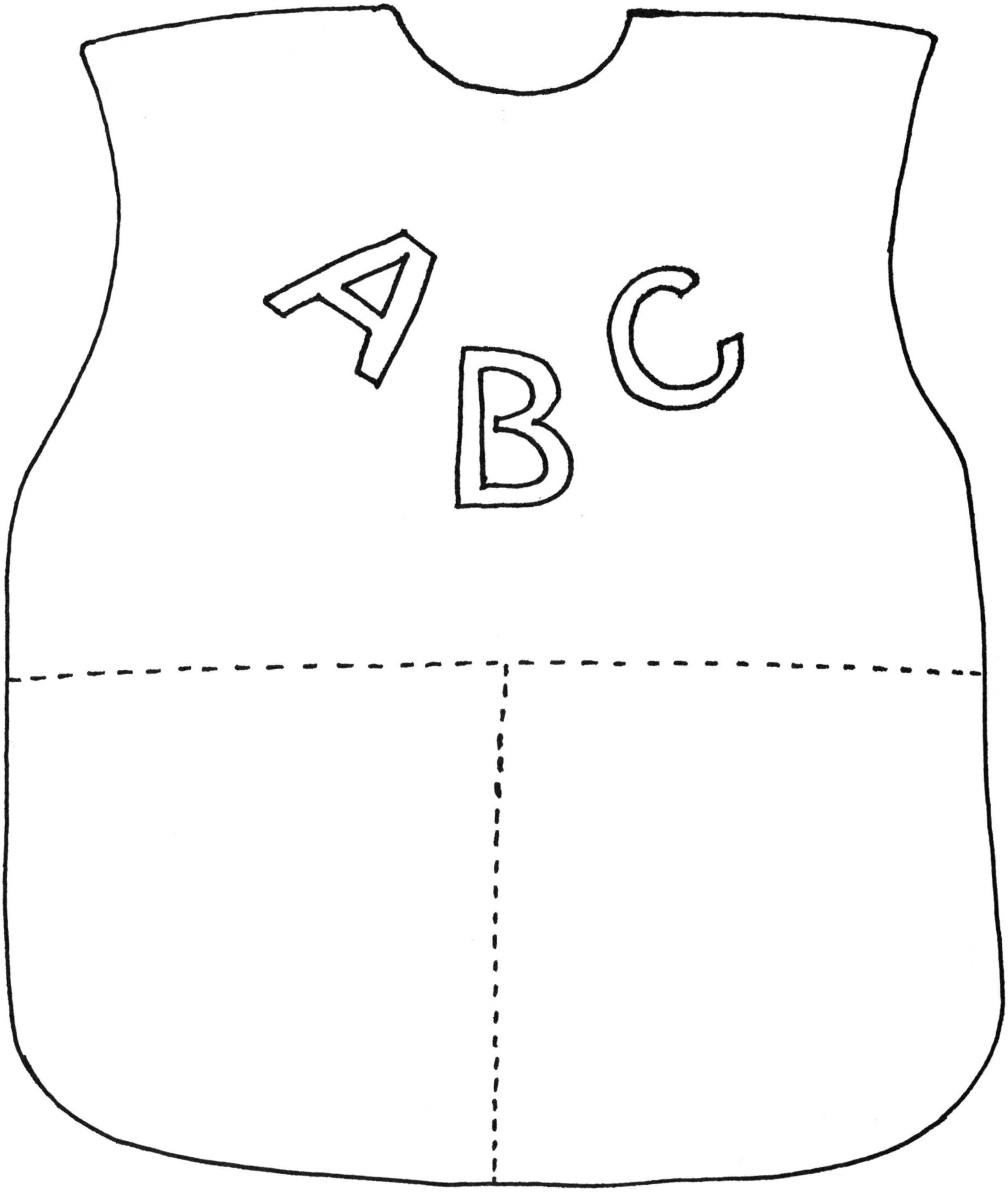
ABC

Dear Parent(s),

To conclude our clothing unit, we are making a closet on _____ .
(Date)

We need your child to bring a small shoebox on that day. We hope this closet will be something your child can play with since the articles of clothing will be removable.

unit 7

BEAR WITH US

This unit will be such fun because everyone loves bears! Children will learn to distinguish between reality and fantasy. All the stories we suggest are fantasy; however, during the Openings you will teach interesting facts about several different kinds of bears. Note the likenesses and differences of brown bears, pandas, and polar bears. Share with the children information on their eating and sleeping habits, coloring, and habitats. Each day, compare and review.

The daily activity plans in Unit 7 include:

- Circus Bear Day
- Teddy Bear Day
- Blueberry Bears Day
- Valentine Bears Day
- Winter Bears Day
- Polar Bear Day
- Panda Bear Day
- Three Bears Day

Circus Bear Day

PREPARATION _____ To the Teacher _____

The circus is bringing a bear to your room today. If you have any circus posters or pictures, hang them around the room to get in the circus mood.

You will need:

- ingredients, supplies, and recipe for Arrival (see below);
- circus pictures;
- three rings taped on floor for Freeplay;
- balance beam or tape for Activity 1;
- old clothes and clown make-up for Activity 2 (see below);
- board game prepared for Activity 3; and
- plastic or cardboard circles for Closing.

ARRIVAL _____ Make an Orange Frosty _____

Since we are spending the day at the circus, let's get in the mood! Turn on some circus music. As children arrive, have them make an orange frosty. Serve animal crackers with it for snack time.

Orange Frosty

1/2 small can of orange juice concentrate	1/2 tsp. vanilla
1/2 cup milk	5 to 6 ice cubes
1/2 cup water	Combine ingredients in a blender for thir-
1/4 cup powdered sugar	ty seconds. Makes 3 cups.

OPENING _____ Circus Talk _____

Use pictures to help the children visualize all the activity that goes on at the circus. Point out the three rings with acts performing in each. Discuss the ringmaster's job of keeping the performers in the right places and the audience informed of what's happening. Animals do many unusual tricks at the circus—bears ride unicycles, tigers jump through hoops of fire, and elephants stand on small stools. Some people, such as high wire and trapeze artists, perform dangerous feats. The clowns' primary role is to make sure everyone keeps laughing. Allow the children to share some of their experiences at the circus.

_____ Story _____

Read to the children one of the following stories: *Bearymore,* by Don Freeman (Viking Press, 1976). *Paddington at the Circus,* by Michael Bond (Random House, 1973). *The True Book of the Circus,* by Mabel Harmer (Children's Press, 1964).

CRAFT _____ Circus Unicycle _____

Before you begin Craft today, talk about what a unicycle is. If you read the story *Bearymore,* discuss that Bearymore rides a unicycle, as do many circus bears. Also talk about tricycles and bicycles. Compare the number of wheels that each cycle has. Which would be the hardest to ride? Why?

Materials Needed:

pencils, scissors, glue	one circle 3″ in diameter
one long rectangle 4″ by 1″	heavy paper
one short rectangle 2″ by 1″	metal brads

© 1990 by The Center for Applied Research in Education

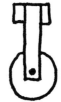

Explanation:
Have the children trace and cut the rectangles. Glue the short rectangle on the top of the long rectangle, as shown. Use the brad to attach the circle to the long rectangle. (Use sturdy paper so the unicycle will work!) If desired, the children can draw a bear and paste it on the seat of the unicycle.

FREEPLAY _____ **Three-Ring Circus** _____

Set up your room as a three-ring circus today. Each Freeplay activity should take place inside a circle on the floor made with masking tape.

_____ **Activity 1** _____

High Wire Artist—Use a balance beam for the high wire. A long piece of masking tape or yarn on the floor will work just as well. Give the high wire artist a ruler to hold (for balance!) and see if he or she can walk the wire. Use the song "High Wire Artist" from the album *Easy Does It* (AR 581), by Hap Palmer (Educational Activities, Inc., Box 392, Freeport, N.Y. 11520), or "Across the Bridge" from the album *We All Live Together,* volume 4 (YMES-0004), by Greg Scelsa and Steve Millang (Youngheart Records, Box 27784, Los Angeles, Calif. 90027).

_____ **Activity 2** _____

Let's Be a Clown—Have available clown make-up for the children to wear. Some old hats, colorful clothes, and big shoes will add to the clown's looks. Use this poem in the center: Recite this poem with the children.

> Close your eyes,   Shake your hands,
> Open your eyes,   Clap your hands,
> Take a look around.   Now dance like a clown!

_____ **Activity 3** _____

Board Game—Take the bears to the circus. Make one game board which is divided into four squares. One square should have a red background with a picture of a clown in it. The second square should be blue with a picture of a high wire artist. The third square should be yellow with a picture of an orange frosty. The fourth square should be green with a picture of a bear riding a unicycle. Also make a color die to use with this game. To do so, glue pieces of felt on a square which has been cut out of foam or styrofoam. Glue a red square on one side of the die, a blue on another side, a green square on another, and a yellow square on the fourth side. Two sides of the die will not have a color on them. You will also need four bears, one of each color, for each child playing the game. These can be cut out of paper, or you can use the teddy bear counters made by the toy company Milton Bradley.

  Object of the game: Try to get each bear to its color destination.
  Procedure: Children take turns rolling the die. If the red side of the die lands face up, that child puts the red bear in the red square. The next child then rolls the die and puts the correct bear where the color die indicates. If a color comes up that the child has already had, or if the side of the die with no color is face up, the child does not get to move a bear.

CLOSING _____ **Circle Game** _____

Use the album *Getting to Know Myself* (AR543), by Hap Palmer (Educational Activities, Inc., Box 392, Freeport, N.Y. 11520). Give each child a plastic or cardboard circle approximately 12″ in diameter as you do either "The Circle" or "Circle Game." Following directions and practicing spatial relationships are the objectives of these two songs. If you do not have the album, you can make up your own set of instructions. (*Example:* Stand beside the circle. Hold the circle above your head. Hop around the circle.)

Teddy Bear Day

PREPARATION _____ **To the Teacher** _____

In advance, send notes to parents requesting that children bring in their favorite stuffed animal today (see p. 174).

The story for today, *Corduroy,* ties in with the Craft and Freeplay.

You will need:

- notes to parents requesting that children bring in their favorite stuffed animal (see p. 174);
- cardboard bear (see p. 175) and clothes for Activity 1;
- folder game prepared for Activity 2;
- bulletin board ready for Activity 3;
- old catalogs for Activity 3; and
- button for Closing.

ARRIVAL _____ **Teddy Bear Fun** _____

As the children arrive with their favorite stuffed animal "friend," let them act out the following rhyme (see p. 174):

> Teddy Bear, Teddy Bear, turn around,
> Teddy Bear, Teddy Bear, touch the ground,
> Teddy Bear, Teddy Bear, turn out the light,
> Teddy Bear, Teddy Bear, say "Good night."

Don't forget to do a verse about kittens, monkeys, or whatever stuffed animals are brought.

OPENING _____ **Introduce Your Friends** _____

Encourage the children to introduce their stuffed animal to the class telling where they got it and what its name is. Categorize the animals according to color, size, old or new, or by their names.

_____ **Story** _____

Read to the children the story *Corduroy,* by Don Freeman (Penguin Books, 1978).

CRAFT _____ **Corduroy** _____

Materials Needed:

Use pattern (see p. 175) to make a paper
Corduroy for each child
buttons
corduroy patches
glue, crayons

© 1990 by The Center for Applied Research in Education

Explanation:
Let the children color their Corduroy. Then they glue on the corduroy patches. Be sure they remember to glue on Corduroy's missing button.

FREEPLAY _____ **Activity 1** _____

Dress-up Bear—Use the pattern (see p. 175) to make a bear out of cardboard. Color it brown. Also make several colors of pants and vests and shoes to fit the bear (see p. 176). Let this be a listening skills activity. Tell the child to dress the bear in, for example, blue pants, red vest, and green shoes. See if the child can remember how to dress the bear without needing the directions repeated.

_____ **Activity 2** _____

Corduroy's Button—This is a Manila folder game. Begin by making a perspective drawing on the inside of a folder (like the one shown) of a department store. This will be the playing board. Divide the store into three floors by adding two horizontal lines. Sketch stairs. Draw an elevator door on the top floor opposite the stairs. Use a dime to trace and make circles (buttons) on each step and across to the elevator door on the top floor. Draw a vertical line beside the store to represent an elevator shaft and trace a vertical line of circles in it. Color the circles throughout the store repeating colors in random order, and add two black dots to each circle so it looks like a button. Draw or use stickers to make one floor the toy department, one the clothes department, and one (the top) the furniture department. At the bottom of the elevator shaft beside a door, draw a little girl waiting for Corduroy. Color the button beside her to include all the colors you have used.

    Directions for play: Each child uses a teddy bear counter, made by Milton Bradley, for a playing piece. Place all plastic bears at the bottom of the stairs on the first floor. Place several buttons of each color used on the playing board in a box. Each child, with eyes closed, chooses one button out of the box and then moves his or her plastic bear to the matching colored button on the playing board. Then the child puts the button back in the box. Children take turns doing this until all children have advanced their bear to the multicolor button beside the little girl. The little girl has her Corduroy, and the game is over.

_____ **Activity 3** _____

Bears for Sale Bulletin Board—Make a bulletin board to look like shelves in a toy store. Have toy catalogs available for the children to cut out pictures of bears to place on the shelves. Discuss why they chose certain bears. What would they name that bear if they could buy it?

CLOSING _____ **Button, Button, Who Has the Button?** _____

Children sit on the floor in a circle. (For a large group, make two circles.) Choose a child to sit in the center of the circle. Choose another child to hold a button. Everyone in the circle holds his hands (palms together) out in front of him. The child with the button keeps his or her hands tightly together and moves around the circle pretending to put the button in several children's hands, but actually giving it to one child. The first child watches to determine when the button is really dropped into someone's hands. All the children keep their hands together until the child who is "it" correctly guesses who has the button.

Blueberry Bears Day

PREPARATION _____ To the Teacher _____

Today it's bears and blueberries! You will be cooking. . .blueberry muffins, of course!
You will need:

- recipe, utensils, and ingredients for blueberry muffins (see below);
- game prepared for Activity 1;
- grease pencil, paper pancakes, and blueberries for Activity 2; and
- fabric squares for Activity 3.

ARRIVAL _____ Muffin Bake _____

Let the children prepare their snack once again—blueberry muffins! As children prepare the
muffins, discuss the color of the berries and where they grow.

Sweet Muffins and Stir-ins

1 egg
2 cups Bisquick® baking mix*
1/3 cup sugar
2/3 cup milk
2 tbsp. vegetable oil

Preheat oven to 400 degrees. Grease bottoms only of 12 medium muffin cups, 2 1/2″ × 1 1/4″, or line with paper baking cups. Beat egg slightly in medium bowl; stir in remaining ingredients just until moistened. Fold 3/4 cup fresh or frozen (thawed and drained) blueberries into batter. Divide batter evenly among cups. Bake until golden brown, 15 to 18 minutes. Yield 12 muffins.

OPENING _____ Blueberry Talk _____

The blueberry is a small, sweet fruit that grows on a bush. People can eat fresh blueberries.
Blueberries are also delicious in pies, muffins, pancakes, syrup, and jam. A blueberry can be
light blue to a very dark blue in color.
    Bears love to find blueberries in the woods and enjoy their sweet taste.

_____ Story _____

Read to the children one of the following stories: *Blueberry Bears,* by Eleanor Lapp (Albert Whitman, 1983). *Blueberries for Sal,* by Robert McCloskey (The Viking Press, 1948, paperback, 1976). *The Blueberry Elf,* by Jane Thayer (Morrow, 1961).

*BISQUICK is a registered trademark of General Mills, Inc., for baking mix; recipe is reprinted with permission of General Mills, Inc.

© 1990 by The Center for Applied Research in Education

CRAFT _____ Blueberry Bushes _____

Materials Needed:

> empty roll-on deodorant bottles
> blue paint
> brown paint
> pencils with erasers
> paper

Explanation:
Using a table knife, remove the ball out of each deodorant bottle. Fill the bottles with brown paint and push the ball back into each bottle. The children use the bottles to paint blueberry bushes. They use the eraser on a pencil to print blueberries on the bushes. Pour blue paint onto a sponge, and the children press the eraser on the paint and print berries on the bushes.

FREEPLAY _____ Activity 1 _____

Blueberries Anyone?—This game is played with a spinner on a circle which you make by using a brad and paper clip. Divide the circle into five equal pie-shaped sections. On one section draw one blueberry, on another section draw two blueberries, on yet another section draw three blueberries, and on two sections draw one bear on each. Each child playing needs a basket, which you make with a yogurt or nut cup by attaching a pipe cleaner handle. Use small blue pom-poms for the blueberries.

> *Directions for play:* Each child has a basket. The object of the game is to pick ten berries without the bear eating them. Children take turns spinning. If the spinner lands on berries, the child takes the amount shown and places it in the basket. If the spinner lands on a bear, the child takes one berry out of the basket or, if there are none, does nothing. The first child to have ten berries in his or her basket wins.

_____ Activity 2 _____

Blueberry Count—Make paper pancakes and laminate them. With a grease pencil, put a numeral on each one or, for older children, write addition or subtraction problems. Make many little laminated blue circles to be the blueberries. Children identify the numeral on a pancake and then count out that many blueberries and place them on the pancake.

_____ Activity 3 _____

Cloth Swatch Match—Glue pieces of different kinds of fabric onto individual cardboard squares. Make two cards of each kind of fabric. (*Examples:* corduroy, velvet, terry cloth, dotted swiss) Put the squares in a box with a small opening for the child's hand. Ask the child to find the matching pairs using only the sense of touch.

CLOSING _____ Music _____

Sing the song "Here We Go Round the Mulberry Bush" substituting the word *blueberry* for *Mulberry.*

Valentine Bears Day

PREPARATION _____ To the Teacher _____

The bears in today's story will tug at your heart. Although the bears are not real, the emotions they express are very real! It's a wonderful way to combine your Valentine's Day celebration and bears.

You will need:

- bread, honey, and cookie cutter for Arrival;
- valentines for Opening;
- hearts and fishing pole for Activity 1;
- felt shapes and sequence cards for Activity 2;
- photocopied pictures of children and paper for Activity 3; and
- five decorated envelopes for Closing.

ARRIVAL _____ Sweetheart Snack _____

Have each child make a sweetheart snack. Using a heart-shaped cookie cutter, each child cuts a valentine from a slice of bread and spreads honey over the heart. Save it for snack time. (Bears like honey, too!)

OPENING _____ Valentine Talk _____

A valentine is a special way to tell someone you care. Usually a valentine has a short rhyme that tells how you feel. It might also have symbols of love, such as flowers, cupids, or hearts.

There are many different stories about how Valentine's Day began. It really doesn't matter how the custom of Valentines started. It's just a wonderful chance to tell someone how much he or she means to you.

Who do you send Valentines to? Who sends you Valentines? What can you do to show someone you love them?

Read some Valentines. Talk about the verses. Perhaps you can make up some Valentine verses with the children.

_____ Story _____

Read _The Valentine Bears,_ by Eve Bunting (Seabury Press, 1983). This story is a wonderful example of love expressed on Valentine's Day. Mr. and Mrs. Bear have never celebrated Valentine's Day because they usually sleep through it. This year, Mrs. Bear decides it's going to be different. When she settles down for her winter nap, she sets her alarm for February 14. The alarm goes off as planned, and both Mr. and Mrs. Bear have a delightful surprise in store for them. (If you are unable to find this book, you might check with your librarian to see if it is available through interlibrary loan.)

© 1990 by The Center for Applied Research in Education

CRAFT _____ Valentine Prints _____

Materials Needed:

>   paper for each child with hearts drawn on it
>   red paint
>   sponge

Explanation:
Draw the same number of hearts as the number of children in your class on a piece of paper 8 1/2″ by 11″. Print each child's name in a heart. Print the following Valentine poem at the top of the page:

>   My friends' fingerprints you see,
>   On this Valentine they made for me!

Make a copy of this page for each child in your class. Place a damp sponge on a styrofoam meat tray. Pour a small amount of red paint on the sponge. Lay all the papers out on a table where the children can reach them easily. The children put their index finger in the red paint and then make their fingerprint on each heart with their name in it (one on each paper).

FREEPLAY _____ Activity 1 _____

Fishing for Hearts—Make a pond full of different colored paper hearts. Attach a paper clip to each heart. Use a pole with a magnet on the end of it to try to catch only the red hearts.

_____ Activity 2 _____

Flannel Board Sequence—Cut out several colors of felt shapes, including hearts. Draw sequence cards showing shapes of those colors arranged in different order. _Example:_ square, heart, circle, heart, square. Ask a child to make the same shape and color pattern on the flannel board.

_____ Activity 3 _____

Sweetheart Bulletin Board—Have the children cut heart shapes from a folded piece of paper. Place a photograph of the child on the heart. (_Or,_ use a photocopied picture of the child. See p. 64.)

CLOSING _____ Five Fancy Envelopes _____

Decorate five envelopes and place one colored shape inside each envelope. (Use the felt shapes from Activity 2.) As you recite the following poem, ask one child to choose an envelope. The child peeks inside and tells you what color the shape is. Repeat the verse and choose another child. When all the envelopes have been chosen, change the shapes in the envelopes and repeat the entire verse until everyone has had a turn.

>   Five fancy envelopes, Looking their best,
>   I wonder what's inside, Can you guess?

(Repeat the verse, each time substituting _four, three, two,_ and _one._)

© 1990 by The Center for Applied Research in Education

Winter Bears Day

PREPARATION _____ To the Teacher _____

You will be talking about the bear essentials today. . . where bears live, what they like to eat, where and why bears hibernate.

    You will need:

- bear stencil (see p. 174), paint, and paper folded for Arrival;
- bulletin board prepared for Activity 1;
- drawing materials for Activity 1;
- wet sand for Activity 2; and
- recipe (see p. 167), utensils, and ingredients for cookies in Activity 3.

ARRIVAL _____ Stencil Painting _____

In advance, fold a piece of newsprint in half for each child. Tape a bear stencil on the inside bottom half of this paper (see p. 174). As the children arrive, have them stencil paint a bear on their paper. (This is part of Craft. See today's Craft for further explanation.)

OPENING _____ Bear Talk _____

Bears in North America live in rugged mountain or forest areas. They have five toes on each foot with a sharp claw on each toe. They cannot see well but have a good sense of smell. Bears can run very fast, but only for short distances. Bears sleep during the coldest parts of the winter. That long period of sleep is called hibernation. They store fat under their skin for warmth and nourishment. Their home is called a den—a shallow cave in a wall of rock. Their favorite foods are honey, berries, insects, and fish. Baby bears are called cubs. Have you ever seen a bear? Where? (zoo, national park, circus)

_____ Story _____

Read to the children one of the following stories: _Beany and Scamp,_ by Lisa Bassett (Dodd, Mead, & Co., 1987). _Buzzy Bear Goes South,_ by Dorothy Marino (Watts, Inc., 1961). _Snow on Bear's Nose,_ by Jennifer Bartoli (Whitman, 1972).

CRAFT _____ Bears in Winter _____

Materials Needed:

    newsprint with bear stencil painted in Arrival

    brown paint

    easels

    paintbrushes

    scissors

© 1990 by The Center for Applied Research in Education

Explanation:
The children painted the bear sleeping in the
cave in Arrival, and they now need to make that
piece of paper look more like a cave. Have them
cut on an arched line as shown in the picture.
Then at the easel they paint the front of the cave
brown.

FREEPLAY _____ **Activity 1** _____

Bulletin Board Mountain—On the bulletin board, put a picture of a tall mountain. Sing the song
"The Bear Went over the Mountain" with the children. It is found on *Let's Sing Fingerplays*
(CMS 688), by Tom Glazer (CMS Records, Inc., 14 Warren St., New York, N.Y. 10007). Since
the song doesn't tell what the bear saw, ask the children to draw what they think it saw. Place
each child's drawing on one side of the mountain on the bulletin board. (You will use this bulletin
board and song in Closing also.)

_____ **Activity 2** _____

Tracks in the Snow—Wet the sand in the sand table and let the children make tracks by press-
ing their hands or feet in it. If possible, ask a park ranger or conservation officer to visit your
classroom. He or she may be able to bring some examples of animal tracks and explain their
differences.

_____ **Activity 3** _____

Bear Paw Cookies—Depending on the length of your school day, you can have the children help
you mix and bake these cookies or only help decorate them. Have the children frost the cookies
with chocolate frosting. Lay five almonds across the front of each cookie to represent the bear's
claws. When their bear paw is finished, children may eat it for snack time.

2 1/3 cups flour

2 tsp. baking powder

1 tsp. salt

1 cup margarine

2/3 cups sugar

1/2 cup chocolate flavored syrup

2 eggs

1/4 cup milk

chocolate frosting

toasted almonds

Chill for one hour. Drop on greased cookie
sheet. Bake at 375 degrees for ten to twelve
minutes.

CLOSING _____ **"The Bear Went over the Mountain"** _____

Use the bulletin board and the pictures drawn in Activity 1. Sing "The Bear Went over the Mountain" and let one child choose a picture of what the bear saw.

Polar Bear Day

PREPARATION _____ To the Teacher _____

Polar bears live where it is cold, so think cold today! Ice cream and ice cubes will help you! You will need:

- recipe, supplies, and ingredients for the ice cream (see below) for Arrival;
- container of water to freeze for Opening;
- game for Activity 1;
- Manila folder game and Pepperidge Farm® fish crackers for Activity 2;
- ice cubes for Activity 3; and
- poem for Closing.

Don't forget the *two* different sized coffee cans. If you make the ice cream in your classroom rather than outdoors, be sure to roll it on a plastic tablecloth. The salt water may leave a white residue on the floor.

ARRIVAL _____ Ice Cream _____

Let's begin this chilly day by making Rock 'n' Roll Ice Cream!

1 cup milk	1 tsp. vanilla
1 egg	1 cup whipping cream
1/2 cup sugar	

Combine all ingredients and pour into a 1-pound coffee can with a tight-fitting plastic lid. Place the lid on the can, tape it shut, and put the can inside a 3-pound can with a tight-fitting plastic lid. Pack the large can with crushed ice surrounding the smaller can. Pour at least 3/4 cup rock salt evenly over the ice. Place the lid on the 3-pound can and tape it securely. Roll the can back and forth on a table or the floor for ten minutes. Open the outer can. Remove the inner can. Remove the lid and stir mixture with a rubber spatula. Scrape the side of the can and replace the lid and tape shut. Drain the ice water from the larger can. Place the smaller can back inside the larger can and pack with more ice and salt. Tape securely. Roll back and forth for five more minutes. This recipe makes about 3 cups of ice cream. Keep in a cold place until snack time.

OPENING _____ Polar Bear Talk _____

Polar bears live above the Arctic Circle where it is very cold. Their shaggy, thick fur is white like snow. They are very good swimmers. Seals are their favorite food, but they eat fish, too. Polar bears cover their black noses with their paws when they hunt because their noses are easy to see in the snow! Have you ever seen a polar bear in the zoo? Were they cooling off in the cold water?

_____ Science _____

Talk about the solid and liquid states of water. Place a small amount of water in a freezer. Check it in Closing to see if it has changed.

_____ Story _____

Read to the children one of the following stories: *Snowy and Woody,* by Roger Duvoisin (Alfred A. Knopf, 1979). *Polar,* by Elaine Moss (Dutton, 1979). *Polar Bear Brothers,* by Ylla and Crosby Newell Bonsall (Harper & Row, 1960).

CRAFT _____ Fluffy Polar Bears _____

Materials Needed:

> bear for each child (see p. 177)
> soap flakes
> bowl, water
> mixer
> black buttons

Explanation:
Use the pattern (see p. 177) to make a paper bear for each child. Put the soap flakes and water in a bowl and whip with mixer until thick. Fingerpaint some of the mixture onto the paper bear until it is white and shaggy. Add a small black button for an eye and a larger one for a nose.

FREEPLAY _____ Activity 1 _____

Snowball Roll—Glue styrofoam packing pieces on a large piece of cardboard to make a snow fort. Cut a small opening at the bottom of the wall. Use the snow fort for the following game: Ask one child to hold the fort in place while another tries to roll a snowball (styrofoam ball) through the opening of the fort.

_____ Activity 2 _____

A Bear's Feast—Open a Manila folder and make one side blue to represent water. Draw a circle on the other side and divide the circle into five equal pie-shaped pieces. In the middle, place a large brad with a paper clip on it to serve as a spinner. Two of the pie shapes should each have a bear drawn in them, two should have a fish drawn in them, and the remaining pie shape should have two fish in it. (If drawing is a problem, you can use stickers).

To begin, give each child five Pepperidge Farm® fish crackers. Place several fish crackers swimming in the water on the Manila folder. Each child takes a turn spinning. If the spinner lands on a bear, the child eats two fish. If the spinner lands on one fish or two fish, the child takes that many fish out of the water. When one child has eaten all his or her fish, with the help of the bears, it is time to begin a new game.

_____ Activity 3 _____

Ice Cube Pass—Have children sit in a circle and pass an ice cube from one to another. Count with the children how many times the ice cube goes around the circle before it is completely melted.

CLOSING _____ Poetry _____

Poetry can be very effective in helping children to develop listening skills, ways of expressing feelings, auditory awareness, and new vocabulary. Share with your class the poem "Bear in There" from the book _A Light in the Attic,_ by Shel Silverstein (Harper & Row, 1981).

Panda Bear Day

© 1990 by The Center for Applied Research in Education

PREPARATION _____ To the Teacher _____

Pandas are black and white; many of today's activities focus on black and white. If you have a stuffed panda or a panda puppet, use it while you read the story.
   You will need:

   • shapes to cut in Arrival (see p. 178);
   • pictures of pandas for Opening;
   • pictures on three-by-five cards illustrating opposites for Activity 1 (see pp. 179–81);
   • color cards for Activity 2;
   • black and white objects for Activity 3; and
   • a black and a white spool of thread for Closing.

ARRIVAL _____ Sharpen Your Cutting Skills! _____

Have children cut two small, white circles (ears) and one large, white circle (face) to be used for the panda bear Craft today. Also cut two small black circles for the eyes and one small black triangle for the nose (see p. 178).

OPENING _____ Panda Bear Talk _____

The giant panda looks like a black and white bear. It is about 3 1/2 to 5 feet long and 3 feet high. Many scientists think that pandas are really big raccoons. The giant panda lives in the mountains of Southern China. It eats young bamboo plants. The kind of bamboo the panda eats grows only in the mountains where pandas live. The pandas couldn't move to another part of China, as there would not be food for them there.
   Show the children pictures of pandas and discuss their coloration and habitat. _Ranger Rick,_ published by the National Wildlife Federation, 8925 Leesburg Pike, Vienna, VA. 21184, and _World,_ published by the National Geographic Society, Washington, D.C. 20036, are good sources.

_____ Story _____

Read to the children one of the following stories: _Milton the Early Riser,_ by Robert Kraus (Windmill Books, Inc., 1972). _Panda Cake,_ by Rosalie Seidler (Parents Magazine Press, 1978). _Poppy the Panda,_ by Dick Gackenback (Clarion Books, 1984).

CRAFT _____ Miss Panda _____

Materials Needed:

   circles and triangle cut in Arrival
   popcorn dyed black
   cotton
   glue
   glue brush

Explanation:
The children glue on the panda's ears. Then they brush glue on the face and put cotton (pulled apart) over the entire face. Put a small amount of black tempera powder in a paper bag along with some popped popcorn. Shake the bag. The children use the colored corn for the panda's ears. Then they glue on the eyes and nose. Caution the children that this popcorn is no longer good to eat.

FREEPLAY _____ **Activity 1** _____

Picture Bulletin Board (Opposites)—Make pictures of opposites on three-by-five cards (see pp. 179–81). (*Examples:* on-off, up-down, etc.) Put half of the set of pictures on the left side of the bulletin board. Children are to find the opposite pictures and place it directly across from the picture on the left. Use black and white as examples since it is Panda Bear Day.

_____ **Activity 2** _____

Color Scramble—Cut out large cards (5″ by 7″) of several colors. Be sure to include black and white! Begin by putting three color cards on a table or chalkboard ledge. Let the children look at and talk about the color cards and the order they are in. Ask the children to close their eyes while you scramble the cards. Then the children open their eyes and try to move the color cards back in their original order. Add more colors to increase the difficulty.

_____ **Activity 3** _____

Patterning—Use black and white objects to make varying patterns (white and black buttons, lace, ricrac, cotton balls, pompons). Lay several objects on a table or sheet of paper to make a pattern. Ask a child to repeat the exact pattern below yours.

CLOSING _____ **Panda Bear!** _____

Show the children white and black spools of thread. Ask them to close their eyes while you hide the spools (or have a child hide them). When the spools are hidden, the children open their eyes and look for them. When they spot one of the spools, they say "Panda," and when they spot the second spool, they say "Bear" and go sit in a designated area. Play for a set amount of time (e.g., three minutes per game) and stop after that much time has elapsed even if not everyone has said "Panda Bear." Hide the spools again and resume play.

Three Bears Day

PREPARATION ———————— To the Teacher ————————————

You will enjoy emphasizing big, bigger, and biggest using the story *The Three Bears.* The story lends itself well to creative drama.

You will need:

- brown paint, oranges, lemons, and marshmallows for Arrival;
- props for acting out the story for Activity 1;
- play dough, bowls, and cornmeal for Activity 2;
- materials for bulletin board for Activity 3; and
- puppets, (see p. 182) shoebox, bear (see p. 175), and lollipops for Closing.

ARRIVAL ———————————— Painting ————————————————

As the children arrive, ask them to paint three bears using an orange, a lemon, and a marshmallow. Cut the oranges and lemons in half. Let the children use the food and brown paint to print circles making bears in three sizes. Two circles, one above the other and made with the orange, will be Father Bear. Two circles, one above the other and made with the lemon, will be Mother Bear. And two circles, one above the other and made with the marshmallow, will be Baby Bear.

OPENING ———————————— Story ————————————————————

Read the story *The Three Bears,* by Paul Galdone (Seabury Press, 1972). While reading, draw the children's attention to the details of the bears' dress, such as hats, aprons, pants, etc.

———————————————— Three Bears Talk ————————————————

Discuss the sizes of the bears in the story and the sizes of the bears the children painted in Arrival. Use the words *big, bigger,* and *biggest* throughout the day. Ask the children if they think the events of the story really could have happened. Should they go into someone's house if no one is at home?

CRAFT ———————————— Three Bears ————————————————————

Materials Needed:

> construction paper
> lace, ricrac
> markers

Explanation:
Children use the materials listed to complete the bear pictures they painted in Arrival. They add facial features and the special clothes the bears wore, such as an apron, hats, or jackets.

FREEPLAY _____ Activity 1 _____

Dramatization—The children act out the story emphasizing the three sizes of the bowls, chairs, beds, and bears. Bring clothes to help children feel the part.

_____ Activity 2 _____

Big, Bigger, Biggest—To teach the concept of big, bigger, biggest, bring three bowls of different sizes and let the children fill them with cornmeal. Through measuring, the children will be able to understand that the bigger the container, the more it takes to fill it. Also have play dough (see p. 55) available and ask the children to make balls of different sizes.

_____ Activity 3 _____

Bear Match Bulletin Board—Make and place three bears of three different sizes on the bulletin board. Make available three beds, hats, bowls, chairs, and pairs of shoes. Children match the sizes of the articles to the bears and place them on the bulletin board with the appropriate size bear.

CLOSING _____ Brown Bear, Brown Bear _____

(You may wish to have half of your group do each of the Closing activities for a time and then switch activities. Waiting for a turn can be difficult, especially at the end of the day.)
   Brown Bear, Brown Bear What Do You See? (by Bill Martin, Jr.)—Have stick puppets or pictures of different colored animals to give to the children as they play this game. (_Examples:_ green frog, yellow duck, brown bear, etc.; see p. 182.) Have five children stand in front of the group and give each of them an animal to hold. The rest of the children remain seated. The first child in line holds the brown bear as the seated children say, "Brown bear, brown bear, what do you see?" The child answers by saying, "I see a green turtle standing next to me" if that is the animal the next child in line is holding. Then the seated children ask the green turtle what it sees. After the child's response, they move on to the next child.

_____ Feed the Bear _____

Use the pattern from Craft on Teddy Bear Day to make a bear (see p. 175). Laminate it or put clear self-stick vinyl on it and glue it to the side of a shoebox that is standing on end. Cut a hole in the top of the box big enough for lollipops that you have made with construction paper circles and Popsicle® sticks. Pass out the different color lollipops to the children. They identify the colors and then feed the lollipops to the bear by placing them in the hole cut in the top of the box.

Dear Parent(s),

Teddy Bear, Teddy Bear, turn around.
Teddy Bear, Teddy Bear, touch the ground.
Teddy Bear, Teddy Bear, turn out the light.
Teddy Bear, Teddy Bear, say "Good night."
Does this rhyme sound familiar to you? We plan to teach it to your child on Teddy

Bear Day, which will be _____ . On that day, we want each
                                 (Date)
child to bring his or her favorite teddy bear or other stuffed animal.

Thanks!

—— WINTER BEARS DAY—ARRIVAL ——

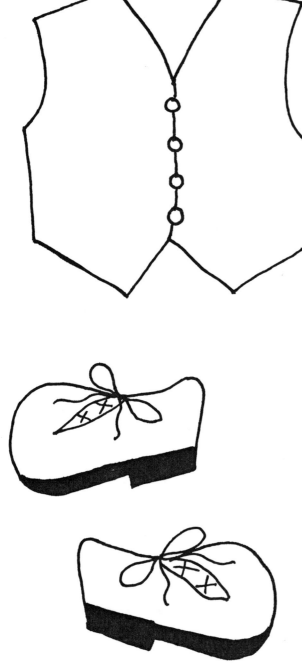

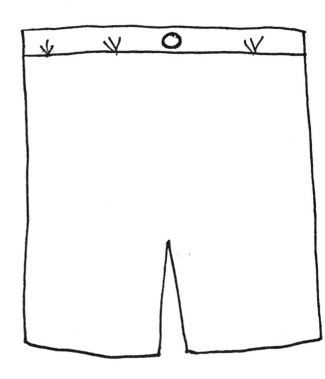

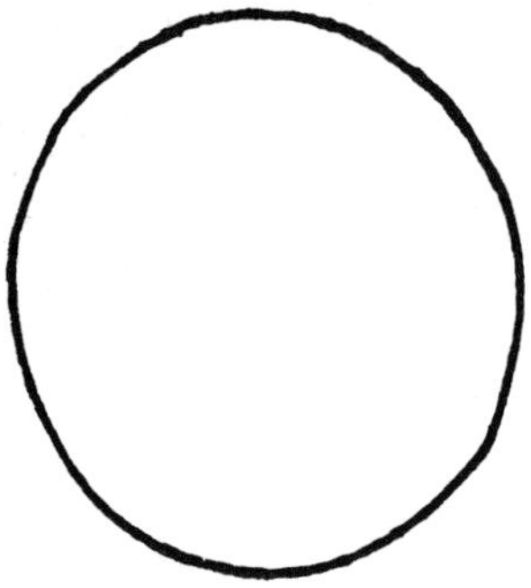

Eyes
(black)
two per child

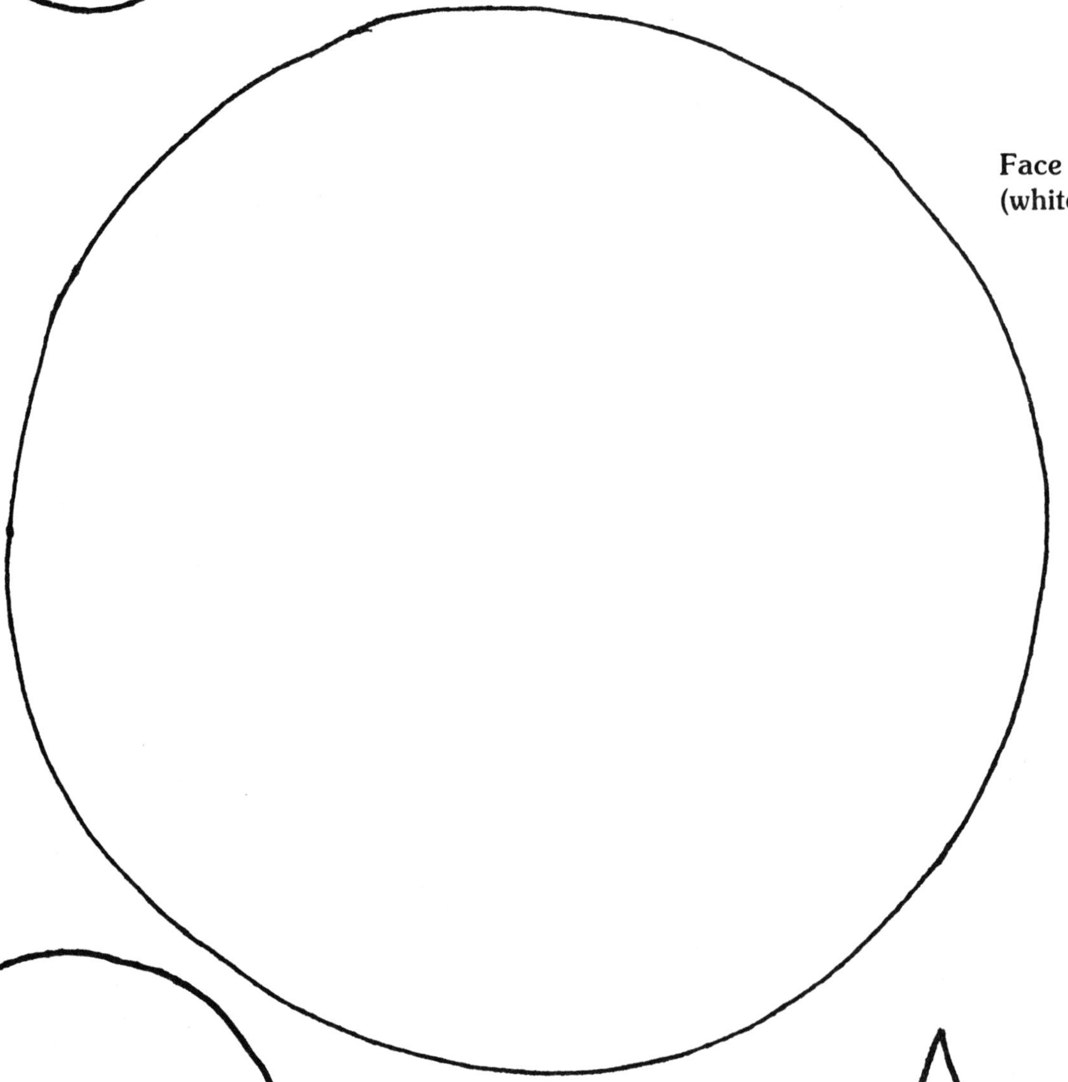

Face
(white)

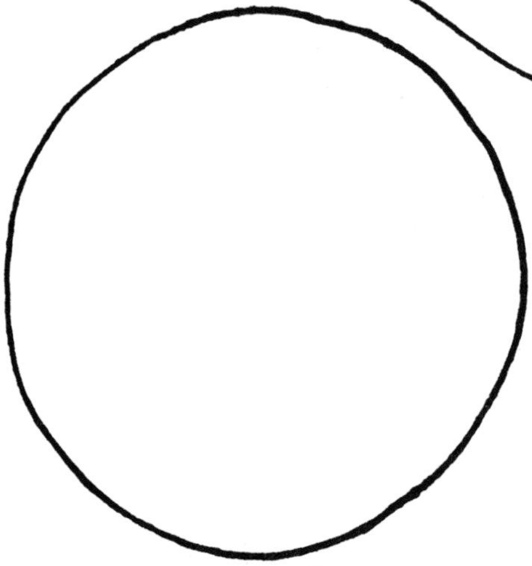

Ears
(white)
two per child

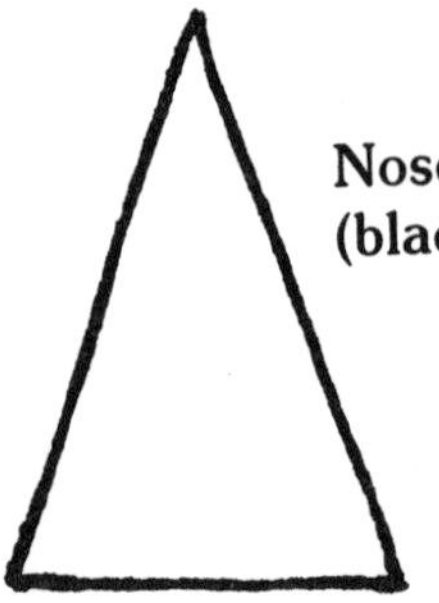

Nose
(black)

day

night

empty

full

happy

sad

low

black

white

in

out

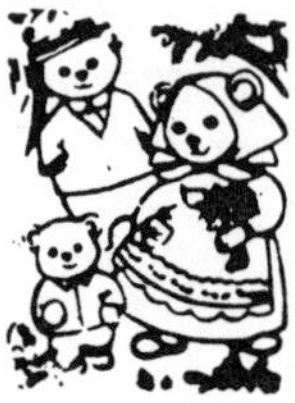

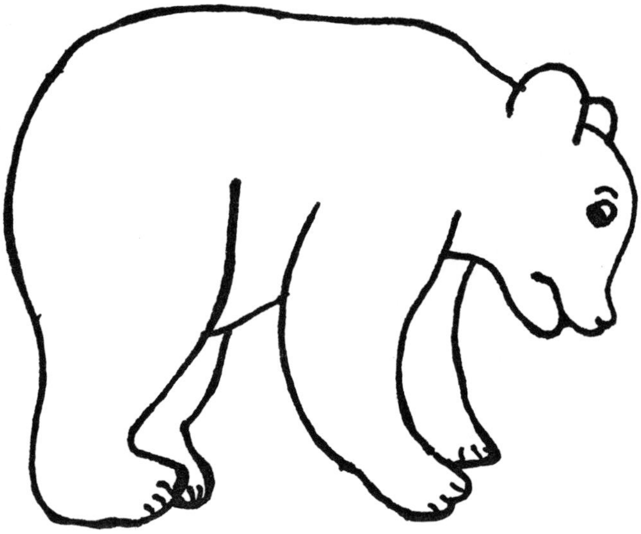

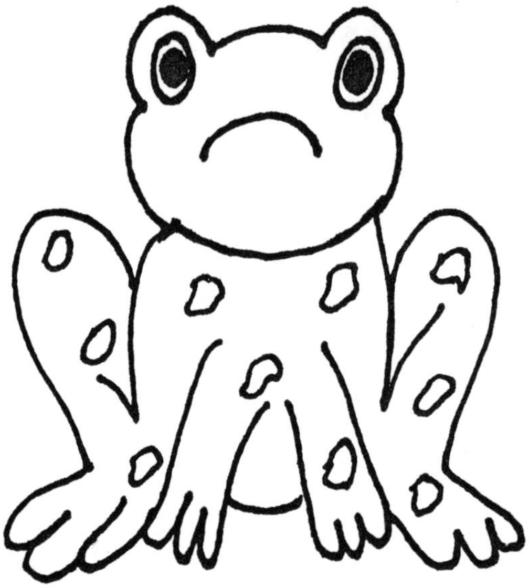

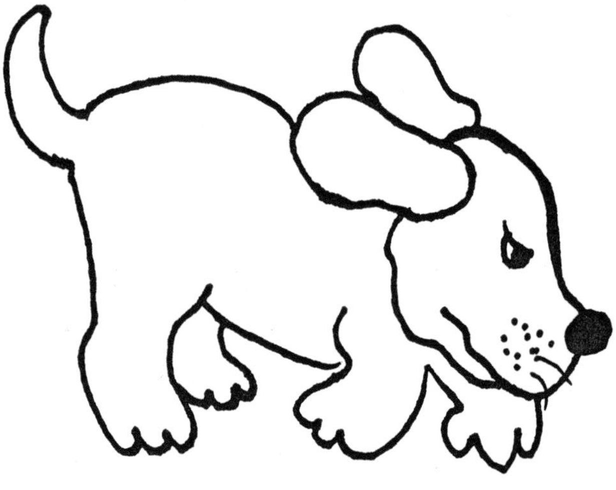

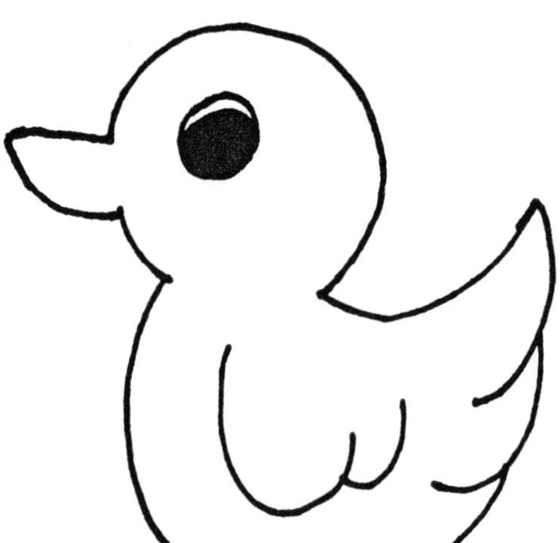

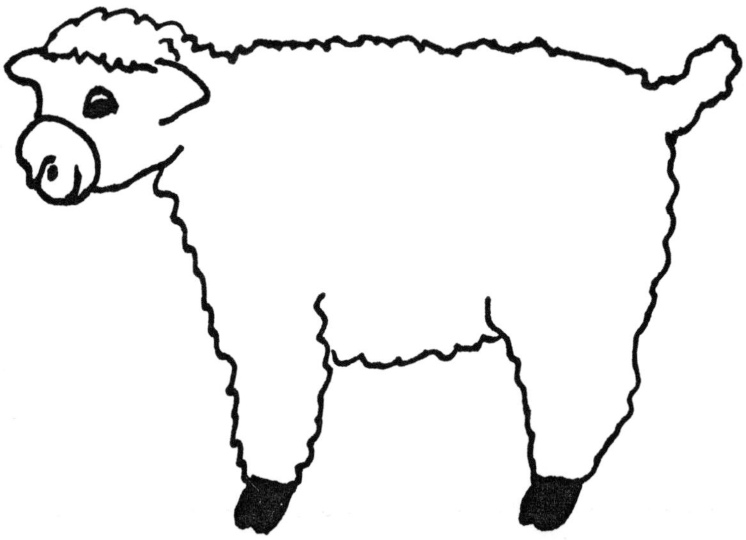

unit 8

OLD FAVORITES

The following eight days will bring back memories of your childhood while you are making memories for your students.

Kindergarten and preschool children delight in singing or saying nursery rhymes. The simple melodies and short verses are so appropriate for young children. Repetition and recall are important skills emphasized at the same time.

Along with singing and creative dramatics, the unit's activities emphasize opposites.

The daily activity plans in Unit 8 include:

- Jack and Jill Day
- Jack and the Beanstalk Day
- Old King Cole Day
- Humpty Dumpty Day
- Jack Be Nimble Day
- The Gingerbread Boy Day
- Hey Diddle, Diddle Day
- The Three Little Pigs Day

Jack and Jill Day

© 1990 by The Center for Applied Research in Education

PREPARATION —————————— **To the Teacher** ————————————————

Jack and Jill went up the hill and then came down! From Arrival to Closing, you will use opposites today. You will start the Old Favorites bulletin board. On each of the following days, you will add one thing to it.
  You will need:

- visuals of Jack and Jill used for the bulletin board and Opening (see p. 200)
- clown faces (see p. 201), box, and beanbag for Activity 3.

ARRIVAL —————————— **"The Opposite"** ————————————————

As the children arrive, let them follow the instructions in the song "The Opposite" on the album *Getting to Know Myself* (AR543), by Hap Palmer (Educational Activities, Inc., Box 392, Freeport, N.Y. 11520). For example, the singer will ask the children to bend backwards and "do the opposite." Then he will tell them to look up and "do the opposite."

OPENING —————————— **"Jack and Jill"** ————————————————

Teach the nursery rhyme "Jack and Jill" to the children who do not already know it, making sure all the children understand the meaning of *fetch* (to get something) and *crown* (top of the head).

> Jack and Jill went up the hill,
> To fetch a pail of water.
> Jack fell down and broke his crown,
> And Jill came tumbling after.

—————————— **Opposite Talk** ————————————————

This is the first of two days when you talk about opposites. Make available many examples of opposites with which the children can experiment. The following examples go well with the rhyme "Jack and Jill": (1) Fasten a paper clip to a picture of a boy and a girl (see p. 200). On another piece of paper, draw a hill. Lay the picture of Jack and Jill on top of the picture of the hill. Let the children use a magnet on the back side of the paper to move Jack and Jill up and down the hill. (2) In a shallow pan, demonstrate that water does not move on a flat surface. Tilt the pan and show that water will roll down, but it can't roll back up. To get water up a hill, we need to carry or pump it.

—————————— **Bulletin Board** ————————————————

This month, you will make a bulletin board that resembles a nursery rhyme collage. Each day, you will put a visual you have made on the bulletin board, or the children will make something to put on the board that reminds them of the rhyme they learned on that day. Throughout the month, you can use this bulletin board to review the nursery rhymes the children have learned. For today, put up the visual of Jack and Jill going up and down the hill.

CRAFT _____ Jack or Jill _____

Materials Needed:

>   one large piece of paper per child with a hill drawn on it
>   photocopied picture of each child (see p. 64)
>   one ice cream stick per child
>   two pipe cleaners per child
>   tape, glue, crayons

Explanation:
Prior to class, cut slits along the top of each hill with an
X-ACTO® knife. The children glue their own picture to the
end of an ice cream stick. Then they wrap both pipe
cleaners around the stick one above the other. Twist each
pipe cleaner one time. Tape the back of each pipe cleaner
for security. Bend the top pipe cleaner up to be the child's
arms and the bottom pipe cleaner down to be the legs and
feet. The children draw grass on the hill and the well at
the top of the hill if they wish. When finished, they insert their puppet through the slit, with
legs on top of the paper, and make their puppet go up and down the hill.

FREEPLAY _____ Activity 1 _____

Jack Says—Play Jack Says as you would play Simon Says using commands that have opposite
words in them. *Examples:* "Jack says stand up/sit down." "Jack says stand inside the circle/out-
side the circle."

_____ Activity 2 _____

I Wonder—Ask the children some of the following questions: Why did Jack and Jill need water?
Did Jill get hurt when she fell? Who came to help Jack and Jill? What did they do after they
fell down the hill? After talking about these things, have the children draw a picture of what
Jack and Jill did after they fell down the hill. You can write a sentence about each child's picture at the bottom of the paper. These pictures will look nice on a bulletin board in your room.

_____ Activity 3 _____

Happy and Sad Clowns—Draw a happy clown face on the side of one small cardboard box and
a sad clown face on the side of another box (see p. 201). The children listen to a statement that
you read aloud and decide if it makes them feel happy or sad. If it makes them feel happy, they
throw a beanbag into the box with the happy clown. If it makes them feel sad, they throw the
beanbag into the box with the sad clown. *Examples:* "Mom brought me a big surprise." "I fell
down and scratched my knee."

CLOSING _____ Story _____

Read one of the following stories: *Big Dog, Little Dog,* by P. D. Eastman (Random House, 1973).
Demi's Opposites—An Animal Game Book, by Demi (Grosset & Dunlap, 1987). *Push, Pull, Empty, Full: A Book of Opposites,* by Tana Hoban (Macmillan, 1972).

Jack and the Beanstalk Day

PREPARATION _____ To the Teacher _____

Jack is little, the giant is BIG. Baking cookies is a fun way to reinforce the concept of opposites. You will need:

- sugar cookie dough, pizza pan, and cookie sheet for Arrival;
- items for planting bean seeds for Opening;
- game prepared for Activity 1;
- L'eggs® containers and gold eggs for Activity 2;
- leaf patterns and photocopied pictures for Activity 3; and
- sequence pictures for Closing (see p. 202).

ARRIVAL _____ Giant and Tiny Cookies _____

Since this is the second opposite day, have the children help you make a giant sugar cookie for the class to share for snack time today and a tiny cookie to take home for someone special. To make the giant cookie, have each child press a small piece of ready made sugar cookie dough into a round pizza pan. Grease the pan well so that the giant cookie will come out in one piece. Let each child break off a small piece for snack time.

OPENING _____ Story _____

Read the story _Jack and the Beanstalk,_ adapted and illustrated by Tony Ross (Delacorte, 1981), to the children. Include some talk about opposites as you read the story. Let the children chant with you "fee, fie, fo, fum. . ." first loud and then soft. Also talk about giant/tiny, mean/friendly, rich/poor. This reinforces the concept of opposites introduced on Jack and Jill Day (see p. 184).

_____ Growing a Beanstalk _____

Plant some bean seeds for the children to observe during the next few weeks. Be sure to plant them in clear plastic cups so the root systems are visible. Conduct an experiment to see which of four conditions is most conducive to growing beans: (1) light and water, (2) light but no water, (3) water but no light, and (4) no water or light. Chart the progress of each beanstalk.

CRAFT _____ A Nest of Golden Eggs _____

Materials Needed:

large piece of paper for each child
straw
oval patterns and small pieces of paper
pencils, glue, scissors
macaroni which has been spray painted gold

Explanation:
Children create the hen's nest by gluing straw on their piece of paper. Then they trace and cut several eggs and glue them on the nest. Finally, they glue the gold macaroni onto the eggs.

FREEPLAY _____ **Activity 1** _____

Climb the Beanstalk Game—Make a beanstalk with a castle at the top. To do so, insert a large cardboard tube in the plastic top of a coffee can with a circle cut in it the size of the tube. Cut leaves for the beanstalk from heavy cardboard or scraps of paneling. Cut slits in the tube and insert the leaves. Paint the container, leaves, and tube green. Attach one small, metal hook to each leaf. Paint a castle on the sides of a small box and attach it to the top of the beanstalk.

You must also make small cards to use with this game. On each card, draw a colored shape. (Cards for older children can contain words or addition or subtraction facts.) Hang one card on the hook of each leaf.

To play the game, the child must identify the shape and color on each card, from the bottom to the top of the beanstalk. If the child makes it to the castle, he or she gets a prize—a sticker to wear or a few fish crackers to eat.

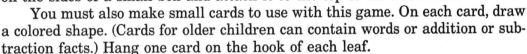
_____ **Activity 2** _____

Match the Golden Eggs—Glue gold foil paper (wrapping paper) to cardboard eggs and cut the eggs into jigsaw puzzles. (Each egg puzzle can be kept in a gold L'eggs® container.) Children try to put the jigsaw eggs together.

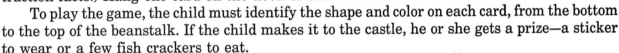
_____ **Activity 3** _____

Beanstalk Bulletin Board—Have each child cut out a leaf and write his or her name on it. The child can glue a photocopied picture (see p. 64) of himself or herself on the leaf. Arrange these leaves to form a beanstalk up the sides of the bulletin board.

CLOSING _____ **Recording** _____

Have the children pretend to be farmers planting beans as they listen to the song "Oats, Peas, Beans and Barley Grow" on the album *Baby Beluga* (SL-0010), by Raffi with Ken Whiteley (Shoreline Records, 6307 Yohge Street, Willowdale, Ontario, Canada MZM 3X7).

_____ **Sequence Cards** _____

Make picture cards to represent the different stages of growing beans (see p. 202): (1) planting seeds, (2) sunshine, (3) rain, (4) tiny plants, (5) plants with blossoms, (6) plants with beans, and (7) beans picked in a bucket. Discuss the proper order with the children, and then mix up the cards and see if the children can put them back in the right sequence.

Old King Cole Day

PREPARATION _____ To the Teacher _____

Today you will crown the bulletin board, play a crown game, and crown the king when you act out the nursery rhyme. Compare the word _crown_ as it is used today to the way you used it on Jack and Jill Day.

You will need:

- the crown and decorations for Arrival;
- game prepared for Activity 1;
- props for Activity 2; and
- game prepared for Activity 3.

ARRIVAL _____ Crowning the Bulletin Board _____

In advance, cut out a crown large enough to cover the top of the nursery rhyme bulletin board. As the children arrive, they can glue on glitter, sequins, and colorful braid or ricrac to make the crown look very regal.

OPENING _____ "Old King Cole" _____

Recite the rhyme "Old King Cole" with the children and then ask the following questions: What is an "old soul"? How old do you think King Cole was? Why did he call for his bowl? Do you always get what you ask for? What's the difference between wishing for something or getting upset when you don't get what you want? If you were a king, what would you call for? What's the difference between King Cole's crown and Jack's crown in "Jack and Jill"?

Old King Cole
Was a merry old soul
And a merry old soul was he;
He called for his pipe,
And he called for his bowl,
And he called for his fiddlers three.

CRAFT _____ King's Royal Robe _____

Materials Needed:

robe pattern (see p. 147)	sequins
purple paper	pencils, scissors, glue
cotton balls	

© 1990 by The Center for Applied Research in Education

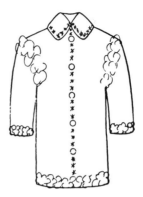

Explanation:
Use the pattern from Coat Day (see p. 147). Have the children trace and cut out a robe from the purple paper. Glue on cotton balls and sequins for trim.

FREEPLAY _____ Activity 1 _____

Bowling Game—Cover ten Pringles® potato chip cans with plain paper. On one can, glue a picture of the king's pipe, on another glue a picture of his bowl, and on the third glue a picture of a fiddle. Two children take turns rolling a ball, trying to knock over the cans. They receive two points for each can with a picture on it that they knock over and one point for each can without a picture. The first child to score five points is the winner.

_____ Activity 2 _____

Dramatization—This is a fun story for children to act out. Have one child be the king and wear a crown and sit in a large chair. Give five other children one of the following objects: a pipe, a bowl, or one of three fiddles. As the teacher and children recite the poem, the children present King Cole with objects. Repeat several times so everyone gets to join the fun.

_____ Activity 3 _____

Putting Jewels on a Crown—Each player needs a crown game board like the one shown. (Shapes should be different colors on each board.) In advance, make cards with colored shapes on them—one shape per card. Also make "jewels" in those same colors and shapes for the children to put on their crowns. Be sure there is a jewel for each shape on the crown. Children take turns drawing a card. If they have a shape of that color, they may put that jewel on their crown. The first player to complete his or her crown is the winner.

CLOSING _____ Story _____

Read one of the following stories: *The King Who Learned to Smile,* by Seymour Reit (Golden Press, 1960). *The King's Tea,* by Trinka Hakes Noble (Dial Press, 1979). *King Wacky,* by Dick Gackenbach (Crown Publishers, 1984).

Humpty Dumpty Day

PREPARATION _____ To the Teacher _____

Humpty Dumpty was an egg! The activities today are centered around eggs. . .real eggs, plastic eggs, hard-boiled eggs, and scrambled eggs. Collect and wash eggshells well in advance of this day. The eggshells add a special touch to the Craft.

You will need:

- strips of red paper and envelopes for Arrival;
- eggs and pie plate or shallow bowl for Opening;
- ingredients and utensils to make scrambled eggs for Activity 1;
- L'eggs® containers and paper eggs for Activity 2; and
- Humpty Dumpty puzzle for Activity 3 (see p. 203).

ARRIVAL _____ Cutting Bricks _____

Have the children cut small bricks from narrow strips of red paper. The bricks that each child cuts should be put in an envelope with his or her name on it and saved for use in Craft.

_____ Bulletin Board _____

Have some of the children cut extra bricks. Use these to build a wall for Humpty Dumpty on the bulletin board. Put the laminated Humpty Dumpty from Activity 3 on the bulletin board when the children are finished playing with it.

OPENING _____ Egg Talk _____

Begin by talking about eggs and what different parts there are to an egg. Use illustrations or real eggs to examine the different parts. You might want to crack open a large and a small egg and compare the size of what is inside the shell. You can also dye some of the eggshells with food coloring or natural dyes such as onions or cranberries. Have a hard-boiled egg available and talk about how it is different from an uncooked egg. A fun experiment to try is letting the children hold an uncooked egg in their palm, wrapping their fingers around it and squeezing it. No matter how hard they try, they will not be able to crack the egg.

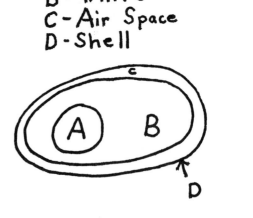

_____ "Humpty Dumpty" _____

First discuss some of the following questions: (1) Why couldn't the king's men put Humpty back together? (2) What would happen to you if you fell off a wall? (3) Where did Humpty live? (4) What was life like in a castle? After discussion, recite the rhyme "Humpty Dumpty" with the children.

Humpty Dumpty sat on a wall,
Humpty Dumpty had a great fall,
All the king's horses,
And all the king's men,
Couldn't put Humpty together again.

CRAFT _____ **Humpty and His Wall** _____

Materials Needed:

   one large piece of paper per child
   one small piece of white paper per child
   bricks cut in Arrival
   oval pattern
   glue, scissors, pencils, crayons
   eggshells

Explanation:
Have the children glue their bricks on the large piece of paper to make Humpty's wall. Then
have them trace and cut out an oval to be their Humpty Dumpty. They add facial features with
crayons. They may also glue some cracked eggshells on Humpty.

FREEPLAY _____ **Activity 1** _____

Scrambled Eggs—Set up a cooking center where the snack is prepared and served today. Let
the children come in small groups and make scrambled eggs and toast. Enjoy!

_____ **Activity 2** _____

Counting Eggs—In advance, put labels with numerals written on them on the outside of empty
L'eggs® containers. Also cut out small ovals to fit inside the containers. The children count as
many ovals to put inside the container as the label indicates.

_____ **Activity 3** _____

Putting Humpty Back Together—In advance, make a large picture of Humpty Dumpty (see p.
203) and laminate it. Then cut the picture into many pieces. The children can pretend to be all
the king's men and try to put Humpty back together again.

CLOSING _____ **Story** _____

Read one of the following stories: *Bad Egg—The True Story of Humpty Dumpty*, by Sarah Hayes
(Little, Brown & Co., 1987). *Septimus Bean and His Amazing Machine*, by Janet Quin-Harkin
(Parents Magazine Press, 1979). *Babar Loses His Crown*, by Laurent de Brunhoff (Random House,
1967).

Jack Be Nimble Day

PREPARATION _____ To the Teacher _____

Jack jumped over (not under!) the candlestick. There will be a jumping contest, lots of candles, and a review of opposites today.

You will need:

- flames cut for Arrival;
- candles of various shapes and sizes for Opening, Craft, and Activity 2;
- tube candle for bulletin board;
- jars for Opening;
- maze cards prepared for Activity 1 (see p. 204); and
- felt candles for Activity 3.

ARRIVAL _____ Fingerpainting _____

Cut a piece of fingerpaint paper in the shape of a flame for each child (approximately 7″ tall). Children use red, yellow, or orange fingerpaint to make the flame glow.

OPENING _____ Candle Talk _____

There are special times when we use candles. On your birthday, you may have had candles on your cake. During some holidays, we burn candles.

A candle is made of wax, which melts when the candle is lit. The part of the candle we light is called the wick.

Recite "Jack Be Nimble" together.

> Jack be nimble,
> Jack be quick,
> Jack jump over the candlestick.

_____ Science _____

A candle needs air for it to burn. To demonstrate that air is necessary, place a glass jar over a burning candle. Ask children to observe what happens. Use three different sized jars (pint, quart, and gallon). The larger the jar, the more air there is, so the longer the candle will burn each time. Explain that once the air (oxygen) in the jar is used, the flame goes out.

_____ Bulletin Board _____

Use an empty paper towel tube as a candle. Wrap colored paper around it and decorate it. Add a fingerpainted flame!

© 1990 by The Center for Applied Research in Education

CRAFT _____ Candle Making _____

Materials Needed:

>   butcher paper with vertical lines drawn
>   every 7 inches
>   flame painted in Arrival
>   display of different candles
>   crayons
>   staples or tape

Explanation:
Mark vertical lines on the butcher paper approximately
7 inches apart. As each child cuts on one line, he or she
gets a rectangular piece of paper to make into a candle.
The children can decorate their candles with crayons.
Display several different candles, including ones of dif-
ferent colors and ones in the shape of numerals or familiar characters. By this time, the fingerpainted flame should be dry and can be attached by stapling or taping.

FREEPLAY _____ Activity 1 _____

Maze Game—Help Jack find his candlestick. Make individual maze cards and laminate or cover
with clear self-stick vinyl (see p. 204). Draw Jack in one corner and his candlestick in another.
Let the children use grease pencils to find the path that leads to his candlestick. Mistakes can
be wiped off with paper towels, or the entire game board can be cleared for another child to use.

_____ Activity 2 _____

Jumping Contest—As the children successfully jump over two candles, move the candles farther
apart and let them take turns jumping again. Have the children recite "Jack Be Nimble" as
they jump, substituting their own name in place of "Jack." Review opposites. . .far/near, long/
short.

_____ Activity 3 _____

Candle Fun—Cut out candles of different colors and lengths from felt. Ask the children to perform the following tasks: (1) Place all the red candles on the flannel board. (2) Place all those
taller than a certain candle on the board. (3) Place all the candles shorter than a certain candle
on the board. (4) Place all candles of one color in sequence from shortest to tallest. Stress opposites. . .tall/short, big/little, hot (flame)/cold (no flame). You will think of many more activities
to do with these candles as you go along.

CLOSING _____ Story _____

Read one of the following stories: *Jack Jump Under the Candlestick,* by Donna Lugg Pape (Albert
Whitman, 1982). *Over-Under,* by Catherine Matthias (Children's Press, 1984). *Fast-Slow, High-
Low, A Book of Opposites,* by Peter Spier (Doubleday & Co., 1972).

Gingerbread Boy Day

PREPARATION _____ To the Teacher _____

The children will be baking their own gingerbread boy cookies as well as decorating a large and a small paper cookie.
  You will need:

- recipe, cookie cutter, and ingredients for Arrival (see p. 205);
- puppets for Opening;
- tape recording of sounds and pictures for Activity 1;
- two pieces of rope for Activity 2;
- large paper gingerbread boy and brown items for Activity 3; and
- different colored gingerbread boys for Closing (see p. 205).

ARRIVAL _____ Gingerbread Cookies _____

Use the recipe provided and have the children help prepare gingerbread cookies (see p. 205). If your daily schedule does not allow time for the dough to chill, prepare it ahead of time. Let each child roll out a small piece of dough and cut out a gingerbread boy to eat for snack time today. Use raisins to add facial features and buttons.

Gingerbread Cookies

1 pkg. instant butterscotch pudding
1/2 cup brown sugar
1 1/2 cups flour
1/2 tsp. soda
1 egg
1/2 cup margarine
1 tsp. cinnamon
1/2 tsp. ginger

Mix all ingredients. Chill dough. Roll out, cut, and add raisins. Bake cookies at 350 degrees for ten to twelve minutes. Yield: one dozen.

_____ Bulletin Board _____

When all the cookies are made, wash the gingerbread boy cutter and have children trace around it on brown paper to make cookies for the bulletin board. Use crayons to add features.

OPENING _____ Story _____

Read to the children the story _The Gingerbread Boy_, by Paul Galdone (Seabury Press, 1975). This story is particularly appealing if told with puppets. The children who aren't holding a puppet can repeat "you can't catch me. . ." as a group. After the story, the puppets can be used to help review the sequence in which the different characters appeared in the story.

© 1990 by The Center for Applied Research in Education

CRAFT ———————————— Gingerbread Boy ————————————

Materials Needed:

> pattern of gingerbread boy (see p. 205) tea bags
> paper large and small coding dots
> scissors, glue, crayons

Explanation:
Have each child trace and cut out a gingerbread boy. They put on small coding dots for his eyes and large coding dots for buttons. They use a crayon to give him a smiley mouth. They use glue brushes to spread glue all over the rest of him. Then they sprinkle tea all over the glue to make him look like a well-baked gingerbread boy!

FREEPLAY ———————————— Activity 1 ————————————

Listening Game—Prior to class, make a tape recording of different sounds that the gingerbread boy might have heard as he was running. (*Examples:* people talking, water running, a dog barking, a cow mooing) Include some sounds not mentioned but which could have been heard (e.g., cars) Pass out pictures of the different things that make those sounds to each of the children. Play the tape. When the children hear the sound made by the picture they are holding, they hold up the picture.

———————————— Activity 2 ————————————

Escaping the Fox—Place two pieces of rope on the floor several inches apart. The children pretend to be the gingerbread boy jumping over the stream to escape the fox. Widen the stream to make the task progressively more difficult.

———————————— Activity 3 ————————————

Bulletin Board Gingerbread Boy—Prior to class, cut out a large gingerbread boy for the bulletin board. Have available as many different brown things as you can find for the children to glue on this big gingerbread boy (sticks, yarn, buttons, lace, ricrac, cloves, peanut shells, material scraps). Glue on gallon milk jug lids for the eyes, and make a mouth with a piece of ribbon or ricrac.

CLOSING ———————————— Name Something Brown ————————————

Have the children name all the brown things they can think of in different categories—animals, foods, toys, things we wear, things in this room, etc.

———————————— Find the Color ————————————

Before class, cut out gingerbread boys in all the colors (see p. 205) mentioned in the song "Hide and Go Seek" on the album *Color Me A Rainbow* (MH-80), by Sharon Lucky (Melody House Publishing Co., 819 N.W. 92nd, Oklahoma City, Okla. 73114). Display these gingerbread boys around the room, and as the children listen to the directions on the song, they can quietly point to the gingerbread boy that is the color mentioned.

Hey Diddle Diddle Day

PREPARATION _____ To the Teacher _____

The cow, the moon, the dish, and the spoon are all kept very busy today!
   You will need:

- moon for bulletin board, paper and yarn for Arrival;
- pictures for flannel board for Opening (see p. 206);
- ingredients and container to make shakes for Activity 1;
- poem for Activity 1;
- Jump the Moon game for Activity 2; and
- suitcase and clothes for Activity 3.

ARRIVAL _____ Bulletin Board _____

Make a large moon for the bulletin board. Each child draws a picture of a moon on a large sheet of paper. Then they glue short strips of yellow yarn on their moon and on the large moon for the bulletin board. (Their moon will be used in Craft.)

OPENING _____ Recording _____

Do some farm activities with "Hey Diddle Diddle." "Grandmother's Farm" on the album _Witches Brew_ (AR 572), by Hap and Martha Palmer (Educational Activities, Inc., Box 392, Freeport, N.Y. 11520) is a fun song.

_____ Recite Poem _____

Have available pictures of a cow, moon, dog, dish, and spoon for the flannel board (see p. 206). Hand the pictures to the children as you recite the poem "Hey Diddle Diddle." The child with the picture mentioned places it on the flannel board.

> Hey diddle diddle,
> The cat and the fiddle,
> The cow jumped over the moon;
> The little dog laughed
> To see such a sport,
> And the dish ran away with the spoon.

_____ Hey Diddle Diddle Talk _____

This poem is a fantasy, which means it could not really happen. Cows cannot jump over the moon, but they can give us milk to drink. Dogs do not laugh, but they wag their tails and bark when they are happy. Cats cannot play fiddles but do enjoy playing with yarn balls and other cat toys. Even though we know all this, isn't it fun to think about a cow's being able to jump over the moon?

CRAFT _____ Jump over the Moon _____

Materials Needed:

    moon with yarn made in Arrival

    glue, pencils, crayons

    yarn

Explanation:
The children lay their paper with the moon on the floor. Recite the first three lines of "Hey Diddle Diddle," each time substituting the names of children in the class. (For example, "Hey diddle diddle, the cat and the fiddle, Nicholas jumped over the moon.") Have that child step over the moon with one foot. Trace around his or her foot. Then the child uses crayons to make his or her foot look like a cow. Glue on some yarn for the cow's tail.

FREEPLAY _____ Activity 1 _____

Milk Shakes—Using large plastic tumblers with lids, have each child make a shake. Offer strawberries, mashed bananas, peanut butter, etc., to flavor the soft ice cream and milk. While the children are drinking their shakes, read them "Shaking" from *A Light in the Attic,* by Shel Silverstein (Harper & Row, 1981).

_____ Activity 2 _____

Jump the Moon—Make one game board that has a moon in the center and squares of colors that form an arch over the moon. There should be twenty to twenty-five squares in the arch. Use only four colors. Also make game cards that have a small square of color on each. Make seven cards of each color, and make three cards that have a dish drawn on them and three cards that have a spoon drawn on them. *Directions for play:* Each child has a cow for a marker. (Use plastic cows from your farm center.) Each player draws a card and moves his or her cow forward to the nearest square of that color. If the drawn card has a dish or a spoon on it, then the player moves backwards two spaces. The first player to get over the moon is the winner.

_____ Activity 3 _____

Let's Take a Trip—Ask the children the following questions: (1) Why did the dish and spoon run away? (2) Where did they go? (3) How did they get there? Let's pretend they were running off to the beach. Name the things they need to pack in their suitcase. Have a suitcase and different items to pack in it. Choose one child to pack for the trip. When the child is finished packing, the other children check to see if he or she remembered to pack everything. Choose other places to go and let a different child pack for each place.

CLOSING _____ Story _____

Read one of the following stories: *The Cow That Got Her Wish,* by Margaret Hillert (Follett, 1982). *The Curious Cow,* by Esther K. Meeks (Follett, 1960). *Daisy,* by Brian Wildsmith (Pantheon Books, 1984).

Three Little Pigs Day

PREPARATION _____ To the Teacher _____

Little children love to huff and puff in this nursery rhyme, and today everyone gets a chance. Fairytale Concentration (Activity 2) gives the children a chance to review all the stories and nursery rhymes they enjoyed during the month.

You will need:

- supplies to build three houses for the bulletin board for Arrival;
- Number Beanbag prepared for Activity 1;
- Fairytale Concentration prepared for Activity 2 (see p. 207);
- ping-pong balls for Activity 3; and
- farm animal pictures for Closing (see pp. 208–09).

ARRIVAL _____ Bulletin Board _____

Have the children help you make three houses for the bulletin board. The houses should be approximately 10″ squares with triangle roofs. Glue straw on one, Popsicle® sticks on another, and styrofoam packing pieces sprayed red on the other. Glue sandpaper on the triangles to make the roofs. As you make the houses with the children, ask them if they can guess what story they are going to hear today.

OPENING _____ Story _____

Read to the children the story of *The Three Little Pigs,* by Paul Galdone (Seabury Press, 1970). Emphasize the differences in the houses. Each of them are made of a different material, which causes each house to be a different color. Bring to class a brick, a stick, and straw. Demonstrate, by blowing, the strengths or weaknesses of each. Help the children understand the story by asking the following questions: Which house was the strongest? What are some ways the wolf tried to trick the pigs? What were the three houses made of? What happened to the wolf in the end?

_____ Pig Talk _____

What are baby pigs called? What is a litter? Where do pigs live? Why do pigs like mud? Do you think pigs could ever really build houses like those described in the story? Do pigs really talk? Baby pigs are called piglets and live on farms. A group of piglets born at the same time is called a litter.

This story is another fantasy, which we all know could not really happen.

_____ Recording _____

Listen to the song "The Three Little Piglets Playlet" on the album *Color Me A Rainbow* (MH-80), by Sharron Lucky (Melody House Publishing Co., 819 N.W. 92nd, Oklahoma City, Okla. 73114).

If this record is not available, choose children to act out the parts of the characters in the story. The rest of the children hold a green, red, or yellow shape (the record refers to the sticks as green). As the houses are built, children holding that color stick raise it in the air.

© 1990 by The Center for Applied Research in Education

CRAFT _____ Easel Paint _____

Materials Needed:

> paint—yellow, red, and green
> easel brushes
> paper

Explanation:
The children paint a house. They may choose red for a brick house, yellow for a house of straw, or green for a stick house. (Use green for the stick house because that color was used on the record in Opening.)

FREEPLAY _____ Activity 1 _____

Number Beanbag—Make a number board on a paper house and lay it flat on the floor. Each child stands behind a tape line and throws a beanbag onto the number board. The child must identify the numeral on which the beanbag lands. If the beanbag lands on a line, the child identifies all numerals that are touched by the beanbag. *Scoring:* Use wooden blocks. For a correct answer, give the child a wooden block with which to build a vertical house. Each child gets seven turns. The child with the tallest house is the winner.

_____ Activity 2 _____

Fairy Tale Concentration—Make two identical pictures on separate cards that tell something about each nursery rhyme learned this month (see p. 207). Place all cards in rows face down. child turns two cards over. If the pictures match, the child keeps the cards and tells which story or nursery rhyme they represent. If the pictures do not match, the child lays them face down exactly where they were, and the next child gets a turn. The game is over when all pairs are identified. The child who has the most matches is the winner.

_____ Activity 3 _____

Huff and Puff—Children blow ping-pong balls between two tape lines on the floor.

CLOSING _____ "Old MacDonald" _____

Children stand in a circle. Place pictures of animals and their babies on the floor in the center of the circle (see pp. 208–09). A child chooses a mother animal and her baby, names them, and then the whole class sings a verse of "Old MacDonald" using that animal.

Make two clowns. Draw a happy face on one and a sad face on the other.

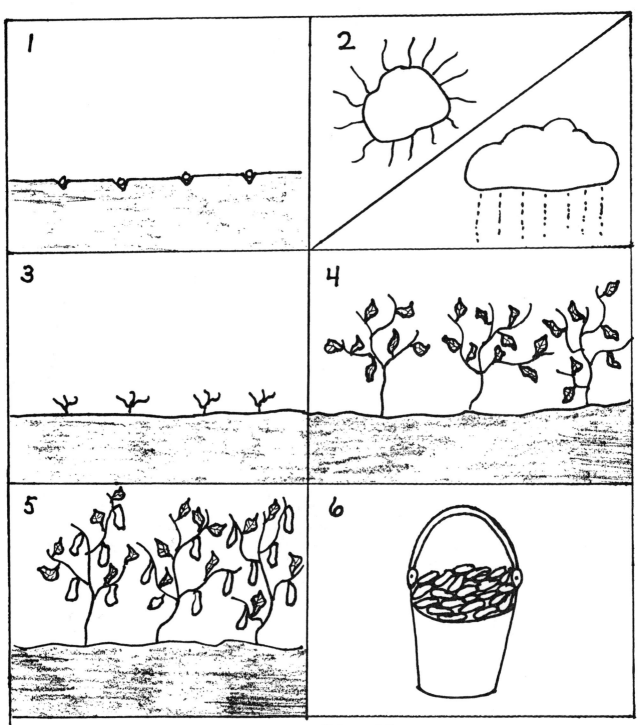

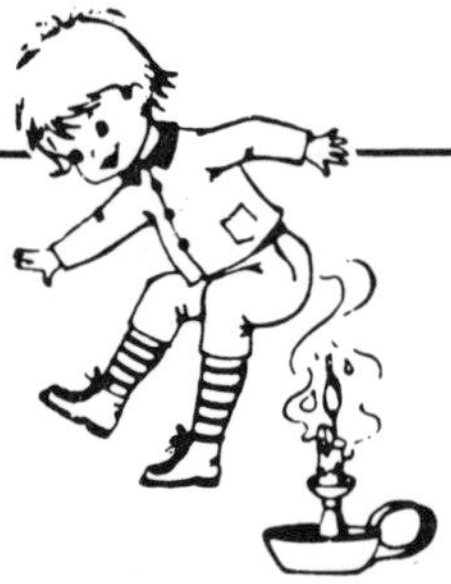

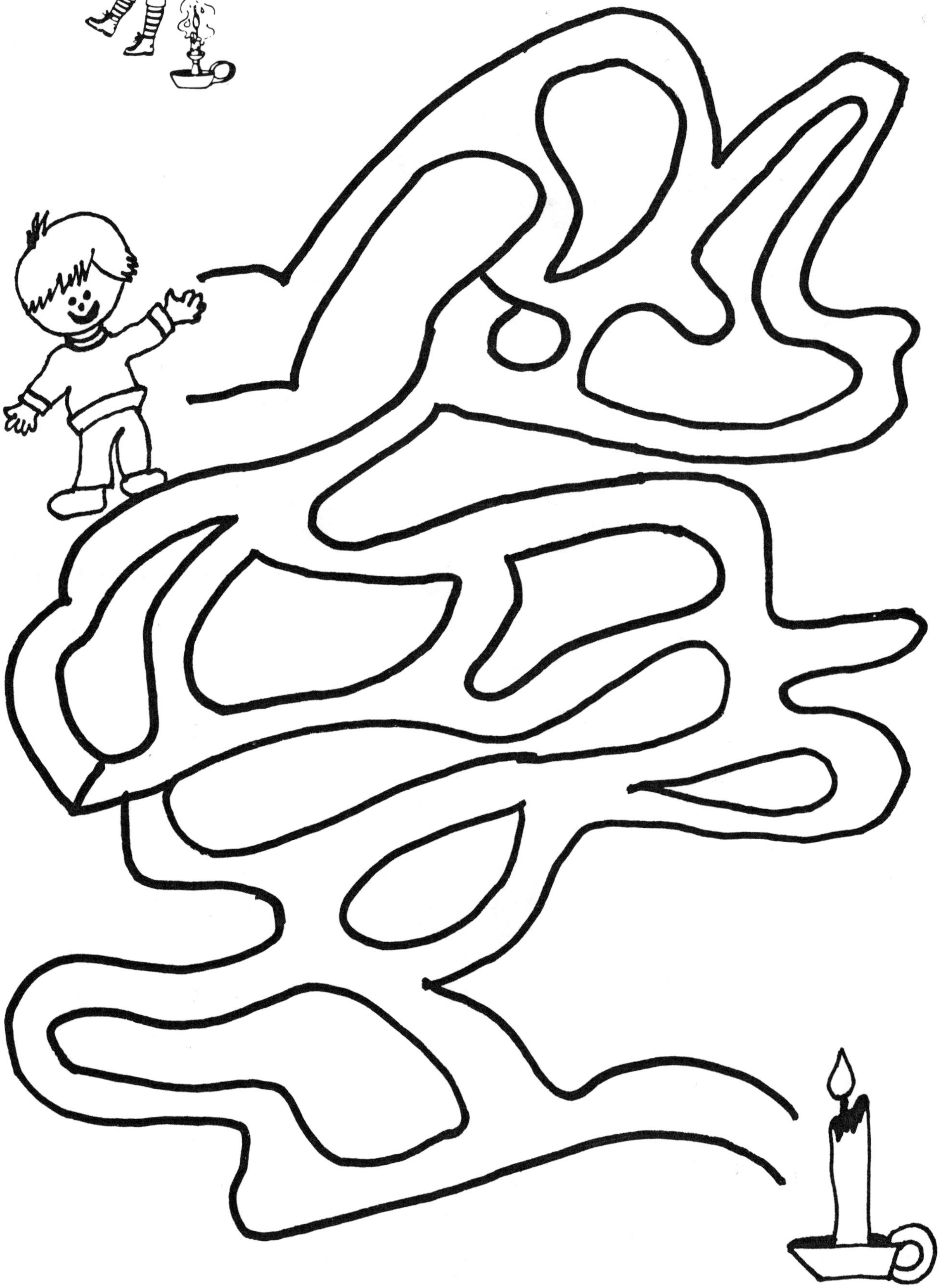

Want to Bake?

Gingerbread Cookies

1 pkg. instant butterscotch pudding

1 egg

1/2 cup brown sugar

1/2 cup margarine

1 1/2 cups flour

1 tsp. cinnamon

1/2 tsp. soda

1/2 tsp. ginger

Mix all ingredients. Chill dough. Roll out, cut, and bake cookies at 350 degrees for 10 to 12 minutes. Yield: 12 cookies

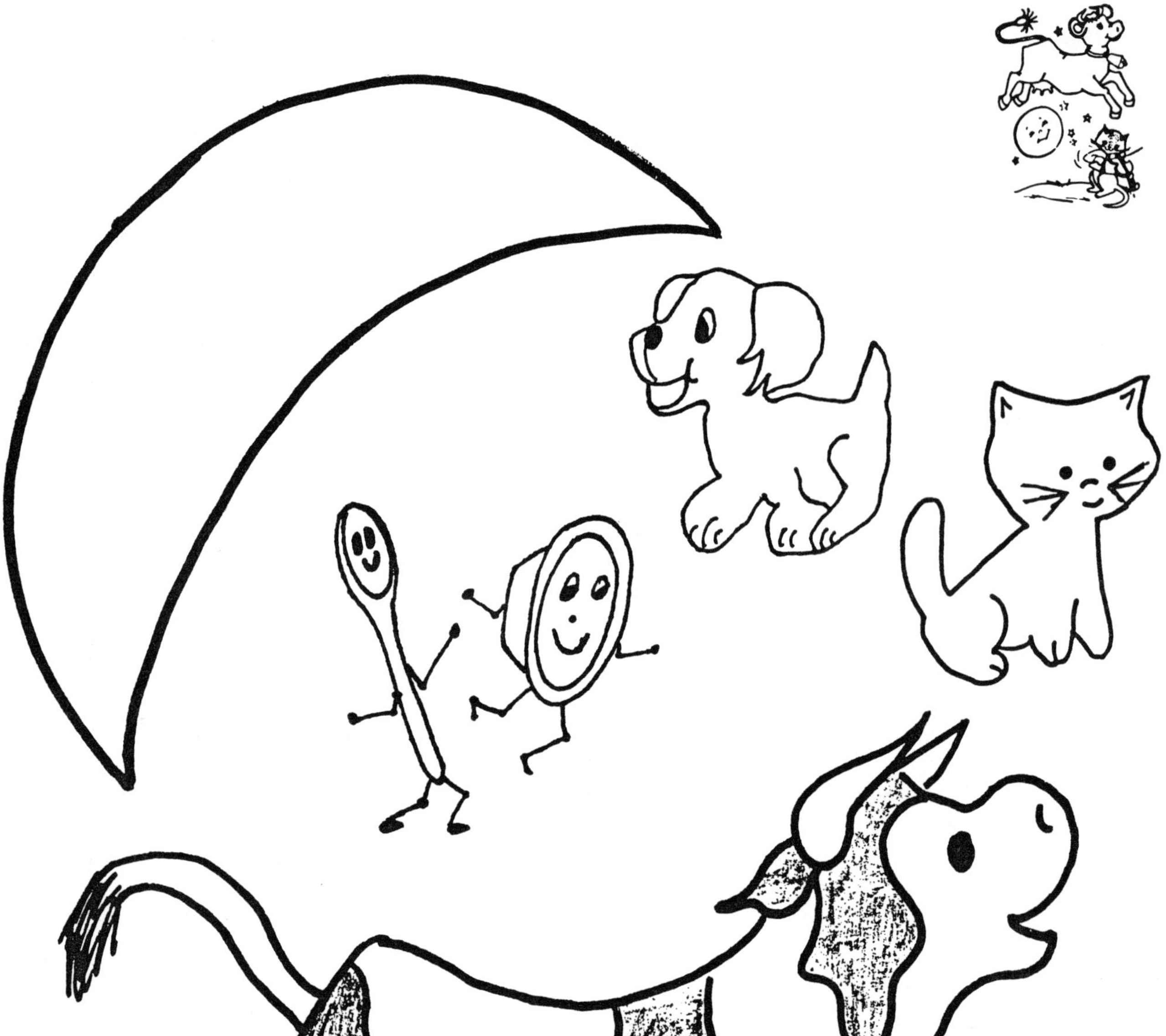

Make two of each card.

Jack Be
Nimble

Old
King
Cole

Gingerbread
Man

Humpty
Dumpty

Hey
Diddle
Diddle

Three Little Pigs

unit 9

THINGS THAT GO TOGETHER

The daily activity plans in this unit require children to think about why two things go together or why they are associated with one another. The activities will stretch children's thinking skills.

As you move through the unit and the children work with a few of the go togethers, they will begin to understand why the two things are associated and possibly think of some other combinations on their own.

The daily activity plans in Unit 9 include:

- Needles and Pins Day
- Spool and Thread Day
- Bat and Ball Day
- Hammer and Nail Day
- Bee and Honey Day
- Slim and Trim Day
- Sand and Sea Day
- Boat and Dock Day

Needles and Pins Day

PREPARATION _____ To the Teacher _____

Each child needs a plastic lid (hair spray, spray starch) for Craft (see p. 228). If you have a quilt (not a family heirloom), this would be a good time to hang it in your classroom. The children will sew quilt squares today.

You will need:

- supplies for pinhead painting for Arrival;
- pin cushion, metal needle and plastic darning needle for Opening;
- burlap squares, needles, and yarn for Activity 1;
- dressmaker pins, oval styrofoam, and numeral cards for Activity 2; and
- darning needles and styrofoam meat trays for Activity 3.

ARRIVAL _____ Pinhead Painting _____

As children arrive, have them decorate a strip of paper to go around a plastic lid. Stick pins with flat heads into corks in the shape of △, ○, □, or ◇. Have children dip the pinheads into the paint by holding onto the corks and then decorate the strip of paper. This paper will be used to complete a pincushion in Craft.

OPENING _____ Needles and Pins Talk _____

Pins and needles are both sharp so that they can be easily pushed into fabric. A needle has an eye through which thread can be inserted. A pin has a head that is either flat or round. Show the children the difference between sharp and dull by using a pincushion, a metal needle, and one of the darning needles from Activity 3.

_____ Song _____

Sing and do the actions of "Here We Go 'Round the Mulberry Bush." Be sure to include a verse saying "we mend our clothes."

CRAFT _____ Pincushion _____

Materials Needed:

> one plastic lid per child (see p. 228)
> decorated strip painted in Arrival
> batting or cotton
> straight pins
> piece of material
> glue

© 1990 by The Center for Applied Research in Education

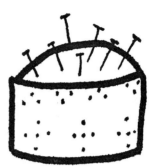

Explanation:
Have the children glue the decorated strip of paper around the outside of the plastic lid. Stuff batting in the lid and cover it with the piece of material by pushing the material in and around the batting. Let the children stick pins in their cushions!

FREEPLAY _____ **Activity 1** _____

Quilting—Cut a 4″ square of burlap for each child. The children can design a quilt square by using large plastic needles and yarn. At the end of the day, glue all the squares onto a large sheet of paper to make a class quilt.

_____ **Activity 2** _____

Pin Porcupine—Make several cards with a numeral on each one. A child picks one card and sticks that many dressmaker pins in an oval styrofoam. See how long it takes to make a porcupine.

_____ **Activity 3** _____

See-through Shapes—Draw shapes on small pieces of paper and lay them on styrofoam meat trays. Children use blunt darning needles to poke holes in the paper along the lines of the shape. Hold the paper up to a window to see the shape outline.

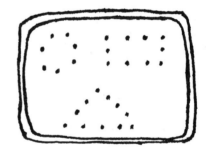

CLOSING _____ **Story** _____

Read one of the following stories: *The Elves and the Shoemaker,* by The Brothers Grimm, translated by W. Andrews (Charles Scribner's Sons, 1960). *Ben and the Porcupine,* by Carol Carrick (Houghton-Mifflin Co., 1981). *The Patchwork Quilt,* by Valerie Flournoy (Dial Press, 1985).

Spool and Thread Day

PREPARATION _____ To the Teacher _____

Check your sewing supplies. You need several different colors of spools of thread. You and the children will be sewing a button on a piece of fabric, so a thimble will come in handy! Activity 1 requires antique spools. If you can't find these, a 3/4″ dowel is a suitable substitute.

   You will need:

- food for the snack for Arrival;
- button, fabric, needle, thread, spools of thread, and fabric swatches for Opening;
- yarn and antique spools for Activity 1;
- game prepared for Activity 2; and
- pattern cards and spools for Activity 3.

ARRIVAL _____ Spool and Thread Snack _____

Spread two round crackers with cheese and place a large marshmallow between them to form the spool. Lay a piece of red string licorice beside the spool to represent thread.

OPENING _____ Spool and Thread Talk _____

While showing the children a spool of thread, explain that the hole is needed so that the spool can fit onto a sewing machine. Thread is used when sewing two pieces of fabric together with a machine or needle. Thread is chosen to match the color of the fabric.

_____ Button Sewing _____

During the Spool and Thread Talk, start sewing a large button onto a piece of fabric. Invite the children to come up one at a time and help sew.

_____ Choose Your Color _____

Divide the class into two groups and have them sit on the floor in two lines facing each other. These two lines should be approximately 5′ apart. All the children in one line receive fabric swatches of different colors. Children in the other line receive spools of thread in colors that match the fabric swatches. There should be one spool of thread and one fabric swatch that match in each line. One at a time, children with the thread walk over to children with the matching fabric. They hand them the end of the thread and return to their place in line, unraveling the thread as they go. They sit down and place their spool on the floor. Continue until all fabrics and threads are matched.

   The children must keep the thread on the floor so others can return to their place in line without getting caught in the thread. (When matching is finished, cut the thread. Do not attempt to rewind it.)

CRAFT _____ Spool Painting _____

Materials Needed:

> paper
> paint
> spools
> spools with wire

Explanation:
The children dip the ends of the spools in paint
and/or roll the spools with wires in paint to make
a design.

FREEPLAY _____ Activity 1 _____

Yarn Winding—Tie yarn to antique spools and have contests to see who can wind yarn around
a spool the fastest.

_____ Activity 2 _____

Spool Garages—Turn shoeboxes upside down and cut
two doors in the side of each one. Stick a coding dot
of a different color above each door. Children roll
spools of thread into the boxes, matching them to the
coding dot above the door.

_____ Activity 3 _____

Spool Stacking—Make pattern cards that show stacked spools of thread of several different colors. Provide the children with actual spools of thread of the same variety of colors. Give children
a pattern card. They stack the spools accordingly.

CLOSING _____ Story _____

Read one of the following stories: *Kate's Quilt,* by Kay Chorao (E. P. Dutton, 1982). *The Quilt
Story,* by Tomie de Paola and Tony Johnston (Putnam, 1985). *The Bedspread,* by Sylvia Fair
(Morrow, 1982).

Bat and Ball Day

PREPARATION _____ To the Teacher _____

You'll be pretending to be at the baseball park all day, so if you or the children have baseball shirts or hats, wear them!

Note the Closing. You need the video, _Tiger Town_, as well as the traditional baseball snacks—hot dogs and Cracker Jacks.®

You will need:

- round sugar cookies, white frosting, and red licorice for Arrival;
- baseball equipment for Opening;
- plastic ball and bat for Activity 1;
- paper, paint, and pencil eraser for Activity 2;
- game prepared for Activity 3; and
- video and food for Closing.

ARRIVAL _____ Baseball Cookies _____

Have children frost round cookies with white frosting and add shoestring licorice for stitching. To stimulate discussion of leather and stitching, have available several baseballs for the children to examine.

If you choose to serve the traditional baseball food suggested in Closing, you can send these cookies home with the children.

OPENING _____ Bat and Ball Talk _____

Allow time for lots of enthusiastic discussion. Children will want to tell about their experiences at the ballpark. Bring in ball equipment for the children to touch and examine. Demonstrate how to hold a bat. Point out the special type of glove a ballplayer wears. The catcher's equipment is the perfect example of how important safety is when playing baseball or any other sport.

_____ Music _____

Teach the chorus of the song "Take Me Out to the Ball Game." The words and music of the song can be found in the book _Take Me Out to the Ball Game and Other Favorite Hits 1906–1908_, edited by Lester S. Levy (Dover Publications, 1984).

_____ Story _____

Read to the children one of the following stories: _Curious George Plays Baseball_, by Margaret Rey (Houghton-Mifflin Co., 1986). _Play Ball, Kate_, by Sharon Gordon (Troll Associates, 1981). _The Littlest Leaguer_, by Syd Hof (E. P. Dutton, 1976).

© 1990 by The Center for Applied Research in Education

CRAFT _____ Easel Painting _____

Materials Needed:

    newsprint folded into thirds   paint and brushes
    easel   words to "Here Is a Ball" (see p. 228)

Explanation:
Teach the children the following poem:
Here is a ball.   (Make a circle with thumb and index finger.)
And here's a bigger ball.   (Make a circle with thumbs and index fingers.)
A great big ball I see.   (Make a circle using arms above head.)
Can you count them? Are you ready? 1...2...3!   (Make each ball as you count.)
The children paint a ball in each section of their paper, making the balls big, bigger, and biggest. Glue the words to the poem (which are typed on a small piece of paper) onto each child's painting.

FREEPLAY _____ Activity 1 _____

Baseball Game—Play a baseball game. For young children, you will need a large plastic bat and a large plastic ball. It may work best to lay the ball on the floor or ground and have the batter hit it. It is difficult for young children to hit a ball in the air.

_____ Activity 2 _____

Eraser Painting—Give children a piece of paper divided into four sections with a numeral in each. With the eraser of a pencil, children paint the correct number of balls in each section.

_____ Activity 3 _____

Scoreboard Game—Make several cards in the shape of a bat, each having a different number of coding dot "balls" on them. The child selects a bat, tells how many balls he or she hit this inning (according to the number of coding dots), and then hangs the bat on the scoreboard. The next child does the same. At the end of the game, count the total number of balls hit in the game.

CLOSING _____ Out to the Game _____

Serve the children hot dogs, Cracker Jacks,® and juice while they watch the video *Tiger Town.* This is an excellent baseball movie for young children. There are other movies available, but be sure to preview because profanity is used in many of them.

Hammer and Nail Day

© 1990 by The Center for Applied Research in Education

PREPARATION _____ To the Teacher _____

If you know someone who would enjoy sharing their carpentry skills, invite him or her to your class. A simple bird house can be built using precut pieces of wood, a hammer, and nails!
   You will need:

- hammer, nails, and wood for Opening;
- wooden hammer, golf tees, and ceiling tiles for Activity 1;
- nails and small ball for Activity 2; and
- modeling compound (see p. 55) and nails for Activity 3.

ARRIVAL _____ Pound-a-Rhythm _____

Be creative! The children are to pound out rhythms with you. Use the side of your fist as a hammer and hold the other hand flat, palm side up. Begin with very simple rhythms. You hammer first, and then the children are to hammer out the identical rhythm. As the children catch on to what you are doing, let them take turns being the leader.

OPENING _____ Hammer and Nail Talk _____

Show the children a hammer and several nails of different sizes. Point out that the head of the hammer is different on each end. One end is used to pound nails into wood, and the other end is used to remove nails. As you are discussing this, pound a nail into wood and then remove it with the hammer.

_____ Song _____

Sing and do the actions to "Johnny Works with One Hammer".

> Johnny works with one hammer, one hammer, one hammer
> Johnny works with one hammer, now he works with two.

(The song continues with numbers increasing until Johnny works with five hammers. The last line says, "Now he goes to sleep.") _Actions_—Hammer with the following body parts as you sing: right arm, left arm, right foot, left foot, head. Hammer with just the right arm during the first verse, adding another body part with each verse until the fifth verse, when all parts are moving at once.

CRAFT _____ Nailhead Painting _____

Materials Needed:

   cardboard shapes to trace
   paper, paint, pencils
   nails with large heads

Explanation:
Children trace a square and a triangle to draw a house. Use a nailhead to paint dots around the outline of the house. (Put masking tape on the sharp part of nail.)

FREEPLAY _____ Activity 1 _____

Pound That Hammer—Using wooden hammers, the children pound golf tees into old ceiling tiles.

_____ Activity 2 _____

Nail Bowling—Set ten nails with large heads upside down about 1″ apart and arrange like tenpins on a surface 4′ long. The child rolls a "jack" ball and counts one point for each nail knocked over.

_____ Activity 3 _____

Tall and Short Nails—Each child needs play dough or modeling compound (see p. 55) and several nails of different lengths. Have the children push the nails into the dough, arranging them from tallest to shortest. Or, the children can combine all their nails and choose one size and push only that length into their dough.

CLOSING _____ Story _____

Read one of the following stories: *Nail Soup,* retold by Harve Zemach (Follett Publishing, 1964). *The Clever Carpenter,* by R. W. Alley (Random House, 1988). *The Tool Box,* by Anne and Harlow Rockwell (Macmillan, 1971).

Bee and Honey Day

PREPARATION _____ To the Teacher _____

Most children have only seen honey in a jar. Bring a honeycomb to class and show it to the children. Compare the taste and texture during snack time.

You will need:

- refrigerator tube biscuits and honey for Arrival;
- flower for Activity 1;
- two large bees and tissue paper for Activity 2; and
- game prepared for Activity 3.

ARRIVAL _____ Biscuits and Honey _____

As children arrive, let them help prepare biscuits for snack time. Use refrigerator biscuits in a tube, and serve them warm with honey, of course!

OPENING _____ Bee Talk _____

The bee is a yellow and black insect. It flies and makes a buzzing sound. It has a lower lip that is long like a tube and that makes it possible for the bee to suck nectar from flowers. Bees use nectar to make honey. There are two kinds of bees—bumblebees and honeybees. The home that bees make to live in is called a hive.

_____ Fingerplay _____

Teach the following fingerplay:
Here is a beehive. (Make a fist with hand.)
Where are the bees?
Hiding away where nobody sees.
Here they come out of their hive.
Let's count them. (Raise fingers one at a time.)
1...2...3...4...5...Bzzz   Bzzz   Bzzz (Wave fingers in air.)

CRAFT _____ Bee and Hive _____

Materials Needed:

play dough or modeling compound for each child (see p. 55)
black pipe cleaners
yellow tissue paper
toothpicks and pencils

© 1990 by The Center for Applied Research in Education

Explanation:
The child rolls the play dough into a long rope and coils it to make a cone shape to resemble a beehive. Twist a 3″ pipe cleaner tightly around a pencil to form a bee's body. Remove the coiled pipe cleaner from the pencil and tuck a piece of yellow tissue through center of the bee's body to form wings. Stick a toothpick through the bee and into the hive to hold it in place.

FREEPLAY ———————————— Activity 1 ——————————————

Find the Flower—Hide a flower in the room. Choose one child to find the flower. The rest of the children buzz loudly as the child gets close to the flower and softly as he or she gets farther away.

———————————— Activity 2 ——————————————

Bulletin Board Bees—Provide the children with two large paper bees and many small squares of black and yellow tissue paper. Children twist the squares of tissue on a pencil top and glue them on the bee to make the black and yellow stripes.

———————————— Activity 3 ——————————————

Take the Bees Home—Cut the bottoms out of five styrofoam cups. Turn them upside down to resemble a hive. Put a different color coding dot on the front of each hive. Make several bees like the ones the children made for Craft, and place them in a honey pot. Have each child draw a card which has a colored numeral on it (e.g., a red numeral 2). The child takes that many bees out of the honey pot and puts them in the hive of the same color.

CLOSING ———————————— Story ——————————————

Read one of the following stories: *Honeybee and the Robber,* by Eric Carle (Putman, 1981). *The BEE,* by Lisa Ernst Campbell (Lothrop, Lee & Shepard, 1986). *Bread and Honey,* by Frank Asch (Parents Magazine Press, 1981).

Slim and Trim Day

PREPARATION _____ To the Teacher _____

Sweatsuits are the order of the day for both you and the children! (See p. 229.)

Winnie the Pooh, in *Walt Disney's Happy, Healthy Pooh Book* (Western Publishing Co., 1977), does a wonderful job summarizing every aspect stressed today. Remember to serve a healthy snack. . .perhaps fruit kabobs!

You will need:

- foods for Opening;
- orange for Activity 1;
- items for game for Activity 2; and
- beanbag and food pictures for Activity 3.

ARRIVAL _____ Aerobics _____

As the children arrive, have them exercise to the song "Wake up—Warm up" from the album *Preschool Aerobics*" (KIM 07740), by Georgiana Stewart (Kimbo Educational, Box 477, Long Branch, N.J. 07740).

OPENING _____ Health Talk _____

Exercise and diet are factors determining how healthy we are. Fruits, vegetables, and dairy products are some of the foods we need to eat every day. Eating too many foods with high sugar content takes away our appetite for nutritious foods that our bodies must have. Show the children two foods—one that is good for them and one that is not. (*Example:* orange, candy bar) Ask the children which one is nutritious and good for them. Continue with several more choices.

Because of TV commercials, aerobics classes, and fitness clubs, children are aware that adults often exercise. Children need to be concerned about fitness and involved in exercise also.

_____ Can You Feel the Beat? _____

Ask the children to lie on the floor. Have them place their index and middle fingers to the right of the Adam's apple just under their jawbone. They will be able to feel their pulse. Check if they are breathing fast or slow.

Stand up and exercise. Repeat checks of pulse and breathing.

CRAFT _____ Totbells! _____

Materials Needed:

> two paper towel rolls per child
> four styrofoam cups per child
> glue, crayons

© 1990 by The Center for Applied Research in Education

Explanation:
Each child makes two totbells. Use crayons to decorate the cups and towel rolls. Dip the ends of the towel rolls in glue and insert them into the cups. When the glue dries, the children can begin their weight lifting program.

FREEPLAY _____ Activity 1 _____

Relays—Divide the children into two teams. Children roll an orange with their nose to a designated spot and back to the next child in line. Repeat until all have had a turn.

_____ Activity 2 _____

Odd Object Out—Place four items on a tray. Children tell which one doesn't belong and why.
Examples: orange, apple, candy bar, banana
         fork, knife, spoon, soap
         sweatband, jogging shorts, tennis shoe, iceskate
         candy bar, cupcake, soda pop, milk

_____ Activity 3 _____

Beanbag Toss—Teach children the following poem:

> I feel fit as fit can be
> When I eat foods that are good for me.

Tape pictures of nutritious and non-nutritious foods on the floor. As children say the rhyme, they toss a beanbag and try to hit the foods that are good for them.

CLOSING _____ Story _____

Read one of the following stories: *Gregory, the Terrible Eater,* by Mitchell Sharmat (Four Winds Press, 1980). *Growing Vegetable Soup,* by Lois Ehlert (Harcourt Brace Jovanovich, 1987). *A Garden for Miss Mouse,* by Michaela Muntean (Parents Magazine Press, 1982).

_____ Exercising _____

Children will enjoy using their totbells while exercising to "Hot Diggity" on the album *Preschool Aerobic Fun* (KIM 7052), by Georgiana Stewart (Kimbo Educational, Box 477, Long Branch, N.J. 07740).

Sand and Sea Day

PREPARATION _____ To the Teacher _____

You and the children will pretend to spend the day at the beach, so have the children come dressed in beach attire and bring a beach towel. (See p. 229.) Serve a simple snack that can be eaten on the beach towel. The illustrations in *A Day At the Beach,* by Mircea Vasiliu (Random House, 1977), will make you feel like you're at the beach even if you're not!

You will need:

- pictures and beach ball for Arrival;
- beach bag (packed) for Opening;
- sand table and plastic containers for Activity 1;
- seashells and tub of sand for Activity 2; and
- Beach Bingo prepared for Activity 3 (see p. 233).

ARRIVAL _____ Beach Ball Fun _____

Display pictures of things we can do at the beach (play in the sand, jump in the waves, etc.). As the children arrive, repeat the following poem:

> We're going to the beach today.
> Do you want to come and play?
> (child's name), (child's name), One, Two
> What do you like to do?

Throw a beach ball to the child as you say his or her name. The child tells you what he or she likes to do at the beach.

OPENING _____ Beach Talk _____

Let's pretend we are going to the beach! What things will we do when we get there? What do we need to take along? Have a packed beach bag containing: towel, beach ball, suntan lotion, sunglasses, hat, pail, and shovel. Caution the children that when playing at the beach, there must be a lifeguard on duty before entering the water. Lifeguards are people trained in water safety and rescue.

_____ Recording _____

Sing the song "They Go Together" from the album *Witch's Brew* (AR 576), by Hap and Martha Palmer (Educational Activities, Inc., Box 392, Freeport, N.Y. 11520). You can make cards to use with this song using the patterns on page 145 and 146.

CRAFT _____ Sand Castle _____

Materials Needed:

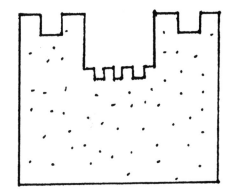

  stencils of sand castles (see pp. 230–32)
  glue, blue chalk, paper
  sand

Explanation:
The child places a stencil on the paper, and brushes
glue inside the stencil. Next he removes the stencil
and sprinkles sand on the glue. Finally he lays the
chalk on its side and draws a sea around the castle.

FREEPLAY _____ Activity 1 _____

Sand Table—The children add water to sand and use various sizes and shapes of plastic containers to make castles.

_____ Activity 2 _____

Finding Seashells—Hide seashells in a tub of sand. Ask the child to find a specific **number or**
kind of shells, compare their shapes and sizes, and count them.

_____ Activity 3 _____

Beach Bingo—Make cards with pictures of things you
would see at the beach (see p. 233). As you call out
each item, the children place shells on the pictures.
The game is over when someone has Bingo.

CLOSING _____ Story _____

Read one of the following stories: _Sand Cake,_ by Frank Asch (Parents Magazine Press, 1979).
Sweetie and Petie, by Katherine Ross (Random House, 1988). _Hide and Seek Fog,_ by Alvin Tresselt
(Lothrop, Lee & Shepard, 1965).

Boat and Dock Day

PREPARATION _____ **To the Teacher** _____

Fill the sand table with water. Float plastic boats of all shapes and sizes. Make a simple dock to tie up some of the boats so the children will see the purposes of a dock.

You will need:

- watercolors and paper for Arrival;
- pictures of boats for Opening;
- game prepared for Activity 1;
- game prepared for Activity 2; and
- fishing poles and fish for Activity 3.

ARRIVAL _____ **Watercolors** _____

Let the children use watercolors to paint waves on the bottom half of a piece of paper.

OPENING _____ **Boat Talk** _____

Boats are used for work and play. Show pictures of different kinds of boats and let the children tell which kinds they have seen. Point out that boats are moved by motors, oars, or sails.

Boats need help to stay in one place—out on the water an anchor is dropped, and on shore they are tied to a dock. Docks are flat platforms built along the shore. People tie their boats to them and use them for loading and unloading. You often see people sitting on the docks fishing.

_____ **Recording** _____

Sing the song "They Go Together" on the album _Witches Brew_ (AR 576), by Hap and Martha Palmer (Educational Activities, Inc., Box 392, Freeport, N.Y. 11520).

CRAFT _____ **Docking Your Boat** _____

Materials Needed:

pictures of waves painted in Arrival
craft sticks, toothpicks
one styrofoam egg carton cup per child
triangle patterns
scissors, glue, paper, pencils

Explanation:
The children glue three craft sticks on the paper painted in Arrival to make a dock. Give each child a toothpick and paper to make a sail. The children trace and cut a triangle and glue it to the toothpick. Then they insert the toothpick into the egg cup and glue it to the paper near the dock.

© 1990 by The Center for Applied Research in Education

FREEPLAY _____ **Activity 1** _____

Manila Folder Game—Draw a picture of a dock on one side of a Manila folder with a path of shapes leading to it. On the dock, draw all of the shapes that are on the path. In the corner of the folder, make a spinner that has each of the shapes, a wave, and an anchor. Make six sailboats by cutting triangle sails from six different colors of paper and gluing them to a toothpick. Insert each sail into a large marshmallow. _Procedure:_ Children take turns spinning and advancing their boats to that shape. If they spin an anchor, they lose one turn; if they spin a big wave, it pushes them back two spaces. The first boat to the dock is the winner.

_____ **Activity 2** _____

Sail the Ocean—Use chairs to make a large boat. Have life jackets for the passengers to wear and telescopes (paper towel tubes) for them to use. Provide a blue sport coat and a hat for one child to wear as he or she pretends to be the captain of the ship. Some experiences on this voyage might include: whale sighting, land ahoy, and rough seas where some of the passengers get wet!

_____ **Activity 3** _____

Go Fishing—Let the children sit on the edge of a table and dangle their feet as they try to catch fish of different colors. Their fishing rods should have a magnet on the end, and the fish should have a metal washer glued on for an eye.

CLOSING _____ **Story** _____

Read one of the following stories: _The Lake Mess Monster,_ by Beverly Komoda (Parents Magazine Press, 1981). _Scuffy the Tugboat,_ by Gertrude Crampton (Western Publishing Co., 1979). _Benjy's Boat Trip,_ by Margaret Bloy Graham (Harper & Row, 1977).

Dear Parent(s),

Please have your child bring in a plastic lid from
an aerosol can, such as spray starch, hair spray, or
spray paint. We will be making pincushions, so any
size will do. Please send the lid on or before

_____ .
      (Date)

Thanks!

BAT AND BALL DAY—CRAFT

See the three sizes of balls I painted!
We learned this rhyme while we were painting.

Here is a ball.
   (Make a circle with thumb and index finger.)
Here is a bigger ball.
   (Make a circle with thumb and index finger.)
A great big ball I see.
   (Make a circle using arms above head.)
Can you count them?

Are you ready?

1. . .2. . .3!
   (Make each ball as you count.)

I feel fit as fit can be
When I eat foods that are good for me.

Proper nutrition and the importance of exercise

will be the topic of the day on _____ .
(Date)

On that day, please dress your child in a sweatsuit or loose-fitting clothing so that we can enjoy an aerobics session.

Thanks!

Dear Parent(s),

We're planning a day at the beach (just

pretend)! On _____ , we would like
(Date)

the children to come dressed in beach attire and
bring a beach towel. Building sand castles,
digging for seashells, and playing beach bingo are some of
the activities we have planned.

Thanks!

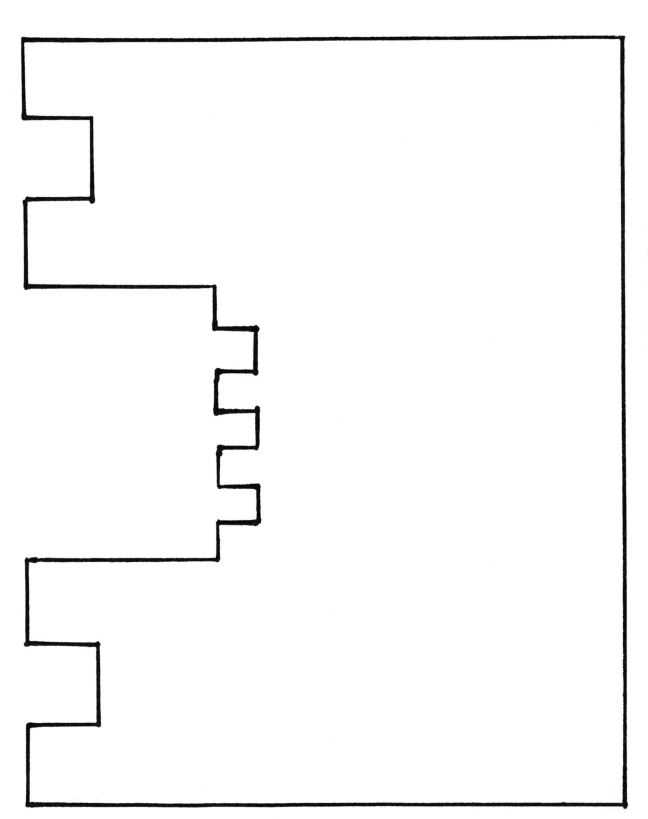

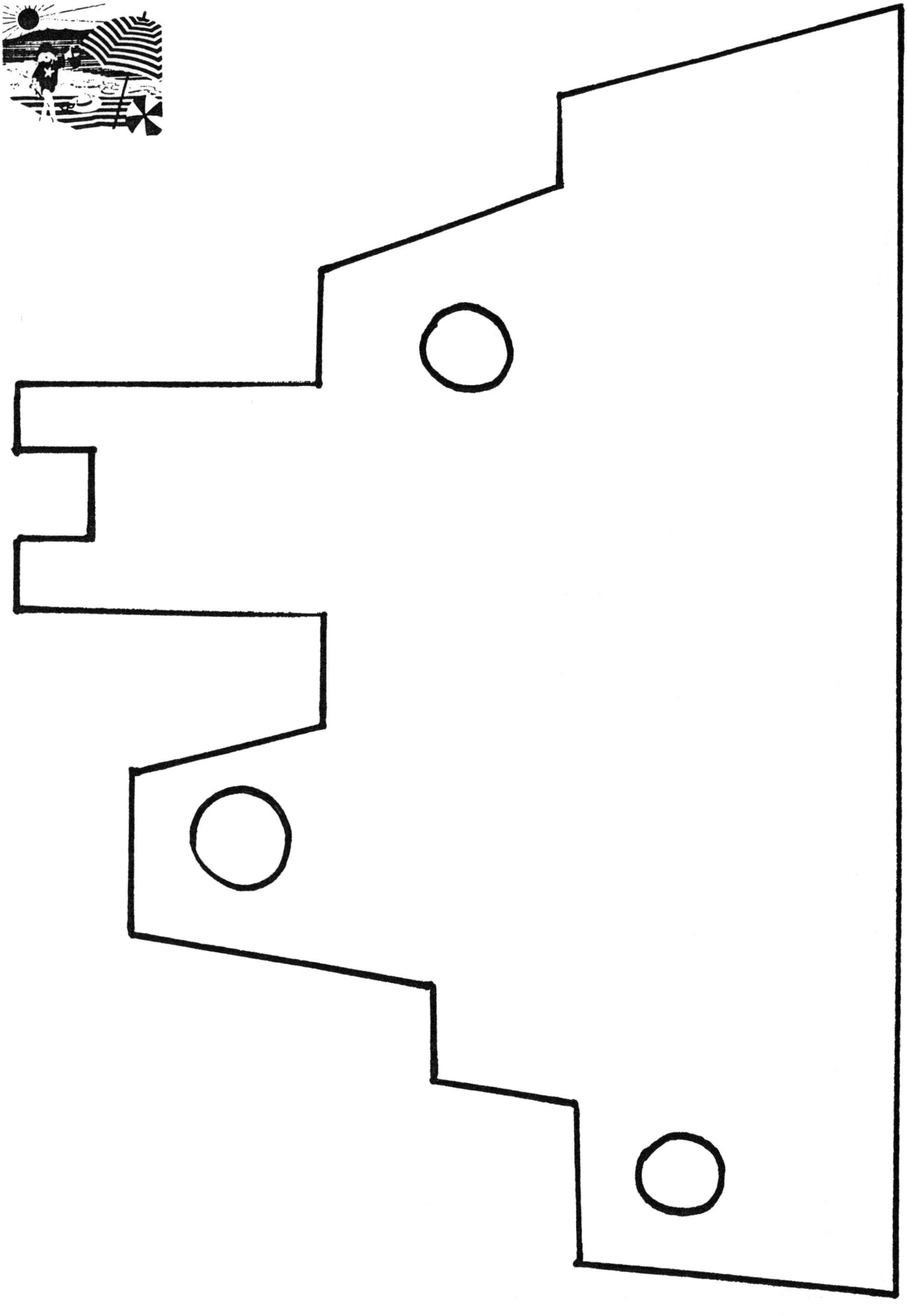

unit 10

SONGS AND RHYMES

Music is an important part of an early childhood program and can be used in a variety of ways.

In this unit, songs and rhymes are used to develop language and listening skills as well as to increase children's attention span.

Children basically enjoy music and should be given every opportunity to do just that. . .enjoy!

The daily activity plans in Unit 10 include:

- Duck Day
- Frog Day
- Bug Day
- Snake Day
- Lamb Day
- Ant Day
- Thumb Day
- Three Men in a Tub Day

Duck Day

PREPARATION ——————— To the Teacher ——————————

During the next four days, the children will learn one verse per day of the song "The Little White Duck" on the album *Little White Duck and Other Songs* (LP 261) Wonderland Records (division of A. A. Records, Inc., 250 W. 57th St., New York, N.Y. 10019). Each verse must be photocopied so every child can have it attached to the daily Craft. Also, on each day you will be working on a mural.

You will need:

- duck cookie cutter or pattern and paper for Arrival;
- pictures of duck body parts (see p. 252) for Opening;
- flannel board pieces (see p. 253) for Opening;
- charts and items for sinking and floating for Activity 1 (see p. 254–55);
- paper for mural and duck for Activity 2; and
- pictures (see p. 252) and plastic eggs for Activity 3.

ARRIVAL ——————————— Cutting ——————————————

Have available a very simple duck cookie cutter. Children can trace around it, cut out the duck, and save it for Craft.

OPENING ——————————— Duck Talk ——————————————

The male duck is called a drake. The female is called a duck, and babies are called ducklings. In the spring, the female duck lays and broods ten to fourteen eggs. After four weeks, the yellow ducklings hatch. Ducks have webbed feet, so they are good swimmers. They eat tadpoles, snails, worms, and plants that they find in the water.

Duck body parts include: bill, wing, webbed feet, and feathers. Show the children pictures of these parts (see p. 252.)

——————————————————— Song ——————————————————

Teach the children the following song:

> There's a little white duck sitting on the water,
> A little white duck doing what he oughta!
> He took a bite of the lily pad, flapped his wings
> and he said, "I'm glad
> I'm a little white duck sitting on the water
> Quack, quack, quack."

(Have a pond and a lily pad on the flannel board. Place the white duck in the pond as you learn today's verse.) (See p. 253.)

© 1990 by The Center for Applied Research in Education

CRAFT _____ Sponge Painting _____

Materials Needed:

> 8 1/2″ by 11″ paper for each child
> duck cut in Arrival
> clothespins
> sponges cut in small pieces
> blue paint
> typed verse for each child

Explanation:
Clip the clothespins to the sponges so the children can dip the sponges in the paint. The children paint the entire paper blue and glue the duck and the verse on the pond.

FREEPLAY _____ Activity 1 _____

Float and Sink—Make two laminated charts, each with a water line (see pp. 254–55). On one chart, draw a picture of a duck on top of the water. On the other, draw a picture of an anchor under the water. Children put items in a tub of water to see if they sink or float and then place them on the appropriate chart.

_____ Activity 2 _____

Pond Mural—Have children color the bottom half of a large mural paper blue. Prior to class, cut out a large white duck. Provide children with scraps of white paper to make feathers. These can be fringed, rolled, or torn. Children glue the feathers on the duck and place the duck on the pond.

_____ Activity 3 _____

Give a Clue—Put pictures of duck parts discussed in Opening in plastic eggs (see p. 252). Children take turns standing before the group and opening one egg. The child gives clues to the group about the picture he or she is holding until someone guesses it correctly.

CLOSING _____ Story _____

Read one of the following stories: *The Hungry Fox and the Foxy Duck,* by Kathleen Leverich (Parents Magazine Press, 1979). *Make Way for Ducklings,* by Robert McCloskey (Viking Press, 1941). *Have You Seen My Duckling?*, by Nancy Tafuri (Greenwillow Books, 1984).

Frog Day

PREPARATION _____ To the Teacher _____

Frog, Bug, and Snake Days give you the opportunity to incorporate some science facts along with the song (see p. 256).

Note the sticky tongue you will need to make for Opening. The children will love it! You will need:

- food and cookie cutter to make a snack in Arrival (see p. 257);
- frog's tongue and breadcrumbs for Opening;
- flannel board pieces (see p. 256) for Opening;
- game prepared (see p. 257) for Activity 1;
- paper for lily pads and frog for Activity 2; and
- Button Count game prepared for Activity 3.

ARRIVAL _____ Finger Jello Frogs _____

Using a cookie cutter, cut frog shapes from green finger jello (see p. 257). Dip small marshmallows in whipped topping to keep the eyes in place.

Finger Jello

4 envelopes unflavored gelatin
3 pkg. (3 oz. each) lime flavored gelatin
4 cups boiling water

Combine gelatin in large bowl. Add boiling water and stir until dissolved. Pour into a 9″ by 13″ pan and chill until set (at least one hour).

OPENING _____ Frog Talk _____

Frogs are amphibians. Nearly all amphibians spend the first part of their lives underwater. When they change into adults, they are able to live on land. Amphibians have smooth, thin, moist skin. Their skin is so thin it lets water in and out. Frogs don't have to drink because they take in water through their skin.

The tongue of a frog is attached to the front part of its mouth and is sticky. The frog can shoot out its tongue and capture its food. Frogs eat insects, minnows, earthworms, and spiders.

Frogs hibernate in mud in the bottom of a pond during the winter. They breathe through their skin. Illustrate a frog's sticky tongue by putting glue on the end of a long narrow piece of paper and picking up bread crumbs.

_____ Song _____

Review the first verse of "The Little White Duck" learned on Duck Day. Now teach verse 2.

There's a little green frog swimming in the water,
A little green frog doing what he oughta!
He jumped right off of the lily pad, that the little duck
bit and he said, "I'm glad I'm a little green frog
swimming in the water, glub, glub, glub."

(Today, add the little green frog to the flannel board.) (See p. 256.)

CRAFT _____ Little Green Frog _____

Materials Needed:

      one basket-style coffee filter per child
      green chalk, scissors, pencils
      simple frog pattern (see p. 256)
      green paper
      verse 2 of the song (see p. 256)

Explanation:
Children use the side of the chalk to color the coffee filter to resemble a lily pad. Tear out a piece to look as though the duck has taken a bite! Next, children trace and cut out the frog. Glue the frog and the typewritten verse on the lily pad.

FREEPLAY _____ Activity 1 _____

From Egg to Frog—(1) Most frogs lay their eggs in fresh water. (2) When tadpoles hatch from the eggs, they swim breathing through their gills. They eat water plants or small insects. (3) The tadpole changes into a frog. (4) It develops lungs, grows legs, and loses its tail. Adult frogs can live on land.

    Draw the four stages of a frog's life along the bottom of a rectangular paper (see p. 257). Draw the same illustrations on four separate cards, and lay them beside the chart. The child matches the stages and clips them onto the chart with clothespins. Then fold the bottom half under so it cannot be seen, and check if the child can put the stages in order. If not, repeat with pictures showing again.

_____ Activity 2 _____

Mural—Work on the mural must continue, so today the children each cut out a free-form lily pad and color one large frog that you have cut out.

_____ Activity 3 _____

Button Count—Provide the children with several laminated frogs, lily pads, and buttons. Write a numeral on each lily pad that tells the child how many buttons to place on the frog's tummy.

CLOSING _____ Story _____

Read one of the following stories: *Bullfrog Grows Up,* by Rosamond Dauer (Greenwillow Books, 1976). *Jump Frog Jump,* by Robert Kalan (Scholastic Books, 1981). *The Caterpillar and the Polliwog,* by Jack Kent (Prentice-Hall, 1982).

Bug Day

PREPARATION _____ To the Teacher _____

Spatter painting supplies are necessary. Directions for making individual spatter painting boxes are found in Arrival. You may want to contact a biology teacher from whom to borrow some bugs for Activity 1.

You will need:

- spatter painting supplies for Arrival;
- flannel board pieces for Opening (see p. 258);
- bug specimens and magnifying glass for Activity 1;
- black paper punches for Activity 2; and
- beanbag and poem for Activity 3.

ARRIVAL _____ Spatter Painting _____

To make the pond for the little black bug, spatter paint by placing paper under a wooden frame 2″ high covered with the screen. Children rub across the screen with a toothbrush dipped in blue paint. Save the paintings for Craft.

OPENING _____ Bug Talk _____

Insects can run, swim, jump, tunnel, crawl, buzz, and even walk on water.

Bugs are one kind of insect. Bugs have three body parts—head, thorax, and abdomen. They have two attennae, or feelers, that come out the top of their head. These help the bug feel, taste, and smell the world. Bugs usually have two eyes and a mouth that allows them to chew or bite their food. All bugs have six legs and at least one pair of wings. Bugs eat leaves, seeds, bark, wood, or other insects.

_____ Song _____

Introduce verse 3 after singing the first two verses.

> There's a little black bug floating in the water,
> A little black bug doing what he oughta!
> He tickled the frog on the lily pad
> that the little duck bit and he said, "I'm glad
> I'm a little black bug floating in the water,
> chirp, chirp, chirp."

(Place the black bug in the pond with the duck and frog on the flannel board.) (See p. 258.)

© 1990 by The Center for Applied Research in Education

CRAFT _____ Little Black Bug _____

Materials Needed:

> spatter painting from Arrival
> one black pom-pom per child
> small coding dots
> black markers, glue
> verse 3 of the song (see p. 258)

Explanation:
Children glue the black pom-pom and verse for today onto their painting. Attach coding dot eyes and use markers to draw legs.

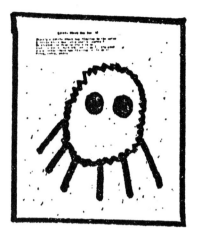

FREEPLAY _____ Activity 1 _____

Scientist at Work—The children look at different kinds of bugs with a magnifying glass. Have them count the legs, examine the wings, find the eyes, etc.

_____ Activity 2 _____

Pond Mural—Have the children paper punch black "bugs" and glue them onto the pond. They will enjoy adding legs with crayons.

_____ Activity 3 _____

Beanbag Game—Children sit in a circle on the floor. Sit in the middle of the circle, holding a beanbag to which you have attached a felt bug. As you toss the beanbag, the children recite this rhyme:

> Look out now, there's a bug on you!
> Say your name so he will shoo!

The child holding the beanbag says his or her name and tosses the beanbag back to you.

CLOSING _____ Story _____

Read one of the following stories: *How Many Bugs in a Box?*, by David A. Carter (Simon & Schuster, 1988). *Clotilda*, by Jack Kent (Random House, 1978). *Billions of Bugs*, by Haris Petie (Prentice-Hall, 1975).

Snake Day

PREPARATION _____ To the Teacher _____

Spatial relationships are stressed in several activities on this day, and some new science facts are introduced. *The Snake That Sneezed,* by Robert Leydenfrost (Putman, 1970), is a story the children will enjoy dramatizing.

You will need:

- coffee filters and blue food coloring for Arrival;
- flannel board pieces (see p. 259) for Opening;
- yarn snakes for Opening and Activity 2;
- obstacle course set up for Activity 1; and
- red modeling compound or play dough (see p. 55) for Activity 3.

ARRIVAL _____ Coffee Filter Pond _____

Have each child flatten a basket-style filter with his or her hands and place it on newspaper. Put several drops of blue food coloring into a glass of water. Children drop the colored water onto the filter until it is completely blue. This will be used as part of Craft.

OPENING _____ Snake Talk _____

Snakes are reptiles. Most reptiles have a thick skin with tough, dry scales. (Dinosaurs were reptiles!) Snakes move by bending their bodies from side to side. We say they "slither." They eat mice, birds, frogs, insects, or rabbits. Snakes do not chew their food. They swallow it whole.

Snakes shed their skin as they grow. Slowly the snake works its way out of its skin until it is shed inside out in one piece.

Many snakes live where it is warm. If they do live where it is cold, they hibernate underground until the weather turns warm.

_____ Song _____

Introduce verse 4 after singing the first three verses.

> There's a little red snake lying in the water,
> A little red snake doing what he oughta!
> He frightened the duck and the frog so bad,
> He ate the little bug, and he said, "I'm glad
> I'm a little red snake lying in the water,
> sssss, sssss, sssss."

(Add a little red snake to the flannel board and have him eat the little black bug as you sing about it in the song.) (See p. 259.)

_____ Spatial Relationships _____

Using the yarn snakes prepared for today's Activity 2 and the flannel board pieces you have been using to teach the song, have the children place the shortest snake beside the lily pad, the longest snake under the green frog, etc.

© 1990 by The Center for Applied Research in Education

CRAFT _____ Little Red Snake _____

Materials Needed:

> coffee filter pond from Arrival
> red fingerpaint
> verse 4 of the song (see p. 259)

Explanation:
Glue the copy of verse 4 onto the coffee filter pond from Arrival. Then the children use red fingerpaint to paint one red snake in the water. (While the children have on their paint shirts, have them paint a red snake on the mural.)

FREEPLAY _____ Activity 1 _____

Dramatization Fun—Children pretend to be snakes as you lead them through situations a snake encounters, stressing spatial relationships. For example: "Let's slither _over_ this big rock (chair)— Oh, here's a nice warm place in the sun (tumbling mat), let's curl up and rest for awhile. Is that sun ever getting warm! Let's slither _under_ this log (sheet elevated by coffee cans) and cool off. Are you hungry? Let's slide _around_ this tree (box) and find something to eat."

_____ Activity 2 _____

Yarn Snakes—Cut pieces of colored yarn into different lengths. The children arrange these snakes from shortest to longest, find all the short snakes, name the colors, and count them.

_____ Activity 3 _____

Play Dough Snakes—Have available lots of red play dough or modeling compound (see p. 55) so the children can make red snakes slithering or coiling.

CLOSING _____ Story _____

Read one of the following stories: _The Snake That Sneezed,_ by Robert Leydenfrost (Putman, 1970). _The Day Jimmy's Boa Ate the Wash,_ by Trinka Noble (Dial Press, 1980). _Crictor,_ by Tomi Ungerer (Scholastic Books, 1969).

Lamb Day

PREPARATION _____ To the Teacher _____

If you know someone who raises sheep, invite him or her to your classroom. Ask the person to bring in some of the items used in caring for sheep, such as shears, blanket, metal comb, etc.
   You will need:

   • wool and paper for Arrival; and
   • animal pictures (see pp. 260–61) and yarn for Activity 1.

ARRIVAL _____ Trace Hands _____

Trace around each child's hand, making sure the fingers point toward the bottom of the page. Save these for Craft. Have wool for children to touch, feel, and smell.

OPENING _____ Lamb Talk _____

The female sheep is called a ewe, the male a ram, and the babies lambs. A group of sheep is called a flock and is taken care of by a shepherd. The sound the sheep make sounds like "baa, baa."
   Sheep are covered with wool that is removed by shearing. The wool is used to make clothing. The sheep need to be sheared so they can be cool in the hot weather.

_____ Song _____

Sing "Mary Had a Little Lamb" and then discuss the problems the lamb caused at school.

Mary had a little lamb,
Its fleece was white as snow;
And everywhere that Mary went
The lamb was sure to go.
It followed her to school one day,
That was against the rule;
It made the children laugh and play
To see a lamb at school.

CRAFT _____ Mary's Lamb _____

Materials Needed:

picture of each child's hand from Arrival
cotton
coding dots, glue, black crayons
yarn bow for each lamb

© 1990 by The Center for Applied Research in Education

Explanation:
Be sure the hand outline is placed so that the thumb is the lamb's head and the fingers are the legs. Children glue on cotton to cover the body, and they glue a bow at the neck. They color the legs and put on a coding dot for the eye.

FREEPLAY _____ **Activity 1** _____

Animal Match—Children match pictures of farm animals and their babies (see pp. 260–61) by placing a piece of yarn from the mother to her baby. Have children name both animals and say the sound they make.

_____ **Activity 2** _____

Shepherd and Sheep—Choose one child to be a shepherd. The rest of the children are the sheep. As music plays, the shepherd leads the flock. Signal for a child or children to go to a designated hiding place. When the music stops, the shepherd counts the sheep and tells how many are missing and who they are.

_____ **Activity 3** _____

Dramatization—Set up chairs as if in a classroom. Lead the children through a dramatization of "Mary Had a Little Lamb." Two children pretend to be Mary and her lamb. The rest of the children sit in the chairs pretending to be in school. As the lamb follows Mary into school, the children look surprised and laugh and play.

CLOSING _____ **Story** _____

Read one of the following stories: *Pelle's New Suit,* by Elso Beskow (Harper & Row, 1929). *Charlie Needs a Cloak,* by Tomie de Paola (Prentice-Hall, 1973). *The Lamb and the Butterfly,* by Arnold Sundgaard (Orchard Books, 1988).

Ant Day

© 1990 by The Center for Applied Research in Education

PREPARATION _____ To the Teacher _____

This day includes a song and a fingerplay that you may want to write on chart paper before class begins. Both review the numbers one through five.

You will need:

- food for snack for Activity 1;
- game prepared for Activity 2; and
- Ants on the Pants game for Activity 3.

ARRIVAL _____ Song _____

Sing the song "Ants Go Marching" as you're marching. This could lead into a game of Follow the Leader.

> The ants go marching 1 by 1, hoorah, hoorah. (repeat)
> The ants go marching 1 by 1.
> The last one stops to chew some gum
> And they all go marching down to the ground
> To get out of the rain—boom, boom, boom.
>
> Verse 2: 2 by 2. The last one stops to tie his shoe.
> Verse 3: 3 by 3. The last one stops to climb a tree.
> Verse 4: 4 by 4. The last two stop to shut the door.
> Verse 5: 5 by 5. The last one says, "Man alive."

OPENING _____ Ant Talk _____

Ants are insects, but they belong to a special group (of insects) called social insects. That means they live in groups and cannot live alone. (Honeybees are social insects, too.)

Ants build and live in colonies. Each colony is ruled by one ant, called a queen. The queen's job is to lay eggs. Most of her eggs hatch into future workers. Every worker has a job to do. Some ants clean, some find food, and some guard the nest or colony. Each ant needs the others to stay alive; they all belong to one family.

_____ Fingerplay _____

Teach the following fingerplay:

Five little ants in an ant hill
Busily working and never still.
Do you think they are alive?
Watch them come out,
1...2...3...4...5.

Make an ant hill by tucking your fingers into your palm and holding your hand palm-side down. Wiggle your tucked fingers to show ants working. Raise your fingers one at a time to count.

CRAFT _____ Marching Ants _____

Materials Needed:

    paper, brown crayons
    black paint, glue, and brushes
    sand

Explanation:
Children draw a small hill on the bottom of the
paper. Cover the hill with glue and sprinkle with
sand. Children dip a finger in black paint and
print five ants marching toward the hill.

FREEPLAY _____ Activity 1 _____

Ants on a Log—Children prepare and eat their snack.
Have each child fill celery pieces with peanut butter.
Put raisins (ants) on top.

_____ Activity 2 _____

Ants in a Jar—Prior to class, make cards with a numeral on each one. The child draws a card
and cuts or tears that many little black ants and puts them in a large glass jar. At the end of
the day, have each child guess how many ants are in the jar. The next time the children come
to school, tell them how many ants were in the jar and whose guess was closest.

_____ Activity 3 _____

Ants on the Pants—Play this game. See Activity 2 of Pants Day (see p. 133) for playing procedure.

CLOSING _____ Story _____

Read one of the following stories: _The Way of an Ant,_ by Kazue Mizmura (Crowell, 1970). _Two
Bad Ants,_ by Chris VanAllsburg (Houghton-Mifflin, 1988). _An Anteater Named Arthur,_ by Bernard
Waber (Houghton-Mifflin, 1967).

Thumb Day

© 1990 by The Center for Applied Research in Education

PREPARATION _____ **To the Teacher** _____

Creative children will especially enjoy making thumbprint creatures in Activity 2. Be sure to display them for parents to see. You will need a supply of large buttons to make castanets.
    You will need:

- hand cookie cutter, paper, and paint for Arrival;
- large buttons and rubber bands for Activity 1;
- paint and sponge for Activity 2;
- game prepared (see p. 262) for Activity 3; and
- puppet stage or table for Closing.

ARRIVAL _____ **Hand Shape** _____

Use a large hand cookie cutter dipped in paint to make a print or trace around each child's hand. Save these for Craft.

OPENING _____ **Thumbkin** _____

Teach the following song sung to the tune of "Frère Jacque":

Where is Thumbkin?

Where is Thumbkin? Where is Thumbkin?	(Hide thumbs of both hands behind back.)
Here I am, Here I am.	(Bring out thumbs one at a time.)
How are you today, sir?	(Wiggle thumb on left hand.)
Very well, I thank you.	(Wiggle thumb on right hand.)
Run away, run away.	(First hide left thumb behind back and then right thumb.)

    After singing the song, encourage the children to examine their own hands and their friends' hands. Discuss similarities and differences.

_____ **Story** _____

Read to the children one of the following stories: *Donald Says Thumbs Down,* by Nancy Evans Cooney (Putman, 1987). *Danny and His Thumb,* by Kathryn F. Ernst (Prentice-Hall, 1973). *The Hole in the Dike,* retold by Norma Green (Crowell, 1974).

CRAFT _____ **Special Hands** _____

Materials Needed:

    hand shape made in Arrival
    paint

Explanation:
Children dip their fingers in paint one at a time and place thumbprint on thumb of hand shape, index fingerprint on index of hand shape, etc.

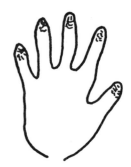

248

FREEPLAY _____ Activity 1 _____

Button Castanets—Individual castanets can be made by looping a rubber band through holes of large buttons. Remember, each child needs two. Review songs children have learned as they tap the rhythm.

_____ Activity 2 _____

Thumbprint Review—Spread a small amount of paint on a damp sponge and let children make thumbprints on a large sheet of paper. Children add features with crayons to make the prints resemble animals that they have been singing about this month.

_____ Activity 3 _____

Pushpin Outline—Make four cards to put on the bulletin board (see p. 262)—one with a hand traced in red, one in green, one in blue, and one in yellow. Mark twenty-five dots on each hand outline (where children will insert pushpins). Make cards with a different number of thumbprints on them. Give each child a small paper plate containing the color of pushpins which matches one hand card on the bulletin board. Take turns drawing a card and counting the number of thumbprints. This tells the child the number of pushpins to put in the dots of the playing card on the board. The game ends when all the dots on one traced hand are covered.

CLOSING _____ Whose Hand Is It? _____

Choose three children at a time to hide behind a puppet stage or table placed on its side, letting only their hands show. The rest of the children try to guess which hands belong to which child.

Three Men in a Tub Day

PREPARATION _____ **To the Teacher** _____

After reviewing all the songs and fingerplays the children have learned in this unit, perhaps moms, dads, and friends could stop by the classroom for a command performance.
    You will need:

- white and blue paper for Arrival;
- soap flakes, egg beater, and bowl for Activity 1;
- bottles and food coloring for Activity 2, and
- washcloths and towels for Activity 3.

ARRIVAL _____ **Mosaic Sea** _____

Provide blue paper for children to tear into small pieces (approximately 1/2″ by 1″). Next they glue these pieces on the bottom half of an 8 1/2″ by 11″ paper. This will be the water for the Craft.

OPENING _____ **Three Men in a Tub** _____

Recite the following rhyme:

> Rub-a-dub-dub,
> Three men in a tub,
> The butcher, the baker,
> the candlestick maker.

Discuss the poem with the children. Ask questions such as: How many men were in the tub? Show me with your fingers. What does a butcher do, a baker, a candlestick maker? Why were they in a tub? How did they get their tub to move?

_____ **Song** _____

Teach the song "Row, Row, Row Your Boat" after you have discussed that rowing may have been how the three men moved their tub. Have the children pretend to row their boat as they sing.

> Row, row, row your boat
> Gently down the stream,
> Merrily, merrily, merrily
> Life is but a dream.

CRAFT _____ Three Men in a Tub _____

Materials Needed:

    sea from Arrival   colored pencils

    cupcake papers   glue, scissors

Explanation:
Make the tub by cutting a cupcake paper in half and
gluing it on the sea made in Arrival. The child lays
his or her palm on the cupcake paper and traces
around three fingers to be the three men in the tub.
Use colored pencils to add facial features.

FREEPLAY _____ Activity 1 _____

Soap Suds Fun—Whip soap flakes and water with an egg beater. Spread the mixture on a table,
letting children draw pictures in the soap. Caution the children that they must keep their hands
away from their eyes. Hands will smell spring fresh!

_____ Activity 2 _____

Seriation—Fill ten bottles of the same size with varying amounts of colored water. Ask children
to arrange the bottles in order. Which bottle has the most water? Which bottle has the least water?

    With a spoon, gently tap the side of each bottle. Which sounds highest, lowest? Play a simple
tune such as "Row, Row, Row Your Boat," "Three Blind Mice," or "Twinkle, Twinkle Little Star."

_____ Activity 3 _____

Sorting Clothes—Have children fold, match, and sort washcloths and towels by color and design.

CLOSING _____ Story _____

Read one of the following stories: _No Ducks in Our Bathtub,_ by Martha Alexander (Dial Press,
1973). _No More Baths,_ by Cole Brock (Doubleday & Co., 1980). _Five Minutes Peace,_ by Jill Murphy
(Putman, 1986).

Duck Body Parts

bill

feather

webbed feet

wing

Little White Duck

There's a little white duck sitting on the water,
A little white duck doing what he oughta!
He took a bite of the lily pad, flapped his wings
and he said, "I'm glad
I'm a little white duck sitting on the water.
Quack, quack, quack."

Flannel Board Patterns

Frog Pattern for Flannel Board and Craft

Little Green Frog (verse 2)

There's a little green frog swimming in the water,
A little green frog doing what he oughta!
He jumped right off of the lily pad that the little
duck bit and he said, "I'm glad I'm a little green
frog swimming in the water.
Glub, glub, glub."

Dear Parent(s),

Using cookie cutters to cut out special shapes can make finger jello a special treat. We used a frog cookie cutter and green gelatin and attached marshmallow eyes by dipping them in whipped topping.

> 4 envelopes unflavored gelatin
> 3 pkg. (3 oz. each) lime gelatin
> 4 cups boiling water

Combine gelatin in large bowl. Add boiling water and stir until dissolved. Pour into 9″ by 13″ pan and chill until set (approx. 1 hr.)

FROG DAY—Activity 1

eggs

tadpole or polliwog

young frog

adult frog

Flannel Board Pattern

Little Black Bug (verse 3)

There's a little black bug floating in the water,
A little black bug doing what he oughta!
He tickled the frog on the lily pad
that the little duck bit and he said, "I'm glad
I'm a little black bug floating in the water.
Chirp, chirp, chirp."

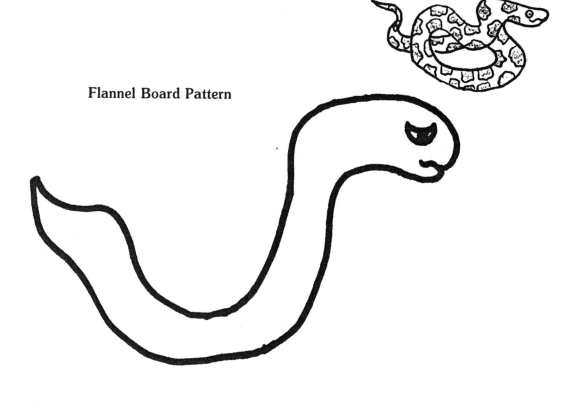

Flannel Board Pattern

SNAKE DAY—CRAFT

Little Red Snake (verse 4)

There's a little red snake lying in the water,
A little red snake doing what he oughta!
He frightened the duck and the frog so bad,
he ate the little bug, and he said, "I'm glad
I'm a little red snake lying in the water.
Sssss, sssss, sssss."

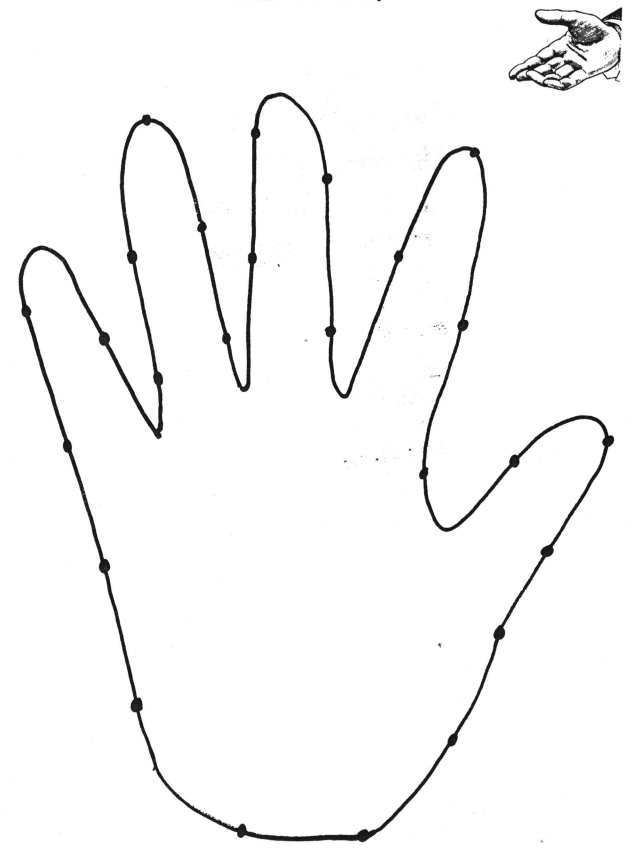